Violence and Piety in Spanish Folklore

Timothy Mitchell

Violence and Piety in Spanish Folklore

upp *Philadelphia* • *1988*

UNIVERSITY OF PENNSYLVANIA PRESS

COVER: Engraving from a late 19th-century edition of the *Testamento de Judas*. Courtesy of Dª Pilar García de Diego.

Library of Congress Cataloging-in-Publication Data

Mitchell, Timothy (Timothy J.)
   Violence and piety in Spanish folklore / Timothy Mitchell.
     p.   cm.
   Bibliography: p.
   Includes index.
   ISBN 0-8122-8093-8. ISBN 0-8122-1262-2 (pbk.)
   1. Folklore—Spain. 2. Festivals—Spain. 3. Spain—Religious
life and customs. 4. National characteristics, Spanish.
5. Violence—Spain—Folklore. 6. Piety—Folklore. I. Title.
GR230.M57 1988
398'.355'0946—dc19   87-32445
                                                        CIP

To Angela and Laura

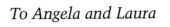

Contents

Acknowledgments

I would like to thank the Graduate School of the State University of New York at Buffalo, the Fulbright-Hayes Program, and the Charlotte W. Newcombe Foundation for their support through several years of research and writing. In addition, the Spanish Ministry of Culture has generously supported the publication of this book through its Program for Cultural Cooperation with United States Universities. I am indebted to Shirley Lease Arora, Julio Caro Baroja, David D. Gilmore, René Girard, and Bruce Jackson for their suggestions and encouragement. I have also benefitted from the comments of Roger Abrahams, Cesáreo Bandera, Diane Christian, Francisco Fernández, Carmelo Lisón, and Alan Soons. I am grateful to the editors of the *Journal of American Folklore*, the *Journal of Religious Studies*, and *Hispanic Journal*, who published earlier versions of certain chapters. Finally, the kindness and constant encouragement of Patricia Smith of the University of Pennsylvania Press made the completion of the task a most rewarding experience.

Violence and Piety in Spanish Folklore

Introduction

Few histories are as fascinating as that of Spain, and the most fascinating aspect of Spain's history may well be its unique and extraordinarily long-lived fusion of violence and religiosity. Incredibly, the way in which the cultural creations of folk Spain have reflected or potentiated this phenomenon has never been examined in a systematic way. Such a systematic study is the main objective of this book, and its objects are legends, beliefs, folk poetry, rituals, fiestas, and popular dramatic representations. The relatively unencumbered insight into social and psychological processes that these sources afford will enable me to suggest a new approach to the general "style" of Spanish civilization, an approach with potentially radical implications for our understanding both of Spain and of Spanish America.

This book is not a folkloristic field study, nor a village ethnography, nor an ethnohistory, nor an ethnophilosophical essay, but a critical synthesis of works that belong to all of these genres. I have availed myself of the insights and perspectives of many disciplines to realize this synthesis. I have striven for historical depth and geographical variety. I have made far greater use of the work of Spanish scholars than is customary in English-language studies of Spanish life.

The result, however, is not a research compendium or a descriptive overview of a field. My study is theoretical in nature and relentlessly pursues a line of inquiry that has not been pursued before:

the role that local or national identity crises and the psychocultural processes they set in motion have played in the deployment of an array of Spanish popular genres. At times I am able to advance my argument by drawing from a sizable number of monographs that have never been examined in the light of any sort of theory; at other times I am forced to adopt a polemicist stance in dealing with popular customs whose understanding has actually been impeded by the profusion of theories brought to bear on them.

To forestall possible disappointment for certain readers, I must state that I am not concerned with relating Iberian folklore and folkways to those of other Mediterranean countries, nor with seeing the bull in terms of animal category systems, nor with interpreting Spanish festivals in the light of frames, fields, liminality, reflexivity, or play messages. Valuable work is already well under way from a structural/symbolic perspective, but the perspective I adopt is dynamic, genetic, and historical. It has been strongly influenced by the work of René Girard, a controversial cultural theorist who ascribes a central place to violence in the morphogenesis of religion and other cultural institutions. In addition, my study can be seen as a contribution to the ever-growing body of research on ethnicity, local identity, and sociocentrism. And in still another way it can be included in a recent field of scholarly inquiry that Hobsbawm has aptly named "the invention of tradition" (1983a, 1983b). But it is not what the study of Spanish traditions can do for these exciting new approaches, but what they can do for the study of Spanish traditions, that remains my leitmotiv.

Above all, I am convinced that a better understanding of Spanish folklore will provide fresh research options for working Hispanists, preoccupied as we generally are with the words and deeds of conspicuous minorities. A broader perspective finds ample justification, even urgency, in the impressive cultural accomplishments protagonized by folk groups in Spain over the centuries. Chief among these, in my view, is the ritual or festive canalization of intercommunity and intra-community violence. This canalization assumes a myriad of forms—from the lynching of Judas in effigy to the feigned combats of *moros y cristianos*—but they all reflect the strife-ridden history of Iberia and they all represent a creative overcoming or sublimation or "working out" of this strife.

This is not to overlook the fact that popular forms that evolved to control violence are intimately related to lethal explosions of it. I harbor no romantic illusions about the origins of much of the material I deal with—fear, prejudice, xenophobia. Spaniards, after all, are "human, all too human." Knowledge of the violent matrix of many rituals is precisely what leads an objective observer to acclaim their prophylactic utility, their aesthetic and emotional sophistication, and above all their success in the maintenance of a genuine moral consciousness.

In one way or another, Spanish folklore is typically "moral lore" as well. As Caro Baroja insists, the Spanish peasant or villager has tended to see himself as residing "at the moral center of the universe"* (1976 : 119). Quite independently of any empirical corroboration, the people of one town have tended to deem that of another less honorable or more shameless a priori. Since a community's moral code is unfailingly bound up with its sense of singularity, whatever expresses the latter affirms the former, no matter how profane or barbarous or sacrilegious it might seem at first. I will supply abundant examples of this phenomenon further on; what I wish to underline now is that patently unethical procedures of moral reinforcement are not only compatible with but actually prepare the way for a "higher" or more self-conscious capacity for guilt, for penitence, and for reconciliation with community and deity.

This process can be observed at work in different genres of collective culture: The festive execution of Judas, a "sacrificial" mode of evil expulsion, provides the setting for a "confessional" mode in which neighbors proclaim their faults and air their divisive secrets in public. Pious legends recount the awesome Oedipal sins of hapless men who nevertheless manage to expiate their guilt and die saintly deaths. The capacity of traditional morality to achieve the salvation of sinners reaches archetypal dimensions in *Don Juan Tenorio*, wherein the man earlier ages condemned to hell is finally rescued by a stand-in for the Virgin Mary.

Anyone who approaches Spanish folk religion in search of mock persecutions and ritual scapegoats, as I did at first, will not be dis-

---

*All quotations from works in Spanish or French, prose or verse, have been translated by the author.

appointed. They are legion. What psychoanalysts call "projection" or what Girard labels "magico-persecutory thought" have been standard operating procedures throughout the ages. Only with time did I come to see that this basic structure invariably breaks down or evolves to include introjective and redemptive elements—ingenuous ones, perhaps, or still magical, but nevertheless indicative of moral progress sui generis and of an unexpected capacity for self-awareness.

Zorrilla's fidelity to the regenerative promise of popular religion in his reformulation of the myth of Don Juan can be cited as the major reason for its eventual "traditionalization." Why this drama can be studied as anonymous collective lore will be clear after a careful investigation of another traditional representation that has been Spain's most dynamic source of folk/mass culture in contemporary times—the bullfight. The tastes that make *los toros* popular can themselves be derived from a complex of social and aesthetic values that have been reinforced year after year, century after century, in Holy Week processions and other cathartic religious dramas. These dramas, in turn, derive their own staying power from a number of social and psychological functions that are best seen against the gestalt of the festal canalization of violence. This can take one of two general forms: 1) Asymmetric ritual violence is unilateral, absolutist, and inseparable from a magico-persecutory mode of thought and behavior. 2) Ritual violence is symmetrical when it involves two or more groups of roughly equal importance who tacitly agree to disagree and act in accordance with what I term the "laws" of rivalry. Both classes of ritual violence conform and confirm the collective identity of the people involved. As it happens, many of the rites and symbols that a traditional community employs to assert its identity have their origins in times of crisis that threatened or seemed to threaten the community's very survival. It is in just such a situation that Spain's first great identity myth comes to the fore—Santiago Matamoros (Saint James the Moor-Slayer), paragon and paradigm of medieval holy warriors. The crucial cult of Santiago exemplifies how a stress-provoked invention of tradition serves to protract the most permanent and ubiquitous modes of group differentiation that anthropologists have uncovered.

Herewith I have outlined, in reverse order, the logic that governs the sequence of the chapters.

The determination of what makes Spain Spanish, the analysis of the national mind or soul, the attempt to define the personality or essence of Spain—these are very traditional pursuits. My attention has been drawn not so much to the self-contradictory diagnoses produced therein as to the process of identity definition itself. And I have been struck by the extent to which Spain's cultural history has been marked by the urge to isolate supposed characteristics of the "race" for purposes of glorification or decontamination, a process that is tantamount to the invention of said traits. This "will to differentiate" can be traced directly to a consciousness of external threat that has little to do with paranoia and much to do with the harsh realities of war and ecological competition that have characterized the Iberian Peninsula from the beginning. Briefly stated, groups tend to recur to violence to differentiate themselves in times of acute stress and, moreover, the symbols that accompany this vehement awareness of self are almost always religious in nature. I set out to establish this crucial axiom in Chapter One.

Piety forged in violence constitutes the ultimate referent of the moral codes that sustain the unity of the group and the honor codes that regulate its dealings with others. The devotion to a patron saint that crystallizes in a moment of crisis soon comes to symbolize the devotees themselves. Cults common to Christendom at large are localized and personalized, idiosyncratic procedures for the eradication of "enemies" grow up alongside, and solemn rituals become expedient vehicles of abreaction. None of these phenomena are uniquely Spanish. But it is in Spain that they can be observed with unparalleled clarity. And it is in Spain that the forms and values of folk religion have exercised such an unrestricted influence over cultural creativity in general.

*   *   *

The Spanish cultural style is an eminently broad-based and popular one. Nevertheless, students of the same have tended to focus on the literary creations of a cultured minority at the expense of the oral or ritual or dramatic creations of cultured but illiterate Spaniards—the majority until recent times. The one area of folklore that has received exhaustive attention from scholars has been the *Romancero* (ballad corpus), precisely because it lends itself so well to the techniques of literary analysis. But why should verbal creations be privileged over ritual ones? Why should individual works be favored over collective ones? Surely a deeply rooted fiesta is no less relevant to Hispanism than a poem or a novel. The people of Spain were "Romantic" long before they were discovered by the paladins of European Romanticism. And they subscribed to the doctrines and techniques of *tremendismo,* affirms Caro Baroja (1969: 156–157), long before the transient literary movement of the same name. Yet for every study of popular tastes, such as Caro's, we have dozens devoted to those of the educated elite. For every study of the values of honor and shame among real Spaniards, we have a score on Golden Age honor plays. Brilliant as Spanish literature has been, it cannot be taken as synonymous with nor as representative of Spanish culture at large.

It is not my intention to devalue or discourage literary scholarship and criticism. I wish only to point out that a well-rounded approach to "Spanishness" cannot be gained through ignorance or underestimation of the cultural values, tastes, and products of the majority. A large part of what we think we know about Spain is based on just such a restricted purview. The blame can hardly be placed at the door of Spanish belletrists themselves, of course, many of whom have shown passionate interest in the popular traditions of their country.

An awareness of the advantages to be derived from a broader understanding of Spain's cultural style has encouraged me to use the word "folklore" in an inclusive, not exclusive, sense. The term can usefully be applied to a large number of phenomena, from the most obscure agrarian dance to a Holy Week procession with thousands of *penitentes,* from medieval legends to nineteenth-century "blind beggar ballads"—in other words, what Spanish investigators currently include under the convenient heading of *cultura popular.* The equivalent term in English would be "the folklore-popular culture continuum" (Narváez and Laba 1986). Inasmuch as cultural behaviors and beliefs themselves resist facile categorization, it is entirely defensible and sometimes vital for a humanistically oriented social scientist to be able to introduce a traditional tale, a chapbook, a popular play, or even an essay by Unamuno to advance an argument.

All the same, the chief novelty of this book does not consist of the methodological liberties taken (which in any case are only relative). It lies, rather, in the sphere of cultural hermeneutics. My study seeks to pick up the gauntlet thrown down, as it were, by a theoretical system that sheds too much light on the Spanish data and accounts too well for the findings of the best scholars to be ignored. The fact that René Girard has never conducted field research nor interviewed an informant has not kept him from illuminating ethnographic texts with brilliant success. Myth and legend, magic and religion, rites and games—Girard has brought all of these into the sphere of his strikingly original "psychologie interdividuelle." He has found a new approach to problems anthropologists and folklorists have grappled with for decades; he has developed the most important theory of myth since Lévi-Strauss; and, full of gaps and oversights as it is, his reading of human aggression is arguably the most sophisticated available and is as relevant to postindustrial societies as it is to primitive ones.

Ideally, the methodological "ethics" of social scientists impel them to account for the phenomena they study in the most pragmatic, economical, and plausible ways possible; they pledge conditional loyalty only to those theoretical concepts that fulfull these criteria. Until now, the *système Girard* has been praised by many, damned by just as many, and put to use by few. I emphasize the word "use," since I am not concerned with demonstrating the overall validity of Girard's theories. Like those of Walter Burkert (1983), they are partially based on unverifiable paleoanthropological reconstruction. But it *can* be verified that victimization is a tremendously dynamic motor of Spanish rituals and folk dramas. And interpersonal and intergroup conflict is *observably* mimetic. And the formal structure of numerous legends and ballads is *demonstrably* persecutory. A "victimage" mechanism does not have to be grounded in paleoanthropology, I contend, to make it a powerful instrument of cultural analysis.

Yet I do not wish to give the impression of forcing the data to conform to a preexisting dogma. In the first place, the Spanish data serve to qualify Girard's "general theory" in important ways. Martyrological lore, for example. In Spain, the openly acknowledged and even flaunted victim has been as fecund a source of mythopoesis as any disguised victim ever was. Marianism presents another problem: merciful as the Mother of God may be, the intensity of Spanish adherence to her cult cannot entirely be accounted for in

Christian terms (cf. Warner 1976, Preston 1982). In the second place, the fact that Spain constitutes an ideal laboratory for the observation of collective violence has hardly gone unnoticed by scholars. One in particular, Julio Caro Baroja, can be legitimately claimed to have "seen it first" in many instances. Though one could scarcely surmise it from reading English-language monographs on Spain, Caro's work is the very foundation of Spanish anthropology, ethnohistory, and folklore studies in the twentieth century. In his 500-plus scholarly publications are to be found most of the facts and phenomena that foreign researchers have later come to be identified with. It is largely due to Caro, in fact, that the field of Spanish ethnography has become the privileged forum for discussion of social violence that it is today. Witchcraft, expulsion rituals, anti-Semitism in folklore and history, scapegoat figures in rural dances, the Inquisition, national identity myths, folk anticlericalism, cathartic festivals of gossip, honor and shame—again and again Caro has broken new ground with his immense erudition and appetite for hard labor. Without his prior analyses, the synthesis I attempt in this book would have been impossible.

Stimulated by Caro's research into the divisive forces in Spanish rural life, a 1974 study by Carmelo Lisón demonstrated the extent to which the moral solidarity of small communities in Galicia was largely the product of the aggression of its individual members—aggression in the form of envy, gossip, evil eye accusations, and pseudo-sacrificial rituals. Stanley Brandes subsequently found derogatory references to Gypsies to be of critical importance in defusing hostilities among the residents of "Monteros" (1980:55–58). In the latest and best ethnography of Andalusia available, David Gilmore amplifies Lisón's Galician findings and argues that

aggression merely needs to be rechanneled, directed, guided by culture at specific internal targets: those whose extranormative or deviant behavior threatens the self-control and cultural uniformity of the group. [1987:27]

Time and again, the Spanish data have led the most reputable researchers to discover the functionality of the scapegoat. They have all seen the "positive" side of victimization, its role in the unification of the community and the maintenance of moral sanctions.

But they have not seen its potence, its sacral structure, and its superb capacity for camouflage, nor do they suspect how much of Spanish collective culture can be derived from it. The time is ripe, in my view, for the definitive deconstruction of the scapegoat mechanism and the rigorous reconstruction of its link to other key social mechanisms of traditional Spain—sociocentrism (Caro), mythomachia and theobiosis (Castro), the warrior fixation (Fernández), the contagion of honor (Bennassar), and several others.

To do all this requires a sophisticated and ambitious theoretical tool to begin with, one that must subsequently be subjected to the crucible of the Spanish data, modified and refined and strengthened. Consider the bullfight, for example, that great craft-art-sport-rite-drama-spectacle that plays havoc with performance genres. Though Carnival or Holy Week or Christmas have been alternately touted as the heart of the ritual year, it is the bullfight-event that comes not once but thousands of times per year all over Spain that has the best claim for such a distinction. No global treatment of Spanish culture worthy of the name can avoid dealing with it. And it is in the bullfight that any theory of pious violence or violence-as-piety has its greatest challenge and its greatest opportunity. As we shall see, the mimetico-mythological structuring mechanism of the bullfight replicates that of the fiestas of Spanish folk religion in its willful albeit unwilling misrepresentation of the facts. We shall also see how the failure to grasp said mechanism has effectively led peasants, poets, and scholars alike into further mythologizing.

Obviously, Spanish folk tradition is more than blood and sand. And it is much more than the sum of its male-centered public rituals, whether the male in question be an animal (bull or cock), a human (their slayer), a god (Jesus Christ), or an effigy (Judas). Although my study deals primarily with persecutory or patriarchal violence and the folk/popular culture engendered thereby, some effort must be made to understand the place of women in this scheme. As it happens, the Spanish people have been extraordinarily devoted to mothers, virgins, wives, and widows, and to the supernatural figures that seem to replicate them or their culturally assigned functions. I have encountered numerous ballads of legendary tough guys whose sense of honor was thoroughly Calderonian but who somehow managed to skirt the consequences with the help of the Virgin Mary or some analogous redemptive female. Many folk rituals feature an organized tug-of-war between rival groups whose object of contention is some miraculous icon of the Mother of God. Bullfighters never fail to commend themselves to María before entering the ring. Young *mayos* literally put their girlfriends and their Virgins on pedestals and proceed to recite verses that mingle the attributes of the first with the second. All of this has even led one anthropologist to picture Spanish folk religion as a vast, mysterious, and all-powerful matriarchal conspiracy (Delgado Ruiz 1986). To better explore Spain's idiosyncratic mélange of honorable violence (pagan? masculine?) and compassion (Christian? feminine?), I have included a chapter on *Don Juan Tenorio,* a popular drama that from my perspective was coauthored by José Zorrilla and the subaltern classes of Spain. It will be seen that the word "machismo" does not even begin to describe the complexities of the patriarchal mind-set.

In the Conclusion I will return to my main thesis and discuss the research paradigms it opens up by reference to the lore and legends produced by Spain's last great identity crisis (1936–1939).

I

The Concept of Sociocentrism

In the beginning was ecological instability, competition among different species—and among different human groups that function like "pseudo-species"—for the same area's resources (Livingstone 1976:156). The Iberian Peninsula, an exceptionally complex and unstable ecological zone, has witnessed thousands of years of such competition. The human geography of Iberia can best be understood, according to Caro Baroja, as an interlocking series of "enemy horizons," inasmuch as the struggle for survival that pits one animal species against another is of primary importance in analyzing enmity among humans—though history serves to diversify levels of struggle and kinds of "booty" (1973:37−38). In this setting of ecological instability and ever-changing modes and motives of acquisitive rivalry, group solidarity enhances prospects for survival. An orderly, cohesive group at peace with itself will compete more successfully for economic/ecological niches. A comforting and entirely functional feeling of in-group unity and superiority is of the essence. Without esprit de corps, a human group does not stand a chance. And it might not even merit the title of "human," if by human we mean the subordination of primate selfishness, undiscriminating sexuality, and brute dominance to cooperation, kinship, morality, and solidarity (Sahlins 1976:64). We do not know the exact means by which primate egocentrism was eventually, albeit imperfectly, brought under control, only that *some* means was found. René Girard's theory of the *victime émissaire* is essentially an attempt to account for the origin of Sahlins's "greatest reform in history." The primeval persecutory mechanism Girard posits might plausibly be described as a sort of cultural (rather than biological) "mutation" that gradually became dominant, since groups in which it occurred would have a distinct survival advantage over others—for hunting, for war, for all activities that demanded consensus. It thus becomes entirely appropriate to examine myths, rites, and moral codes in terms of their ability to stifle potentially destructive competition inside a group in order to make it more competitive in the ecosphere. The irony of the human condition is that such aggression is not really stifled, but *displaced*—onto other groups.

In an ideal world, each human community would be secure in its cultural identity, willing to content itself with a discrete body of lore and customs, predisposed to display a broadminded tolerance for the idiosyncrasies of other communities. In practice, very few peoples arrive at such a healthy relativism. Societies are typically absolutist. People employ their expressive culture, sacred and secular, to glorify themselves and to denigrate others and their sacred or secular expressive culture. "Mythoclasm," as defined by Harry Levin (1960: 106), "starts in the denunciation of myth as falsehood from the vantage point of a rival myth." All over the world, myths and other forms of folklore do the bidding of their ethnocentric possessors.

W. H. Jansen has shown how what he calls the "esoteric-exoteric factor" cuts across most of the traditional folkloric genres. "The esoteric applies to what one group thinks of itself and what it supposes others think of it. The exoteric is what one group thinks of another and what it thinks that other group thinks it thinks" (1965: 46). Though this definition is admirably general and inclusive, Jansen limits its application to modern industrial societies and their oral traditions of *blason populaire,* that is, ethnic humor and slurs. He concludes that such traditions form around groups that are isolated from others for religious, linguistic, or professional reasons, and adduces migrant fruit pickers as a conglomerate example (1965: 49).

Universal as it is, *blason populaire* is only the tip of the esoteric-exoteric iceberg. It is true that isolated groups tend to attract the finger-pointing lore of other groups. But it is equally true that the slings-and-arrows of daily *contact* can be highly productive of differentiating signs and symbols. Moreover, the "tale of the tribe" must compete not only with the tales of other tribes but with other tales *within* the tribe. Even so-called simple societies are composed of—and divided by—households, kinship groups, clans, clubs, age-groups, and sex-specific associations. Herein lies a methodological pitfall of the word "tradition," which often implies the idea of a consensus in the "traditional" group regarding its history and/or beliefs. This consensus might not exist in reality, or may have been arrived at only after years of intra-group rivalry and "logomachy." J. L. Fischer has succinctly summarized the problem:

As long as different interest groups in a society covertly and effectively challenge each other in important spheres of practical culture (political position, economic privilege, etc.), disagreements in mythology (expressive culture) will continue, serving the functions not only of expressing the practical disagreements in less serious form but also, to a certain extent, of keeping the practical disagreements in the field of attention and of justifying the different points of view.   [1963:252]

Thus the mythic motifs that form the stock of a particular oral tradition constitute the visible means of support of intra-community status-seeking. But this ongoing game of one-upmanship can get out of hand, and real battles will ensue. One band will then persecute another, or two bands will engage in the mutual persecution of a civil war. In short order I will explore the role of folk/popular culture in the propagation or rationalization of violence, as well as the role of violence in the elaboration of new beliefs and customs that become "traditional" over the course of time. But for now it must be pointed out that the mythico-political footballs Fischer refers to do not usually lead to grave degrees of divisiveness nor bring the community to the brink of self-destruction. Expressive culture possesses at least four "automatic brakes" that serve to counter the destabilizing tendencies that it so aptly fosters.

   1) In the first place, myths and slurs that function to put an outgroup in its place always serve to simultaneously reconcile the

members of an in-group with each other. And since any person normally belongs to several in-groups at once, organized according to
age, sex, lineage, clan, and so forth, the threads of this unifying reconciliation run all through the fabric of society. People divided by
one tale tradition are usually united by another. This is especially
true if the tale tradition deals with the defects of some third group.
The stock suspicions found by Jansen to accumulate around mar-
ginal or isolated groups ought to be seen, I believe, in terms of their
value in unifying less isolated groups. It is not that the enemy of
my friend is my enemy; rather, it is the enemy that makes him my
friend in the first place.

2) Second, there are other categories of folk culture that do not
lend themselves to wrangling quite so readily as the verbal genres
do. Here I am referring chiefly to ritual, which tends to be inclusive, not exclusive, and seeks to bind rather than sunder. Many
anthropological theorists have noted, despite their differing vo-
cabularies or emphases, that participative drama seems to require
harmony and good will among participants for magico-religious
efficacy. Rites underline shared values, beyond the omnipresent
give-and-take or push-and-shove of everyday life.

3) Third, though it is clear that folklore can maintain or exacerbate preexisting rivalries, it is equally true that it can be cathartic.
If certain divisive tendencies are expressed and given vicarious
fulfillment in tales or jokes, instead of being ignored or repressed,
society as a whole may benefit in the process. In some communities, dominant groups will permit and even encourage symbolic
contestation of their power as a safety valve ultimately serving to
enhance their supremacy (Lewis 1976:141–142). This is not to
suggest that catharsis is merely a manipulatory mechanism, however; it seems to be at work quite unconsciously in the many varieties of folk rites and games that employ mock or real violence to
achieve the sense of group harmony mentioned above. Blood sacrifices, pseudo-bellicose sportive competitions, and the raucous celebrations and effigy-burning of Carnival would all fit into this
category, wherein the capacity of folk culture to foster discord is
cannily turned against itself for the benefit of all. I will return to
the subject of popular violence; here I wish only to underline its
ubiquity, its normality, and its paradoxical role as promoter and ap-
peaser of the aggressive impulses present in the community.

4) There is, finally, one very basic way in which the clannish tendency of folk culture brings about inner harmony by simply being itself. The eternal jockeying for position, the urge to have the last word in the ongoing community war of words, and the disputes over the ultimate status of this or that mythic episode remain intact but lose their sting when the dialectic logic of ethnocentrism is carried one step further: when the quarrel-ridden community coalesces into one large, huddled in-group vis-à-vis another large, threatening out-group on the other side of the mountain. The proverbs and tales that bespeak this "higher" or more-inclusive level of intercommunity rivalry greatly contribute to a sense of intracommunity belonging. Since the dawn of time, apparently, enemies have worked wonders for the community of friends. This banal but crucial phenomenon is essential for understanding the expressive culture of peoples all over the world; its special relevance to Spain is a matter of historical record. When in Spain, Caro Baroja has affirmed (1973:37), the ethnographer's first task should be to determine the "enemy horizon" of the particular group he intends to study. In other words, tell me who your enemies are and I will tell you who you are.

In a publishing career that spans half a century, Caro has repeatedly called attention to the intense localism of Iberian peoples. Apart from the heritage of enemy horizons referred to above, he has investigated the passionate regionalisms that criss-cross the political map, the artificiality of the Spanish State itself, and the traditional distrust and even hatred that divide neighboring towns in rural areas. Most importantly, Caro was the first to attempt a systematization of the vast quantities of expressive culture that these localistic passions have produced. *Sociocentrismo* is the word he settled upon to refer to the capacity to believe that the group one happens to belong to is the best of all possible groups (1957:264). An individual's background, education, and modus vivendi determines the particular size of the group that best elicits this capacity for belief—neighborhood, town, county, province, region, and so forth (1957:266). The in-group will then favorably compare itself with the corresponding out-group on physical, geographical, linguistic, moral, occupational, religious, artistic, and/or historical grounds (1957:269–270): "We" are stronger and more handsome than "they"; we enjoy a superior climate; we speak correctly and without an accent; our women are more virtuous; our products are more valuable; our patron saint is more powerful; our singers and dancers are more talented; our history is more glorious. The intensity of sociocentric feelings grows as the groups involved become more exclusive. Caro attributes the potency of the most local varieties to the simple fact of their staying-power: many villages and towns have been around for two thousand years, while regional "kingdoms" or the nation-state itself are more recent and consequently less binding creations (1957:273–275).

Following Caro's concerns, H. M. Velasco has constructed a provisional motif-index of what he calls "sociocentric texts"—the proverbs, nicknames, songs, and stories that people of one area employ to characterize the peculiarities and alleged flaws of those in a neighboring area. Concentrating on both Castilles, Extremadura, and Andalusia, Velasco outlines more than a dozen major categories of *exovaloración* and cites abundant examples for each one (1981:90–106). Sociocentric texts cast aspersions on the intelligence of the out-group, generalize about comical physical traits shared by its members, or make fun of its linguistic idiosyncrasies; they can refer to the men of a nearby town as thieves and to their women as whores; they can recommend against acquiring a wife or husband or any other good there:

En Cedillo, buenas muchachas,   Cedillo has pretty girls,
y en Lominchar son mejores,   in Lominchar they're better,
pero llegando a Recas   but when you get to Recas
son tronchos de coliflores.   they're real cauliflower stalks.
        [Velasco 1981:91]

The civic monuments, churches, and patron saints of other towns easily lend themselves to the same procedures. As a convenient rule of thumb, it might be said that anything that *can* be mocked *will* be mocked. Sociocentric texts often eschew a binary us-them classification in favor of a distributive scale that takes account of several groups at once, arranging them in either descending order of merit or in terms of their role in the local ecosystem. Competing sociocentric texts mirror the currents of interaction, matrimonial exchange, and commerce that unite all of the towns in a certain area into one system or "world." Each little community constructs its own worldview where all is valorized, moralized, and socio-centralized; the anthropologist takes a relativist overview of them all to find a dense network of role-playing (Velasco 1981 : 106).

The different sectors of the folk world may mock and deride each other, at least in private, but they need each other all the same. Lisón Tolosana has emphasized the many rites and customs that provide the necessary social lubricant, with the patronal or pil-grimage festival as prime examples (1980: 85–100; 1983: 43–83). And he too has endeavored to systematize Spanish sociocentrism and in the process has formulated six generators of cultural speci-ficity with Latin labels and universal applicability (1983 : 96–99). Apart from the primordial familial-local factors he groups under the category of *communitas*, Lisón's *principia individuationis* in-clude the *corpus historicum* of a group, through which its past is commemorated and constantly revalorized; its *corpus mysticum*, including icons, cults, credos, and the like; its *corpus linguisticum*, a multifaceted and all-powerful determiner of singularity; the *cor-pus consuetudinarium*, including everything from architectural styles to kinship systems, modes of property ownership, uses of power, and relations between the sexes; and the group's *corpus symbolicum*, that quintessential category of emotional, psycholog-ical, and ideological factors that conforms a particular "cosmovi-sion" on any of several levels of abstraction and "materializes the ethos and pathos of the group" (1983 : 98).

Sociocentrism includes but is certainly not limited to Jansen's esoteric-exoteric factor, *blason populaire*, or what nineteenth-century Spanish folklorists called *dictados tópicos*. It is a more ac-curate term than ethnocentrism. It bespeaks the continuity be-tween localism and nationalism and can substitute for every word that relates to any level of in-group differentiation or the feelings that accompany it—clannishness, partisanship, chauvinism, paro-chialism, "community pride," factionalism, sectarianism, tribal vi-sion, xenophobia, esprit de corps, or, naturally, enemy horizon. To the degree that we are functioning members of a society, we are all sociocentric. All kinds of expressive culture, from folk to "high," exemplify this truism. At the same time, the systematizing efforts of Caro, Velasco, and Lisón demonstrate that the notion of socio-centrism lends itself to ever more rarified planes of analysis. But I have not cited them to celebrate the human classificatory instinct or because I consider the definition of sociocentrism to be an end in itself. The structural or typological examination of the ways in which one group defines itself in opposition to another group is just the banal but necessary point of departure for my investigation. It is imperative to establish at the outset that 1) human groups consciously employ expressive culture for purposes of differentiation; 2) religious symbols and moral codes figure prominently in this veritable "will to differentiate"; 3) violence can be either the occasional outcome or cathartic instrument of sociocentrism; and 4) the Iberian Peninsula constitutes a privileged laboratory for observing the interaction of these phenomena.

The study of European local traditions has become a major scholarly enterprise, and major scholars have expressed surprise at the resilience of such traditions (Badone 1987:185–186). The definitions and categories proposed thirty years ago by Caro Baroja have oriented many subsequent investigations of sociocentric lore and customs. Caro was the first to emphasize that these forms of folklore are hardly innocuous and that "in Spain they have contributed to the unleashing of civil wars and similar catastrophes in fully contemporary times" (1957:271). Community solidarity is often a mere consensus of hatred that manifests itself in regular, even mechanical ways (1957:282–291).

Further consideration of Spain's turbulent history suggests that episodes of violence have not only been triggered by folklore but have been the fertile *source* of new forms of it. In order to explore how Spain's sociocentric traditions got started in the first place, however, it will be essential to approach the notion of tradition itself from a fresh perspective.

Crisis and the Invention of Tradition

There are dozens of studies that document how folklore and popular culture can be employed to exacerbate social conflict and assist the process whereby more-or-less peaceful modes of sociocentric differentiation slide into violent ones. Such studies tend to put the emphasis on the use of folklore for propaganda: torn from their natural context, traditional proverbs or beliefs are cynically exploited by charismatic leaders or dictators for their own ends. The rise of Nazi Germany is well-covered scholarly terrain that patently reveals how the same body of politicized folklore can be used to justify the interior violence of persecution and the exterior violence of war. Wolfgang Mieder (1982) has described how German folklorists sympathetic to the dogmas of National Socialism resurrected anti-Semitic sayings of the Middle Ages to stir up persecutory zeal among the masses. Léon Poliakov (1974) has abundantly documented the double utility of the Aryan myth in fomenting violent elimination of domestic out-groups and in whipping up war fever among the "real Germans" of the in-group.

But the Third Reich is only one, admittedly spectacular, example among many. The Bolsheviks used folklore for purposes of agitation (Denisoff 1969), so did the Chinese Nationalists (Wang 1965), so did the Italian Fascists (Simeone 1978). Linenthal (1982) has described the extent to which traditional martial myths were evoked by Vietnam-era "hawks" to justify their stance.

The nationalistic movements of this century and the last constitute an ideal paradigm for the study of "manipulatory" applications of expressive culture; even when they do not lead to violence, such movements are typically motivated by an identity crisis of some kind. Lisón observes that it is usually some critical event or imbalance between one society and another that sets the differentiating "engines" to work at a higher velocity than usual (1983:99). The disequilibrium can be precipitated by any of a number of social, economic, or political events and the precise nature of the response will vary accordingly. As Hobsbawm points out, the mere existence of groups seeking to defend or revive tradition signals a break in it (1983a:7–8). The ideology of the "traditionalist" groups will determine which particular reading will be brought to bear on the traditional symbols of singularity. In general, some item already present in the community's composite cultural identity will be exalted as a metaphor for this identity, a symbolic flag to rally around in defense of difference (for example, Mohandas Gandhi and his spinning wheel). Regardless of the degree of conscious manipulation attending to its use, the strategy always works toward the same end: the consolidation of an "us" against a "them." Above all, defining symbolism is designed for use, not rational speculation (Hobsbawm 1983b:268–269; Lisón 1983:100–101).

Many folklorists have expressed uneasiness with the way in

which popular traditions are taken advantage of by the promoters of nationalistic or ethnic differentiation. Barre Toelken is one who has voiced such concerns:

Many of the emerging countries, especially in central Europe, following years of domination by outsiders, have tried to express and retain their own sense of ethnic unity by purposely collecting, archiving, and disseminating to their own people certain key aspects of their own folklore. In this venture, often certain features are considered less important while others are given a focus beyond what would have originally been theirs under normal traditional circumstances. . . . There is always the chance under these conditions that the real traditions in folklore will finally be subordinated to political ends, and that has sometimes happened, lamentably.   [1979:361–362]

Toelken goes on to cite Hitler as the most sinister exponent of this tendency, and includes commercial applications of folklore as another lamentable albeit less vehement form of manipulation (1979:362).

Toelken is not the first folklorist to employ the common denominator of manipulation to connect propagandistic uses of folklore with mercantile ones. The Soviet Union and the United States constitute classic illustrations, says Alan Dundes, of one or the other of these manipulatory modes (1965:309). Dundes acknowledges a tendency among folklorists to accept only the materials of nondeliberate treatment as truly traditional (1965:309). This purist point of view was consistently defended by Richard M. Dorson, always at pains to distinguish the genuine "folklore of the folk" from the "pop kitch" or "fake lore" of industrial man (Dorson 1960:86), supposedly tainted with profit-seeking and mass-media intervention.

The propriety of such distinctions has been seriously called into question by Richard Handler and Jocelyn Linnekin (1984), who argue that, ironically, both folklorists and propagandists can come to share a "commonsense" but fallacious concept of tradition

in which those aspects of social life that are considered traditional are endowed with (or reduced to) the status of natural things. . . . Traditions thought to be preserved are created out of the conceptual needs of the present. . . . To posit a distinction between genuine and spurious traditions is to overlook the fact that social life is always symbolically constructed, never naturally given.   [1984:280–281]

Like Toelken, Handler and Linnekin refer to the deliberate staging of folk customs and crafts for purposes of ethnic consciousness-raising, but find no cause for lamentation therein. They use the word "traditionalization" to refer to events wherein certain items taken to represent past tradition are selected out and "newly contextualized," thus bringing about a fresh awareness among performers and spectators regarding their own group identity (1984: 280). An analysis of nationalistic, scholarly, and rural reformulations of identity symbols in Montreal and Hawaii leads Handler and Linnekin to conclude that

The opposition between a naively inherited tradition and one that is consciously shaped is a false dichotomy. . . . The origin of cultural practices is largely irrelevant to the experience of tradition; authenticity is always defined in the present. It is not pastness or givenness that defines something as traditional. Rather, the latter is an arbitrary symbolic designation, an assigned meaning rather than an objective quality. [1984:285–286]

Handler and Linnekin demonstrate, I think convincingly, that the word "tradition" is misleading if it connotes 1) bounded essence, 2) immutable heritage, or 3) unconscious or naive handling of identity symbols. The possibility that "real traditions in folklore will finally be subverted to political ends" concerns Toelken (1979: 362), but Handler and Linnekin would deny the existence of any real traditions to be subverted. Their arguments bear directly on the issue of violence and sociocentrism.

It is not the case that folklore leads a tranquil life in "normal traditional circumstances" until hotheaded nationalists come along to exploit it; so-called manipulators only protract the divisive tendencies already present in folklore. Earlier I mentioned the methodological faux pas of taking tradition to imply consensus. Fischer demonstrates that any tradition is subject to constant manipulation, each in-group striving for status, jockeying for economic privilege, wrangling with other groups, and seeking to arrange expressive culture in accordance with its own self-glorifying point of view (1963:26off). The folklore of sociocentrism has always been propagandistic and manipulatory *avant la lettre*. Even commercial uses of folklore begin with the folk: communities that specialize in a particular agricultural product or skilled trade have often relied entirely on the oral dissemination or even exaggeration of the virtues of said good or service (the superb swords of Toledo, the unexcelled beans of León, the peerless sunflower seeds of Tarancón, etc.).

Sociocentrism is one with consciousness of a collective self; this group self-consciousness simply becomes more intense in times of crisis. Nowhere is this more evident than in the crisis cults, revitalization movements, and millenarian uprisings that numerous anthropologists and historians have explored. It is within this sphere of inquiry that the reworkings of folk tradition made by European fascists take on a different perspective. "In the retrospective eye of history," observes Weston La Barre (1972:260), "Nazism was yet another nativistic cult, complete with xenophobic myth and a paranoid messiah." True cultural relativism cannot point a finger at Hitler without simultaneously pointing out that all sociocentric uses of folklore carry the seeds of violence within them, and without recognizing the kinship of all reformulators of tradition, whether they be the Brothers Grimm, Gandhi, or Goebbels. The concrete historical circumstances of a given society, the ways in which its in-groups have typically characterized themselves with regard to out-groups, and the exact nature of the precipitating crisis will determine what sorts of personalities emerge to carry out the work of "traditionalization." Therefore, it is not so much a question of investigating how psychopaths dupe gullible masses but of exploring the potential for violence that inheres to symbolic differentiation itself.

In any case, the autonomy enjoyed by the archetypal demagogue is relative; he may be cynical but his power nevertheless depends on "telling the people what they want to hear." Lies, especially big ones, must be believable. And the masses predetermine the standards of credibility, in accordance with needs they can feel if not understand (Hobsbawm 1983b:307). There is imitative interplay between leaders and followers in times of crisis, particularly so when the leaders are of the "charismatic" variety. For La Barre, "Charisma is only shared unconscious wishes and symbolic thought-paradigms in leaders and communicants" (1972:48). Mimesis is of the essence, as René Girard has insisted in his own studies of crisis situations and their violent outcomes (1972:62–248; 1978a:9–214; 1982:7–146). It is these shared reactions to stress that form the backdrop for the creative recastings of old sociocentric tales and adages during times of crisis. Crisis focuses every-one's attention on the identity process—what is it that makes us different from and better than those others? Crisis threatens ac-cepted signs of group identity and stimulates conscious reworking of them.

Defining symbolism need not be mere *bricolage*, however; cre-ativity in the interest of sociocentrism is not confined to an artful reshuffling of a limited number of cards. New cards, new elements enter the picture. The needs of people under pressure may cause them to develop new beliefs or myths or practices. But not all cri-ses are created equal; perhaps they are not equally creative. Would a cross-cultural comparison of the spontaneous creations of groups caught up in the throes of crisis reveal any basic patterns?

Folk legends constitute an ideal terrain for observing how crisis and violence influence sociocentric creativity, especially in the case of historical or pseudo-historical legends that are believed, ac-cording to Linda Dégh (1972:74), because they contrive to contain verifiable facts while preserving an illusion taken to be factual. In comparing legends to fairy tales, Max Lüthi has argued that the legend

looks fixedly at the inexplicable which confronts man. And because it is monstrous—war, pestilence, or landslide, and especially often a numinous power, be it nature, demons, or spirits of the dead—man becomes small and unsure before it. [1976:24]

The rapid propagation of essentially similar illusions during times of stress can be understood in terms of their ability to reassure a frightened group of people (Kluckhohn 1966:37), and this reward-ing feeling of reassurance is carried on by the legend. Typically, stress brings people into contact with the sacred; fear encourages the irruption of the numinous in the form of ecstatic visions or in the guise of supernatural helpers. The war-torn lands near Israel have witnessed the contemporary birth of legends that recount epi-sodes of miraculous aid received during battles (Ben-Ami 1978). At least three different towns in northern Spain claim to be the site of a miracle that took place during the War of Independence in the first years of the nineteenth century, when Napoleonic troops in-tent on defiling the local parish church were struck dead by the

Santo Cristo de la Cama (Andújar Espino 1966). The origin of the
Arthurian legends superbly illustrates the mythogenetic fecundity
of crisis, struggle, and defeat. For historian Gerhard Herm, the tales
of Arthur document "how an epoch of history came to an end, how
a dream was dispelled, how a culture died—and how it went on
living just the same" (1977 : 277). In this case, the invention of tradition was carried out by the folk poets who mediated between the
chaos of a dying Celtic culture and the creation of Arthur-as-culture
hero. Attuned to the innermost psychic needs of their fellows,
caught up as they all were in the slow destruction of their traditional way of life, the Celtic Bards fashioned the reassuring legends
that later fabulators would recast in secular and chivalric terms
(Campbell 1968 : 405 – 570). Here one thinks of Gilbert Durand's
definition of the imagination as the faculty that negates the negative by proposing an image of something better (Durand 1968 : 109).
La Barre devotes considerable attention to the relationship between
cultural chaos and the emergence of a new messiah, prophet, or un-
dying savior (1972 : 197 – 355). The pattern repeats the career of the
culture hero who is often

a protector, champion, or some great war hero of the past. Having helped
men, he is now departed. But he is not dead. At some crucial time of great
stress in the future, when enemies come to destroy the tribe and its way of
life, he will come again to help the people.   [1972 : 200]

The bandit-heroes glorified in folk traditions from Poland to
China exemplify a similar wish-fulfillment, caused not so much by
one acute crisis as by a chronic substratum of crisis—hunger, poverty, exploitation. According to Hobsbawm (1959 : 24), "the bandit-
hero is merely a dream of how wonderful it would be if times were
always good." But peasants do not always play the role of passive
victims achieving vicarious satisfaction through tales of Robin
Hood, Diego Corrientes, or other popular champions. The violence
and fury of peasant uprisings set more active forms of symbolic justification in motion, and real charismatic leaders will then become
"legends in their own time." Emiliano Zapata was such a leader.
His exploits are still sung in dozens of *corridos* and his eventual
return is still taken for granted by landless peons in southern Mexico. The Mexican Revolution was enormously fertile in terms of

cultural innovation in general—ballads, art, literature—a tremendous effort in defining symbolism, dedicated to the construction of a new national identity. The subsequent "institutionalization" of the revolution has furthered the "traditionalization" of its expressive culture. The United States itself is no stranger to the process.

The miraculous legends of wartime, the tales of Arthur and other once-and-future saviors, and the lore of culture heroes, bandit-heroes, and revolutionaries all exemplify the creative power of violence—violence that, in every case, is the continuation of socio-centrism by other means. All crises, perhaps, no matter what their objective causes, tend to become identity crises for the afflicted societies. Stress-provoked "folk work," to borrow Stanley Hyman's phrase, aims at shoring up a group's threatened sense of mastery or righteousness. When cultural items of the past are insufficient to assuage current fears, new folk work will be carried out; and in time the lore created thereby will become the accepted identity signs of the community involved. What in one mythogenetic moment serves to console a distraught group ("our hero is not dead, we too will rise again") may in another epoch or another epic serve as a badge of self-esteem and superiority—not necessarily for the same group ("we are the true inheritors of those manly virtues of old"). The inevitable stage of literary/artistic stylization will only be interrupted by a new crisis, newly spilled blood to water the tree of sociocentric differentiation.

Enough has been said for now in the way of theoretical exposition and numerous examples from Old and New World ethnographic literature have been adduced. The Spanish phenomena can now be approached with a provisional but viable framework in mind. It will be seen that certain fundamental traits of popular piety in Spain correspond quite closely to the patterns of crisis-induced mythogenesis discussed above. At the same time, the legend of Spain's greatest supernatural culture hero, Santiago Matamoros, will serve to demonstrate that the concept of "inventing traditions" is as relevant to medieval history as it is to modern. The same legend will also lead me to modify certain formulas advanced by the investigators of crisis cults. New insight will be gained, furthermore, into the role social mimesis plays in the development and deployment of identity symbols.

2

The Legacy of Santiago

Santiago Matamoros constitutes the charter myth of Spanish identity in general and the prototype of the hundreds of different saints that affirm identities in communities all over Spain.

To begin with, the lore of Santiago and its accompanying cult constitute a tradition invented during one of the more critical moments of a centuries-long crisis known as the *Reconquista*. The tiny, primitive Christian kingdoms in the north of Spain literally had their backs to the sea while the Moors dominated the rest of the peninsula; the "enemy horizon" could not have been more clearly drawn from 711 A.D. onwards. The descendants of the vanquished Goths, divided among themselves by jealous squabbles and dynastic in-fights, desperately needed not only some powerful symbol of unity but also some sign that God was on their side after all. Américo Castro's study of the rise of Saint James the Moor-Slayer covers every detail of this classic invention of tradition under duress and the renewed consciousness of identity it wrought.

Santiago's shrine arose to face the Mohammedan Kaaba as a display of spiritual force, in a grandiose "mythomachia" or struggle between myths. The city of Santiago aspired to rival Rome and Jerusalem, and not only as the goal of a major pilgrimage. If Rome possessed the bodies of Saint Peter and Saint Paul, if the Islam that had submerged Christian Spain fought under the banner of her prophet-apostle, Spain unfurled the ensign of a most ancient belief, magnified in an outburst of defensive anguish, and unmeasurable in any rational way. The presence of a powerful race of infidels over almost the whole face of Spain would necessarily enliven the zeal to be protected by divine powers in the Galicia of the year 800. [1954:147]

The antecedent folk tradition had gradually erased the evangelical distinction between Saint James the Greater and Saint James the Less (or the Just); Santiago, the composite result, was held to be the very brother of Christ and came to be endowed with a thaumaturgic martial invincibility modelled (unconsciously) upon the thundering divine twin Castor (Castro 1954:136−145). The "discovery" of his relics in Galicia came at a particularly opportune time for the embattled Asturian-Leonese kingdom, though the functional category of miracle-working warrior-saint was already filled in the kingdom of Navarre by no less a personage than Michael the Archangel. Caro Baroja notes that Saint Michael, armed to the teeth, had appeared on a mountain top in Aralar shortly after the loss of Spain to the Saracens; the Archangel had made similar apparitions elsewhere in Europe in equivalent moments of stress and his relics (!) were treasured in a number of early medieval monasteries (Caro 1974b:200−202). Never pictured without a lance in his hand and a dragon at his feet, the archangelic knight quickly became the preferred identity sign of the first monarchs of Navarre (1974b:203). The legend relates closely to others of a darker and more tragic tenor that I will discuss in another chapter.

Like the more dynamic bellico-religious symbol of Santiago, the legend of Saint Michael was a stress-provoked reworking of traditional lore that answered to the basic logic of sociocentrism—group self-definition in opposition to another group. Castro sees this "mythomachia" but is also at pains to emphasize that the case of Santiago was defining symbolism *in imitation of* the other group, for

the belief emerged out of the humble plane of folklore and assumed immeasurable dimensions as an answer to what was happening on the Moslem side: one war was sustained and won by religious faith, to be opposed (not rationally, of course) by another fighting faith, grandly spectacular, strong enough in turn to sustain the Christian and carry him to victory. In the same way that the Moors had been unconsciously imitated in many aspects of their existence, a correlation was also established with respect to the military use of religious beliefs. [1954:131−132]

Fire, in other words, is most properly fought with fire. The invention of tradition as a function of rivalrous social mimesis can be grouped with the element of leader-follower mimesis discussed earlier; the reader is asked to retain both varieties in mind. Santiago serves Castro as a major example of the symbiosis between Christians and Moors—and Jews—so rich in consequences for Spanish culture. He is quick to point out the same dialectic of opposition and imitation in other traditionalization processes—Bernardo del Carpio in Spain and King Arthur in Britain (1954: 149–150).

As I mentioned earlier, La Barre considers the early Welsh tales of Arthur to have been an imaginative but essentially vain variety of wish-fulfillment, the impractical "ghost dance" of a moribund culture (1972: 270–271). La Barre insists that crisis cults in general are to be seen as wildly anti-adaptive decompensations under stress that do not attain homeostasis for the "desperately dreaming" culture because they speak to the Pleasure Principle rather than to the Reality Principle (1972: 374–379). That the legends of Santiago and Saint Michael sought to restore cultural homeostasis is clear enough—one reassuring myth arises in opposition to (and in imitation of) a threatening one. The Archangel was venerated quite consciously as the devil's counterpoise in Christian psychostasis (Caro 1974b: 200). But the "compensating" cult of Santiago diverges sharply from the formula advanced by La Barre in that it *worked*. Far from being the maladaptive pipe dream of a doomed race, Santiago Matamoros was the highly adaptive fighting tool of a society of warriors whose irrational invention was rewarded from the very start by the Reality Principle: with Santiago on their side, the Christians won battles. Only its practical and efficacious results can account for the extraordinary growth of the cult throughout Spain and Europe, a success story that can be traced directly to the troglodytic state of medieval military technology. Morale was of the essence: a knight or soldier who knew himself to be shielded or at least assisted by a potent supernatural ally was bound to do better on the battlefield (Castro 1954: 149).

Secondary varieties of sociocentrism clustered around this sacral/martial nucleus. Since Santiago was held to be none other than the brother of Christ, hence a higher-ranking apostle than Peter, the prelates of Galicia had ample grounds to dispute the Pope's supremacy over the Church for nearly three centuries (1954:132–134). The Sepulcher of Compostela became the sole source of international prestige for the kings of Christian Spain, lacking as they were in the cultural refinement and technical prowess of the infidels (1954:158–163).

Saint James the Moor-Slayer becomes Castro's formidable hermeneutic tool for the elucidation of Spanish history, civilization, and psychology; for without Santiago, "the history of Spain would have been entirely different" (1954:130). Studying this myth we come to understand how, unlike the learned or contemplative varieties of religiosity that prospered in other nations, "medieval Spanish Christianity was more productive of holy wars, propaganda, and thaumaturgy" (1954:157).

Even historians who do not share all of Castro's conclusions agree that peace was never so rewarding as war for Spanish Christians (Bennassar 1985:109). Spaniards invented both the word and the concept of Crusade, and the crusading spirit continued to shape Spanish history long after the last Turk was driven from the Mediterranean. For Alvarez Arenas, the Spanish martial spirit is simply indistinguishable from Spanish religiosity (1972:130–132). Fernández Suárez considers the "warrior fixation" to be a fundamental fact of Spanish life—the taste for life in a warring band, to be more exact, where each man imagines himself the protagonist of a glorious epic (1961:194–195). "To do what one feels like while serving God, this is the great dream of the Spaniard" (1961:196). This divinely sanctioned belligerence is one of several national fixations that all depend in one way or another on a primitivistic, almost infantile emotionality for which Fernández Suárez has little sympathy (1961:317–324).

An understanding of Spain's multisecular symbiosis of violence and piety is crucial to an understanding of the conquest of the New World, the wars of the Counter-Reformation, the spontaneous uprising against Napoleon, the Carlist revolts of the nineteenth century, and the bloody Civil War of 1936–1939, as will be abundantly clear from any historical account or analysis of these conflicts. The cross of Christ has been assimilated to the dagger and sword hilt throughout centuries of fratricidal crusades. To adopt a Skinnerian vocabulary, the positive historical conditioning that martial piety received during the *Reconquista* was subsequently reinforced by an intermittent schedule of historical contingency—resulting in the extinction, not of the behavior, but of the enemy.

Saints and Sociocentrism

The legends of Santiago and Saint Michael provide important insights into the functioning of popular religiosity in Spain. The saint (including the Virgin or the Christ) can be considered a basic building block of Spanish sociocentric folklore. The beliefs, rites, devotions, and festivals that express and confirm the identity of a particular community almost always flow from the cult of one miraculous being or another—and are likewise inseparable from the hundreds of shrines and sanctuaries that William Christian has studied in such depth (1976). Saints' legends typically involve 1) the discovery of a sepulcher, relic, or icon and 2) the clearly expressed preference on the part of the magical object for a specific location; sanctuaries are not founded, but "develop" when further miracles attract popular devotion (1976: 56–59). The demand for such miracles grew steadily during the seven centuries of the *Reconquista*. Increasing ecclesiastic centralization of the canonization process led to increased "discoveries" of miraculous icons of the Virgin; María supplied the tremendous demand for divine protectors in the reconquered areas (1976: 60–62). In subsequent centuries, a new layer of Christocentric devotion fused with the earlier strata of sanctuaries dedicated to the martyrs and María (1976: 71–73); this fusion—that multiplied the images of the latter as a *Mater Dolorosa*—presents a number of fascinating theoretical problems that I will deal with later. From the fourteenth to the nineteenth centuries, continual waves of drought, disease, plague, and pestilence maintained the demand for saints who could "specialize" in the prevention or cure of such collective and individual maladies (1976: 71–74). For every local crisis, it seems, there was a compensatory crisis-cult response.

Needless to say, the faithful did not expect something for nothing. Any favors rendered or miracles worked by a given divine sponsor were repaid with interest in the form of fasting, fiestas, vows, charitable contributions, processions, *exvotos**, and the like. In many cases, promises made centuries earlier in return for liberation from some plague are kept without a murmur by the late twentieth-century descendents of the promisers. Folk religion in Iberia comprehends the relationship with the saint as a contract whose unwritten but binding clauses spell out the rights and obligations of the parties involved. If the people keep their side of the bargain, they have every reason to expect the saint to keep his, and even to sanction his infractions. The people of Peralbillo (Ciudad Real), for example, were obliged to toss the icon of San Marcos into the river when he refused to heed their repeated requests for rain (Ramírez Rodrigo 1985 : 347). When the Child Jesus, special patron of the fishermen of the Albufera (Valencia), had somehow allowed the catch to slacken off in the most favorable season, the fishermen went to the church and turned the icon around to face the wall, just as they might have punished a real child, and were heard to utter prayerful threats like

Look, if you don't behave you're going to get a beating! Look, if you don't work the miracle for us . . . we won't give you the fiesta! Look, a two-peseta firecracker and that will be it!   [Sanmartín Arce 1982 : 59]

The fiesta is, to be sure, the major clause in the contract that binds a community to its supernatural protector. According to Gómez Tabanera, failure to hold the fiesta as usual "might very well produce individual or collective sentiments of culpability" (1968 : 164). Maldonado considers Spanish folk religion and Spanish fiestas to be one and the same phenomenon (1975 : 193). Lisón affirms that a community generates a fiesta as the quintessential means of dramatizing, sublimating, and sacralizing its own social structure (1983 : 77–79).

Few fiestas are as useful as the *romería* for understanding the relationship between saints and sociocentrism in Spain. The *romería* can be defined as a small-scale pilgrimage in which the inhabitants of a given locality journey in a body to a sanctuary to celebrate the

---

*any token or offering hung near an icon in memory of the miracle.

festivity of the supernatural protector housed therein. Sometimes the local community will converge at the shrine with other nearby towns that share the devotion; occasionally the fiesta assumes provincial proportions. Inside the basic framework of town, sanctuary, and the road in-between, a *romería* can harbor a wide variety of behaviors. Sometimes the sacred image is brought home to visit the local parish church; other images "travel" to spend a few days in each of the towns under their protection. Masses and other pious rites, dancing, singing, and food-sharing are common denominators. The circumstances of the journey itself promote all manner of socializing, including flirtation and matchmaking. Different sorts of commercial exchange typically grow up around the *romerías* as well. Sanctuaries are almost always situated in mountainous zones of great natural beauty with abundant supplies of water from springs or fountains. *Romerías* nearly always take place in the springtime when the aesthetic appeal of the shrine's locale is enhanced. Finally, unlike many other folk rituals in Spain, the *romería* has actually increased in popular appeal since the 1960s (Christian 1976:86–105; Lisón 1983:70–83; González Casarrubios 1985:60–66, 79–80; Rodríguez Becerra 1985:87–103).

In nearly every case, a *romería* can be traced to the solemn vow made by a community in a moment of crisis. The famous *Romería de la Milagra* of the mountains of Toledo, for example, has its beginnings in the disastrous drought of 1778. One day the desperate inhabitants of Hontanar and Navahermosa brought out their respective icons in "emergency" processions; just when they happened to converge at a certain crossroad it began to rain and the crops were saved. The thankful villagers erected a monumental crucifix (mimesis of the crossroad) and later a shrine on the site of the miracle and have met there to hold a yearly fiesta ever since (González Casarrubios 1985:80). In Pozuelo de Calatrava (Ciudad Real), Our Lady of the Saints is honored with a *romería* on the first Saturday of May for having freed the people from an epidemic of cholera in the middle of the nineteenth century (1985:79). In nearby Puertollano, three cows are sacrificed and stewed in thirteen caldrons, one for each of the survivors of a medieval plague who instituted this festivity of the Santo Voto (1985:86). These examples can be multiplied ad infinitum.

Lisón arrives at his definitive formulation of sociocentrism in Spain via an exploration of the *romerías* of rural Zaragoza, Huesca, and Teruel (1983:43–83). The one held in honor of Our Lady of Bruis serves as a model of them all: Each of the ten villages in the district of La Fueva (Huesca) enjoys the protection of its own private saint and the differentiation symbolized thereby, but all set out one day each year to gather at the hermitage of the Virgin "whose mantle covers all" (1983:76). In effect, the 13,000 hectares of La Fueva comprise a distinct climate and ecosystem and a complex little world of commercial conflicts and interdepenency that the yearly *romería* sanctifies and integrates into one overarching "mystical map" (1983:70–78). The peasants' rigorous fidelity to the Virgin and the transcendence they confer upon the sojourn at her sanctuary surely respond to something more powerful than the guilt feelings mentioned by Gómez Tabanera.

If cults of local saints have their origins in times of grave crisis, new crises can bring about new forms of devotion in ways that closely parallel the "invention of tradition" discussed earlier. The *Cristo de la Salud* in Valencia provides a splendid demonstration of this process, carefully documented by Sanmartín Arce (1982:58–66). Traditionally, the people of the Albufera had enjoyed the favor of two "specialized" patrons: the Child Jesus, mentioned earlier, was expected to assure plentiful fishing by the timely manipulation of winds and waves; the *Cristo de la Salud* was charged with the prevention and cure of the contagious fevers that periodically decimated fishermen, rice-growers, and the population in general. This Christ was credited with a number of miracles and was even said to have intervened in the choice of the advocation *"de la Salud"*—of health (1982:59–61).

Changing times have wrought changes in these devotions. The fevers have disappeared, mass tourism has replaced fishing as the dominant source of income, many young people have married outsiders and now reside elsewhere, and the great lagoon of the Albufera has been polluted by industrial waste. The cult of the Child Jesus has consequently declined in importance, to the point that the fishermen no longer share the expenses of the fiesta as before and hardly participate in the traditional procession. In contrast, that of the *Cristo de la Salud* is now the *fiesta mayor* and convokes the massive attendance of those who have moved elsewhere as well as those who stayed. The traditional cult has been adapted to respond to a very nontraditional crisis:

The problem is no longer the east wind or the west wind. The Child Jesus no longer has to exercise his power over the movement of the water. It is the water itself that is sick, contaminated, and as if it were a new kind of plague to be dealt with, the whole town embarks and carries the *Cristo de la Salud* to the center of the lake on the eve of His fiesta.   [1982:63]

It is not that the people of the Albufera are ignorant of the objective causes of the lake's sorry state. On the contrary, they seek to enlist Christ's support in persuading the authorities at Valencia to finance the necessary waste treatment plants. But the community has another ailment that parallels the first, for the ecological and socioeconomic changes undergone since the 1960s were inevitably accompanied by an identity crisis, which the renewed cult of the Christ of Health has already begun to heal. It is not that all of the people who now operate hotels and restaurants wish to return to the fishing boats and the harsh standard of living of before, but all the same they are not disposed to part with the lake and its cultural legacy as identity symbols. In transporting their icon to the middle of the Albufera in a festive floating procession, the people reaffirm their "ownership" of the lake and everything it symbolizes—their fathers and themselves (1982:65). To paraphrase Handler and Linnekin (1984:280), the "past" thought to be preserved is actually being created out of the emotional and conceptual needs of the present.

At the close of the celebrations in honor of the *Cristo de la Salud*, the outgoing *clavarios*, managers of the fiesta, challenge the incoming ones for the next year "to see if you can outdo us." And in this way, year after year, the fiesta of the *Cristo* grows and creates new rituals, while a new way of life comes into being with a still uncertain blend of new and traditional values.   [Sanmartín Arce 1982:65]

Thus, the forging of identity culture does not imply the end of intra-community rivalry, but its shrewd utilization. As in countless other fiestas throughout Iberia, the most flagrant forms of imitative one-upmanship paradoxically enhance the overall unity of the group and the greater glory of its saintly symbol of singularity. What begins in crisis grows through competition. And different levels of integration (the neighborhoods of a single town or the towns of a single province) utilize or subsume different degrees of competition. Or, as Lisón puts it, "a different fiesta corresponds to every metamorphosis of the 'us'" (1983:82).

A cumulative logic of differentiation and integration can be abstracted from the festal data presented here. A *romería* is like a machine whose input is local singularity and whose output is singularity at the district or provincial level. The spiritual map of Spain that Christian has drawn is nothing more nor less than the overlapping areas of population that sanctuaries of different magnitudes can agglutinate (1976: *separata*). To put it another way, the mystical *communitas* that the villages of the Albufera, the Fueva, or any other ecosystem can achieve during one or two days at the sanctuary would be inconceivable without the day-to-day gestalt of localistic identity affirmation.

Once the intimate relationship between saints and sociocentrism has been established, behaviors that might otherwise be branded sacrilegious become comprehensible. The same Virgins who showed a keen awareness of municipal boundary lines when making their first miraculous appearances eventually come to rival one another (in folk poetry) in the same manner as the groups that believe in them (Caro 1957:288; Lisón 1980:92; Velasco 1981: 102). The same holds true for groups whose self-definition is a function of class-consciousness:

In the famous procession in Seville during Holy Week, the escort of a Virgin from a poor parish would glare with ferocity at the Virgin from a rich church in a fashionable quarter. The Archbishop of Seville himself remarked that "these people would be ready to die for their local Virgin, but would burn that of their neighbors at the slightest provocation." [Thomas 1961:36]

Velasco devotes an entire section of his "motif index" of Spanish sociocentric texts to those that exalt the privileged relationship a given village enjoys with its mystical protector (1981:102–103). A clear-cut will to differentiate is at work in the texts that an in-group employs to concomitantly praise its saint over others and tacitly praise itself for having merited such heavenly favoritism. The devotions of other communities are routinely mocked—generally as a means of mocking the folly or credulity of the devotees:

San Blas de Huete,	Saint Blas of Huete,
que por sanar a uno	for every one he cured
mató a siete.	he killed seven.
[Caro 1957:289]	

A certain village was so proud of its supernatural protector and so determined to adorn him with every possible virtue that during the annual procession the villagers would sing

¡Viva, viva San Fulano,	Long live Saint So-and-So,
nuestro glorioso patrón!	our glorious patron!
Confesor, obispo, mártir,	Confessor, bishop, martyr,
Virgen y madre de Dios.	Virgin and mother of God.
[Caro 1957:289]	

This hoary Castilian joke has been adopted and adapted by dozens of communities to make fun of their neighbors' excessive piety. One's own is no laughing matter. Small wonder, then, that a patronal festival can include real skirmishes between locals and outsiders as an unprogrammed side-effect of the festivities (Lisón 1983:79).

Ethnologists and theologians alike agree that the cult of patron saints has been the most potent and decisive vehicle of local identity Spain has known. In the darkest ages of Spanish history, observes Sáinz Rodríguez, when there was not the slightest glimmer of mysticism or "higher" forms of spirituality, the people never stopped trusting in their saints (1980:307). From the cult of *Santiago Matamoros* in the ninth century to the cult of the *Cristo de la Salud* in the twentieth, the same elements appear over and over again: conflict and identity crisis; the supernatural protector as a function of the enemy horizon or the local ecosystem; sociocentric self-affirmation; mimetic diffusion, mimetic rivalry, and the invention of tradition. None of these processes functions in Spain without the intervention of folklore and without the consonant production of folklore—in the form of rituals, beliefs, legends, fiestas, or wisecracks. Not all Spanish folklore is to be traced to some past episode of violence or crisis, nor, presumably, will all Spanish folklore be susceptible to violent utilization. But those forms of folklore that relate most intimately to the unity of the group do indeed evince such origins and susceptibilities.

3

From Feuds to Fiestas

Earlier, in my discussion of the "automatic brakes" that serve to counter the destabilizing tendencies that sociocentric folklore so aptly fosters, I referred to the cathartic effects of rituals that employ mock or real violence to achieve a sense of *communitas* for the people involved. Such rituals are extraordinarily common in Spain. Generally speaking, they occur in a festal context and take the form of 1) rivalry or combats, and 2) scapegoating. Both varieties are equally amenable to artistic elaboration and the *communitas* that flows from one or the other never lacks an aesthetic component, which raises a number of fascinating questions that must be deferred. The priority at this point is to examine the structure of rivalry and scapegoating rituals and to ask how they might have become "operational" in the first place. Are these festal procedures for the control and containment of violence to be derived from the same identity-crisis matrix as the miraculous wartime legends or the compensating cults of saints discussed earlier?

An affirmative answer to this question could be reasoned along the lines of Girard's victimage theory and his distinction between "original" and "ritual" violence. Girard argues that *violence originelle* always takes place in the midst of a single group, serving, as it were, to "lay down the law" for all, stifle the acquisitive rivalry inherited from the primates, and provide effective means of channeling off aggression (1972 : 369–371). Original acts of violence are gruesomely genuine, but their subsequent mythic elaboration and/ or ritual "imitation" necessarily reflect the group's fundamental incomprehension (*méconnaissance*) of the victim whose death brought them peace and order (1972:135–178). Original violence was intestine and spontaneous; ritual violence is programmed and expulsive—to the point that two groups may come to serve a "sacrificial" function one for the other (1972:370).

Girard maintains that we do not understand the role of ritual in simple societies because we do not understand the problem that vengeance constitutes for them, vengeance understood as the violent reciprocity of households or bands locked in a no-win vicious circle, each striving vainly to have "the last word" (1972:34). It is Girard's hypothetical *victime émissaire* who converts the vicious circle of mimetic rivalry into the vicious circle of ritual expulsions (1972:141). But the dynamics of vengeance is not done away with, but displaced. Banished from the sphere of intra-community relations, it returns "with a vengeance" to haunt (or to regulate) relations between communities. The eternal, seemingly pathological cycles of vengeance between certain human groups ought to be read, affirms Girard, as the obscure metaphor of each side's internal penchant for violence effectively projected outwards (1972:417).

In his superb study of feuding in Montenegro and other tribal societies, Christopher Boehm affirms that

those groups that develop a more effective means of controlling retaliatory homicide will have the better chance of surviving biologically and of continuing the same form of social organization.   [1987:230]

Whereas *osveta* or blood revenge was nothing less than the moral law governing relations between Montenegrin clans, it was simply unthinkable *within* a clan, since "a clan, by definition, could not owe itself blood" (1987:105). The same cultural logic obtains with every other group Boehm examines (1987:219). Feuding can only exist between groups with distinct identities and it functions to reinforce the same. The principles of mimetic alternation and one-upmanship are explicitly voiced in folk definitions of *osveta* (1987:51–63), and the same principles can be seen to structure an elaborate system of feuding rules that Boehm describes in terms of open-

ing moves, middle games, scorekeeping, and conflict management
(1987:91–142). Some insult to a group's "keen and compelling
sense of honor" typically sets the whole process in motion (1987:
103). Honor, understood as the collective property of a clan, is indeed the ideological smoke screen for blood feuds throughout the
nonliterate world (1987:219).

Where Girard posits a preconscious and automatistic victimage
mechanism as the structural core of feuding cycles, Boehm ex-
plores the sophisticated, pragmatic, and wholly lucid decisions of
tribal game-players and problem-solvers. They coincide in seeing
the control of violence as the foundation of the moral standards of
the community.

However they come about, and whatever the degree of reflexivity
attending to them, these cyclical and circular vendettas generate
vast bodies of folklore concerning the origin of the bloodletting,
the characteristics of the traditional foe, and, naturally, the superior virtue of the side one happens to be on. There are many studies
that deal with vengeance and feuding in relation to the oral traditions of "feudal" societies. Byock (1982) identifies feud as the
dominant form of social organization in medieval Iceland and in-
troduces the "feudeme" as the basic structuring unit of the sagas
that mirrored this social organization. Dorfman (1969) found that
all major and minor medieval French and Spanish epics derived
from a basic pattern of four "narremes"—the family quarrel, the
motive (insults, thefts, murders, inheritance struggles), the act of
treachery, and the punishment. In comparison with such studies of
feuding and verbal lore, the connection between feuding and festivals has been relatively neglected.

Medieval feuds constitute the ideal point of departure for analyzing the peculiarly combative character of festal rivalries in Spain
and, as will be seen, these ritualoid activities are inseparable from
the moral standards that hold sway inside the groups involved.

The Catalyst: Collective Honor

Vergüenza, translated inadequately as shame, stood at the heart of
the moral code of every feudal in-group. Caro adduces from an ex-

amination of medieval laws and customs that *vergüenza* included
everything from respect for parents, elders, kings, and laws to modesty, honesty, and piety (1964:415–417). The internal *vergüenza* of
an in-group was a necessary condition for obtaining honor—but
not a sufficient one, for in the decidedly un-Christian ethos of medieval Christian society, honor was something that was best obtained with sword in hand. Moreover, honor was not an individual
but a collective affair, the stakes in an ongoing competition between households or blood lines, each striving to be worth more
(*valer más*) than the other. "In a society erected upon this base,"
observes Caro, "there is constant and obsessive struggle to obtain
whatever 'honors' that exist, which later become the hereditary as-
sets of a lineage" (1964:420). Unfortunately, ignominy is just as hereditary, and leads inexorably into the vicious circle of *venganza*
(vengeance), with agnates and their allies anxious to launder their
good name whenever and wherever it has been affronted. Once polluted by dishonor, blood can only be washed with blood.

Thus, competition for honors in warfare and honor-motivated
cycles of revenge comprised the two sides of a single coin of mimetic rivalry, as well as the fecund source of epics, legends, ballads,
and the novels of chivalry that remained popular in Spain long after
their demise in other parts of Europe. During centuries of struggle
with the Moorish lineages to the south and east, Spain's Christian
clans competed for distinctions on the battlefield. These honors
were obtained in a relatively objective manner: there was no better
way to prove the value of your blood than by spilling that of the
enemy. Once territories had been reconquered, feudal families
settled down to form a relatively stable society of feuding families
that were jealous of their honor, touchy on questions of privilege,
and perennially engaged in tournaments, hunts, and judicial disputes. Sarasa Sánchez (1981) has argued that all these "rites," including the vengeance cycles, functioned to maintain the aristocratic
"myth" of honor and blood superiority vis-à-vis the other estates of
the medieval social pyramid. That disputes among groups can form
a ritualoid system that ultimately consolidates all of them as a
caste apart may seem paradoxical but accords entirely with the
logic of sociocentrism I discussed in Chapter One.

Between 1480 and 1530, however, the old rustic honor feuds lost

their relevance under increasingly powerful monarchs who be-
stowed "honors" for specific services rendered. Rivalry continued
and was even exacerbated in the new cortesan and bureaucratic environment, but the result was a slow, irreversible decay of both the
group solidarity that had characterized the feuding families of old
and the moral basis of that solidarity. "A ferocious individualism
seems to have seized men towards the end of the Middle Ages,"
writes Caro (1964:424). Fathers began to struggle with their own
sons, brothers with their own brothers, each convinced of his own
superior "worth" (1964:424–426). The stage was now set for the
appearance of nasty characters like Don Juan who acted out their
criminal fantasies against the backdrop of a godless, free-floating
brand of "honor" that was more of a curse than a boon. By the beginning of the seventeenth century, the aristocratic honor code was
literally beyond good and evil, no longer a question of morality but
of unbridled ambition and envy. Bennassar asserts that the obsession with honor served to maintain a permanent atmosphere of
violence in many Spanish provinces—and over a period of centuries (1985:206–209).

The link that was gradually forged between honor and blood-
purity was to have far graver consequences for Spain than the sexual misconduct of Golden Age rakes. The blood of the noblest
families could be besmirched if it were revealed that some distant
ancestor had been a *cristiano nuevo* (Jew converted to Catholicism) or, even worse, a *judaizante* (relapsed convert). For those
who possessed it, wealth eventually became the universal solvent,
capable of washing or concealing the stains of public or private *vergüenza* and of buying any new honors or offices placed in circulation
(Caro 1964:432–440; Bennassar 1985:200–204).

The final paradox in the ideological evolution of honor was to be
the rehabilitation of the very class of people who had never waged
an ostentatious feud, never distinguished themselves on any
battlefield, never enjoyed the prestige of wealth, and who had never
(this was the crux) incurred suspicion of racial impurity: the folk.
The majority of the population, in other words, the peasants, the
laborers, and the villagers, eventually came to be thought of as the
ultimate reservoir of an old-fashioned concept of honor that had
everything to do with God-given integrity and nothing to do with
worldly status-seeking.

Caro emphasizes two aspects of this vindication of the once-despised *villano*. To begin with, the corpus of proverbs known as the *refranero* demonstrates that Spain's peasants had never abandoned the basic virtues of prudence, modesty, and piety and had seldom been taken in by the vanity of the "honors" that their social betters competed for (1964:427–428). Secondly, this critical or "corrosive" quality of the folk idea of honor was most powerful when it assumed collective form, when an entire town acted in unison to defend its group honor against the affronts of some aristocratic "villain" (1964:442). Some of the best known works of Spain's Golden Age theatre dramatize such exercises in popular solidarity.

It goes without saying that strong sentiments of collective honor can have extremely negative side-effects for those who do not belong to the honorable collectivity—outsiders, minority groups, etc. Popular pride can lead to the popular terrorism I will discuss at length in Chapter Four. But the crucial point is this: we obtain a true picture of the nature and effects of the Spanish "honor code" when said code is reinserted in its natural context of group self-definition vis-à-vis another group.

Though modern studies of honor in Spain and other Mediterranean countries acknowledge that it is a collective value, they typically focus on its implications for the individual members of a given community. Pitt-Rivers, for example, has investigated honor as a function of the sex role expectations for men and women in Andalusia (1979:41–82). Honor for most men, he asserts, is closely associated with valor, masculinity, and sexual potency. Honorable women are supposed to be timid, modest, and pure. Other values such as honesty and loyalty are not sex-specific (1979:44–48). The structural correlation between honor and shame that holds sway among the folk tends to break down among aristocrats and criminals, for whom honor is essentially a matter of innate or violently earned priority (1979:29). In any case, and in any social class, the readiness to recur to violence is the ultimate mainspring of a real man's honor (1979:27). David Gilmore argues that Pitt-Rivers has "overblown the combative element in Andalusian culture to the point of caricature" (1987:128); and other studies have questioned the extent to which women really behave as the "official" culture imagines they should (Brandes 1980:97–114; Juliano 1986:49–54). Be that as it may, Pitt-Rivers is at pains to show how honor constitutes the hermeneutic key to Andalusian social values and social interaction in general. The norm of courtesy, for example, helps everyone to save face in public no matter what they might think about each other in private (1979:42).

Nevertheless, there is a class of people to whom courtesy is commonly denied: the shameless. There are people whose dishonorable reputation has been demonstrated beyond the shadow of a doubt by their habitual shameless conduct: petty thefts, beggary, and promiscuity in the case of women. They are considered outside the moral boundaries and in this way are associated with Gypsies, who are considered shameless by nature. [1979: 42–43]

Considered by whom? Gypsies do not consider *themselves* to be shameless. In fact, the masculine and feminine ideals of honor and *vergüenza* that Pitt-Rivers isolates are strictly observed in Gypsy communities. When the limits of a group's courtesy are discovered to be the same as the limits of the group itself, it might well be asked which came first. Do Gypsies provoke fear and loathing because they are dishonorable or because they are Gypsies?

The sociocentric texts studied by Caro (1957), Velasco (1981), and others would seem to indicate that the values dear to an in-group are systematically defined as what the out-group lacks, any out-group, be it the minority confined to a certain neighborhood or the entire population of a nearby town. Earlier I mentioned the satirical couplets that local clients of one patron saint use to mock those of another. The supposed amorality of the other community is an equally ubiquitous theme. Quite simply, the men of a neighboring village are portrayed as thieves and their women as whores—always in an aesthetically pleasing, easy-to-remember formula:

Alba de Tormes,	Alba de Tormes,
baja de muros	low walls
y alta de torres;	and high towers;
llena de putas	full of whores
y más de ladrones;	and of thieves even more;
mira tu capa	watch out for your cape
dónde la pones,	wherever you leave it,
que padres e hijos	for the fathers and sons
todos son ladrones.	are all thieves.

Or:

Badajoz,	Badajoz,
tierra de Dios,	God's country,
échase uno,	one lies down,
se levantan dos,	two get up,
y andan los cornudos	and the cuckolds
de dos en dos.	go around in couples.
[Caro 1957:285–286]	

Just as *vergüenza* was the necessary but insufficient condition for honor among the feuding feudal families discussed earlier, moral standards are safeguarded in contemporary rural communities as the precondition for their collective honor. How the moral code gets established in the first place is another matter. But it is clear that there is no honor without *vergüenza* and no prestige without honor. And here is where the local saint or Virgin or Christ comes into the picture once again: the good name of a town is inextricably linked to the good name of its exclusive supernatural benefactor—inside an inter-town competitive framework that in turn fits into the structure of ritual reciprocity of the church-year calendar. The patronal festival is the best means a town has for "showing off"—not only the intense nature of its piety and the heavenly favor it enjoys, but also the visible signs of that favor (its agricultural products, its artisans, its young men and women, and its general prosperity). This showing off is for:

1) domestic consumption—the community reinforces its singularity;
2) domestic status-seeking—different subgroups rival each other during fiesta time to establish which is more devout, more daring or athletic, more modern, more traditional, etc.; and
3) intercommunity status-seeking—hospitality is a prime value in rural Spain and fiestas are the prime context for exhibiting prestigious, potlatch-like generosity (Maldonado 1975: 285–287).

Hence, individual status-striving is cannily channeled into a redistributive ethic of hospitality. Ritualized rivalry mimics mimesis, transforming acquisitiveness into expenditure.

With the exception of Caro Baroja, anthropologists and literary scholars have tended to see group honor as a sort of allegorical extension of individual honor, when in fact the first is the historical and the structural origin of the second. Honor is a collective concept whose collective uses control the personal ones as long as an overall ritual framework remains intact—be it feuding or fiestas. When one overlooks the group aspects of honor, one overlooks the group control of honor's excesses.

Fiestas attract outsiders, especially *fiestas mayores* (those held on or near the feast day of the supernatural protector). They constitute ritual recognition of a basic fact of life: no town is an island. Communities need each other's goods and services as much as they need to feel, each in its own way, "the center of the moral universe" (Caro 1976:119). The exoteric denunciation of another town's "thieves" and "whores" only makes sense in terms of a system of commercial and matrimonial exchange, while the esoteric glorification of local saints integrates itself into the ongoing comparative system of patronal festivals (Velasco 1981:93–94, 102–103). Velasco has formulated a "principle of noncoincidence" that accounts for the order in which fiestas are held in a given regional subculture, since detailed field studies reveal that neighboring towns never hold their celebrations on the same day—even (or especially) during the summer months when the overall temporal distribution of *fiestas mayores* reaches its peak (1982:16–17). This unconscious logic of complementarity is wholly compatible with the logic of sociocentrism:

Non-coincidence makes possible a movement of people from one town to another with the intention, precisely, of participating in the fiestas, which turn into authentic contexts that favor friendships or inter-community marriages or activate confrontations and dissensions that wind up delineating two groups: the locals and the strangers.   [1982:18]

Smith points out that "the festival is often the context for the other genres of folklore" and therefore constitutes "a major class of folklore, one that may include within itself almost all the others as subclasses" (Smith 1972:168). Since these subclasses of folklore (dance, drama, costume, music, etc.) are each in its own measure an expression of the community's "will to differentiate," it would be appropriate to regard the fiesta as a kind of supersociocentric text. And one that cannot be considered apart from an "intertextual" system of comparison-rivalry-cooperation.

Fiestas promote the sort of displacement found in feuds, the mutually advantageous, ritualoid reciprocity that does so much for the inner unity of the bands involved. Some fiestas are even the collective creation of several towns and serve as the agreed upon context for both peaceful discussion of differences and out-and-out exchanges of fisticuffs (Lisón 1980 : 94 – 100). An example: Every summer, the people of a dozen villages that share common pasture land (and therefore common concerns) in the Sierra de Alava, Basque Country, gather at a shrine in honor of the Holy Trinity.

At the sanctuary, each town first hears Mass, celebrated by its own priest; but the morning ends with a solemn Mass attended by all. It is the day of fraternity among the towns of the Sierra. The food and the country-style festivities contribute to reinforce bonds of unity. Nevertheless, the ritual has a surprise in store. On the next day, the young men of the Sierra get together in the same place as the previous day's confraternity, next to the sanctuary, where they divide into bands and settle their differences with blows. In this way they practice a cultural canalization of disorder, its regulation and control, inasmuch as the very real aggression is mediated by rules which confer upon it a certain sporting character.   [Lisón 1980:96]

Just as individual status-seeking is governed and directed into productive channels by festal hospitality, festal feuding keeps individualistic "honor" within bounds. It is more than likely that each young Basque subscribes to the canons of virile, valiant honor that Pitt-Rivers or San Román find among male Andalusians or Gypsies; nevertheless, he does not fight in his own name but as a member of his group. Collective pride is the sustaining force in ritualized rivalry of all kinds, in regular and regulating systems of reciprocal one-upmanship among similar-sized groups of any geographical or ethnic provenance.

Don Juan is not, therefore, a trustworthy paradigm of honor in Spain, but of something else, some malady akin to the metaphysical desire that seizes the characters of certain novels (Girard 1961). In the final analysis, Don Juan cuts a pathetically comic figure in his obsessive urge to "dishonor" young women and their families. What prevents the folk ideology of honor from becoming "literary" in this sense are its firm links with the group's moral code on the one hand and the prestige of its patron saint on the other. These links guarantee that any outburst of violence will be a matter of consensus, not caprice.

As Lisón points out, it is a methodological error to speak of the ethnocentrism of Iberian communities without referring in the same breath to their many rituals of integration (1980:99–100). To harp upon the Spaniard's exaggerated sense of honor without mentioning Spanish culture's built-in controls is to make a similar mistake. Not individualism, but sociocentrism, is the matrix of honor in Spain.

The Laws of Ritual Rivalry

Notwithstanding the awesome variety of ritual and ritualoid confrontations that animate fiestas in Spain, a number of basic patterns can be distinguished. A brief survey of these patterns, whose generality moves me to express as a set of informal "laws," will serve as an introduction to *moros y cristianos*—the curious and extraordinarily widespread dance/drama/fiesta that reenacts the greatest feud in Spanish history.

The "law of parallel size" can be formulated first. For antipathy between groups to achieve ritual manifestation, the groups involved must be of approximately the same social, economic, or demographic importance (Caro 1957:279). In Navarre, for instance, the town of Vera considers itself to be the rival of Lesaca, but not of Echalar, Yanci, or Aranaz—these letter being too small to incite competitive feelings. Vera itself is further subdivided into two similar-sized neighborhoods that replicate the inter-town rivalry on a scale that is not necessarily less intense (Caro 1957:276–277). This law can be extended to include the many communities whose members celebrate the fiesta by dividing into two groups based on sex or into married and single individuals of the same sex.

The second law, which will come as no surprise to the reader, holds that religious symbols will be the dominant vehicle of these parallel confrontations. In Almonáster (Córdoba), the festival of the Holy Cross brings out the latent rivalries between the "rich" neighborhood of El Llano and the "poor" one of La Fuente. In reality the

economic disparities are slight compared to the "will to differentiate" of each *barrio*. The opposition is essentially ceremonial,
hereditary through matrilineal ascription, and entirely directed towards the construction and decoration of a cross. In nearby Bonares,
no fewer than twelve crosses vie with one another in representation
of the twelve streets of that locality (Rodríguez Becerra 1985 : 127–
128). In the famous *"Pinochada"* of Vinuesa (Soria), the ritual war
that pits women against men has a sixteenth-century icon of the
Virgin as its ostensible bone of contention (Caro 1984a: 237–240).
In the city of Huete (Cuenca), the traditional antagonism between
the *barrios* of Atienza and San Gil is magnified and sanctified in
their respective cults of saints. The residents of the first neighborhood are known as *juanistas*, since their patron is San Juan, while
the others are called *quiterios* owing to their devotion to Santa
Quiteria. The feast day of the saint (May 6th or May 22nd) constitutes an authentic explosion of group honor and self-affirmation for
his or her protégés. And here there is no ritual integration à la
Lisón, either; no one even goes to see the rival group's fiesta. Outsiders who have gone to both fiestas have discovered that the participants dress in the same way, sing the same *loas* in honor of their
patron (with the appropriate substitutions), and dance the same
galopeos—with one variation: *juanistas* dance with their arms up
in the air, *quiterios* with arms down. The sense of singularity that
blooms in May is of the perennial type, to the point that until re-
cently no female *juanista* was permitted to marry a male *quiterio*
and vice-versa. Historians disagree as to the original cause of
Huete's festal endogamy. Some say that during the *Reconquista*
the *barrio* of Atienza came to be populated by Jews and that of San
Gil by *moriscos*. Others trace the problem to the Jesuits and
Franciscans who settled in one neighborhood or the other and gradually infused their own rivalry into the people (González Casarrubios 1985 : 81–85; Caro 1957 : 279).

The third law holds that ritual rivalry leads to better fiestas. The
fiesta of the *Cristo de la Salud* discussed earlier provides a clear
example: one year's festal managers challenge their successors to
do better, and they do (Sanmartín Arce 1982 : 65). It is doubtful that
the crosses fabricated in great secrecy by the people of Almonáster
or Bonares would be so lavishly baroque without the spur of com-

petition (Rodríguez Becerra 1985 : 126). In his study of Andalusian fiestas, Rodríguez Becerra finds that the ones organized by municipal authorities are invariably surpassed in popular enthusiasm, funds raised, and general brilliance by those organized by rival confraternities (1985 : 83). Honor is at stake in every case, the collective honor that knows no sharper inducement than competition and no fitter showcase than the local religious festival.

The fourth general rule follows from a consideration of the first three and their exemplifications: ritual rivalry can be an end in itself. Lisón is surprised to find that even the tiniest hamlets find some motive for division at fiesta time (1983 : 78–79). History of a more-or-less legendary variety is usually brought into action to explain the origins of a particular manifestation of ceremonial feuding (Caro 1957 : 278), but the prevalence of such behaviors and their tenacity can hardly be attributed to blind automatism nor to "objective" differences in the groups involved. Nothing might seem more arbitrary than the spectacle of *juanistas* dancing hands-up and *quiterios* dancing hands-down, but arbitrariness is in the eye of the beholder, not the participant, for whom such details could not be more significant. All of which suggests that the consciousness of opposition itself must be psychologically satisfying. And if this is so, it matters little if the festal competitions end in a stand-off, in the real or token victory of one side over another, or in the happy unicity of ritual integration. In any case there is de facto unanimity, since 1) groups mutually agree on the object to be contended for (the sacred icon, top honors in the cross contest, etc.), or, 2) where there is no object, the structure of rivalry itself constitutes the tacit agreement (the endogamous *barrios* of Huete).

The set of laws outlined above can be seen in action over the entire spectrum of Spanish fiestas. In addition, they help to account for the transformations that mainly rural fiestas undergo in an urban milieu and how, over the years and especially during periods of industrialization, certain manifestations of popular piety retain the power to consolidate a group's identity—even when group and identity have changed drastically. This is no small task. It is a gaping leap from the country masquerades where as few as five villagers hold the fiesta for themselves (Caro 1963 : 294) to the present-day *Romería del Rocío*, which was attended in 1985 by nearly a million people (*El País*, 31 May 1985, p. 14). Can one speak responsibly of a traditional religious fiesta with such multitudes? Certainly not in the traditional sense of the word "traditional," whose inadequacies were reviewed and condemned earlier. Patterned sociocentric competition, however, can theoretically take in ever larger numbers of people through the selective manipulation of the identity signs that orient their antagonism. Herein lies the advantage of this concept over other festal elements scholars have specified—sacred time, yearning for paradise, mystical transgression, or deity archetypes (Leach, Eliade, Bataille, Durand). These may not be so durable and may not survive the rural-urban transit with the same vigor as the flexible laws of ritual rivalry. At least this is what I hope to demonstrate by recourse to one of Spain's archetypal festal events.

Moros y Cristianos

"*Moros y cristianos*" is the generic name given to the main activity of the *fiestas mayores* in hundreds of towns or cities in Valencia, Andalusia, Aragón, both Castilles, and Galicia (in descending order of ubiquity). It flourishes in both isolated mountain villages and burgeoning industrial centers. It is a curious blend of piety, patriotism, and popular theatre, and there is always a literary text that structures or at least accompanies the festal text. The plot is remarkably uniform from place to place: people playing the part of Moorish soldiers conquer the Christian fort or castle (erected for the purpose in the town plaza) on one day, and on the following the Christians counterattack and "reconquer" the disputed territory. The genesis of *moros y cristianos* has little to do with the real *Reconquista*, however. The ritualized confrontations may be remotely derived from the rhythmic military maneuvers of mercenary Swiss pikemen of the sixteenth century, and are certainly connected to the *soldadescas* of the seventeenth and eighteenth (Caro 1984a: 116–117). These paramilitary brotherhoods, often divided into rival "companies," were originally organized to parade in the processions of Holy Week, Corpus Christi, or All Souls' Day. They eventually degenerated into little more than roving bands of drunkards armed with swords and ear-rending drums—so goes the contemporary calumny—and were finally outlawed (Ramírez Rodrigo

1985 : 360–361). Their more respectable Golden Age counterparts, dancers with the moral and nationalistic theme of Christians against Moors, were enormously popular and usually hired themselves out for the baptisms, weddings, and birthday parties of the aristocracy (Caro 1984a : 131–138).

These factors help to explain why, unlike representations of the Passion or the Nativity, *moros y cristianos* is an intemporal, freefloating affair that can become attached to any fiesta, including the *romería*, under any sort of advocation (González Casarrubios 1985 : 155). What remains to be explained is the intensity of the identity symbolism that anchors the *moros y cristianos* drama in a particular community on a particular date. The real "star of the show," as it turns out, is the local patron saint, and the aggression of the invaders is typically motivated by their desire to capture his or her miraculous icon. Larrea Palacín underlines this aspect in support of his argument that *moros y cristianos* constitutes religious theatre with a pre-Christian ideology, harking back to the days when every town had its genius loci and the conquest of the town meant the conquest of its god (1968 : 348–349). In keeping with the perennial Spanish tendency to identify the *patria* (fatherland) with the *patria chica* (home town), even the great Santiago was often supplanted in his Moor-killing duties by local warrior saints and their cults (Mijares 1968 : 221–225).

In referring to the rapid proliferation of popular plays featuring Christians and Moors during the Golden Age, Carrasco Urgoiti describes the manner in which the motif of the sacred icon came to be inseparably welded to the theme of the loss and recovery of the *patria chica* (1963 : 487–490). In contrast to those who criticize the plays for their alleged deprecatory attitudes toward Moslems, Carrasco finds that in the majority of cases a traditional script's glorification of the Christian band does not involve contempt for the Moorish one (the actors are all Christians in any case). Rather, the Moors are portrayed in the festal and literary texts as noble warriors who simply do not possess an authentic mode of supernatural protection.

They loyally served and commended themselves to Allah and the Prophet, whose protection failed them; then, in the acid test of a military encounter, the fallaciousness of their beliefs is definitively demonstrated vis-à-vis the truth of the Christian faith.   [1963:477]

The utilitarian criteria whereby authenticity=efficacy is very much in keeping with the religious cosmovision of peasant communities (Wolf 1966:101), which in turn represents a primary form of socio-centric thought. At the conclusion of the festal battles, the baptism of the Moorish general (or king or captain) and his troops ritually integrates them into the one true in-group and completes the moral/patriotic lesson of the drama. But military victory is not the exclusive way to demonstrate that the Christians have God on their side. In Maqueda (Toledo), fierce fighting gives way to a dialogue between the Christian and Moslem kings, who agree to throw dice for possession of the Virgin. Not luck, of course, but divine providence wins the appropriately named Virgin of the Dies for the Christians and brings about the conversion of their foes (González Casarrubios 1985:153–155).

In the core or nucleus of *moros y cristianos* can be found the by now familiar elements of cathartic expulsion, sacrificial evocation of enemy horizon, and ritualized combats centered on fetishistic possession of some mana-laden icon. The script used to organize the folk drama and program the timing of the Moorish attack, Christian retreat, Christian counterattack, and Moorish capitulation, largely made up of stylized orations, parleys, and posturings, represents an initial layer or "ring" of development. The scripts themselves are veritable conglomerates of older and newer phases that reflect both the core phenomena and the collaboration of more educated segments of the local populace, sometimes over many generations.

The versification and style of the parleys usually reflect the literary tone of a given epoch, as well as diverse examples, superimposed as if in tiers, of the poetic modalities that have succeeded one another since the twilight of the Golden Age up until Modernism.   [Carrasco 1963:477]

Other rings of an historical nature superimpose themselves upon these literary accretions. For example, many of the *comparsas* or companies that participate in the fiestas under the Christian banner derive from the civil wars of the nineteenth century that divided the nation into Liberal and Absolutist factions (Lisón 1980: 147–148). Such anachronisms, which seem to trouble no one, provide further evidence of the ongoing creative process that consciously or unconsciously instills fresh relevance into the most "traditional" cultural artifacts.

The rings of political, military, and literary history have now been augmented by others that reflect Spain's phenomenal economic development. The industrious cities of eastern and southern Spain have thrived, and new *comparsas* have obliged the older ones to make room for newly prosperous societal components. In some cities the festal budget runs into the millions of dollars (Sanmartín Arce 1982:53). *Moros y cristianos* as it exists today faithfully mirrors modern class divisions, hierarchies, and current styles of conspicuous consumption. During the festal period—which now comprises a complex series of dances, dinners, benefits, concerts, private parties and public parades—the members of different *comparsas* rival each other in a free-spending, potlatch-like jockeying for social position. Family preferences for or attachments to a particular *comparsa* are strong and durable; the "desertion" of some son to a company other than the one his forefathers served in can provoke genuine family crises (Lisón 1980:150–152). The four laws of ritual confrontation that I outlined above are strikingly borne out: two mock armies of parallel size, each drawn up into parallel-sized mock regiments, rival each other via religious symbols to concoct opulent celebrations that express and maintain a satisfying sensation of symmetrical difference.

It would appear that in most places the fiesta is no longer "about" the superior magical efficacy of the local patron saint or the reassertion of an in-group's moral standards through the ritual expulsion of an out-group. This sacrificial element in the festal drama of *moros y cristianos* may seem a mere holdover or survival from a more rustic or emotionally primary phase. Nevertheless, an examination of the fiesta in its current spectacular guise—especially in cities like Alcoi (Alicante)—reveals that the inner dynamics of sociocentrism has not been supplanted but reinforced. The in-group/out-group battle lines are now drawn up not only between Christians and Moors but also inside the two great camps. Prosperity and urbanization do not bring acquisitve rivalry to an end—

they amplify its scope. The "enemy horizon" is still there in the neighbor to impress, the colleague to outspend, the competitor to outshine. If one Moorish *comparsa* hires a camel, another must rent an elephant, and another two elephants, and so on. There are still "differences" to settle, as in the case of Alava's *romería*/boxing match or Huete's *juanistas* and *quiterios*. Group identity, self-esteem, and "honor" are still at stake. The groups involved in the staging of *moros y cristianos* have become quite diversified but so have the ceremonies and symbols that mediate their status-striving. Sanmartín Arce contrasts the sensual elegance of the Moors, as shown by their clothing, banners, animals, and music, with the austere militarism of the Christians and their accoutrements; but the ultimate significance of these opposed value systems lies not in the victory of one over another but in "the recreation of their mutual dependence" (1982:58). Here is one more confirmation that rivalry is its own reward, as stipulated by law #4.

Moros y cristianos is really not "about" Moors and Christians, it is about the ritual canalization of group honor. It has always been about that. To paraphrase a Spanish proverb, the old wine of sociocentrism has ended up filling the new wineskins of spectacular urban festivals. And, just as the jousting tournaments and feuds of the medieval nobility cemented the collective prestige of their estate, the festal ritualization of social rivalries under the colorful banners of Christians and Moors ultimately functions to consolidate the pride of the whole city in its genius loci.

The common denominator of war, feuding, festal rivalry, and the expressive culture they generate is the principle of mimetic reciprocity. Having overcome an initial identity crisis, the praxis of ritualized rivalry enables the logic of sociocentrism to proceed in dialectic fashion, cannily uniting (often by subdividing) ever-larger in-groups vis-à-vis ever larger or more distant or more abstract out-groups. But there is another great principle that is equally vital for understanding piety and violence in Spain. Caro carefully distinguishes the cases of local antipathies that are governed by parallel or evenly matched oppugnancy from those that reflect a one-sided attitude of prejudice or scorn (1957:278). In order to account for the origins of this unrequited variety of collective antagonism, which has been at least as productive for Spanish folklore as the reciprocal variety, we must return to the initial matrix of crisis. Events as disparate as natural catastrophes, prolonged famines, invasions, or some form of acute culture shock can provoke such levels of anxiety that the unifying or cumulative dialectic of ritual becomes unequal to its task. Intestine rivalries escalate, envy and spite give way to fear and loathing, and an episode of difference-settling violence becomes likely. Thus far I have dealt with the creative aspects of symmetrical violence; the mythogenetic power of asymmetric violence remains to be discussed.

4

Folklore and Persecution

In dealing with persecutions and the lore they produce, point of view is everything. The logic of sociocentrism aims at enhancing a group's notion of its own worth and rectitude; it will permit the group to feel persecuted, but hardly to see itself as persecutory. Traditional narratives like the lives of the martyred saints reveal an in-group consolidating itself in spite of, and sometimes because of, the unjust and vicious persecutors of an out-group. Yet we have no record of a Roman narration celebrating the inglorious murder of innocent scapegoats; the closest thing we have is the account by Tacitus of Nero's politically expedient decision to blame the Christians for the fire of Rome (*Annals*, 15.44). But Tacitus hardly considers the Christians to be innocent victims, but "criminals who deserved extreme and exemplary punishment" in general, since they possessed "a most mischievous superstition" (Kagan 1975: 362). This suggests that any folk legend told from the perspective of a victimizing in-group would probably portray events in a way that would obliterate any hint of wrongdoing on its part. What the folklore of the victims might describe and elaborate as an unjust persecution would logically be depicted as an entirely legitimate and even necessary act from the viewpoint of the victimizers.

For René Girard, the expressive culture of certain periods of European history abounds in examples of disguised or "mystified" persecution; the (mis)representations, furthermore, conform to a standard pattern (1978a:176–214; 1982:7–36). As defined by Girard, "persecution texts" are accounts of real acts of violence, either collective or possessed of collective resonances, that are drawn up from the perspective of the basically naive victimizers and consequently affected by characteristic distortions (1982:18). Hundreds of historical tracts, judicial chronicles, and folktales from the Middle Ages and the Renaissance describe "just" punishment meted out to culprits (usually Jews, Gypsies, or witches) whose heinous and unnatural crimes had brought about some catastrophic situation (plague, floods, crop failures, and so on). Standard histories of the Black Death or medieval Jewry normally include examples or citations of these accounts. When Girard first formulated his concept of persecution texts, he made it clear that oral texts are to be included in the definition (1978a:182).

Girard finds that these oral and written texts share four principal "stereotypes": 1) The first, and the one that puts the others in motion, is the presence of a social crisis whose causes vary but whose representation remains remarkably uniform; indeed, the crisis is one with *l'uniformisation* or *l'indifférenciation* (1982:25) that weakens institutions, threatens hierarchies, poisons families and friendships, and reduces society to a kind of Hobbesian war-of-all-against-all. 2) Terror seizes human groups so afflicted, who blindly assume, says Girard, that the strictest interdicts or taboos of society must have been violated in order to have provoked the catastrophe. The crisis that erases social and familial differences must have been caused—so runs the unconscious logic—by *crimes indifférenciateurs* of a violent, sexual, or religious nature (1982:26–27). The second stereotype includes any and all of the archetypal crimes that someone will be blamed with. 3) The third involves the process whereby the malignant party is identified. Any sort of ethnic, religious, or purely physical abnormality will do, and one trait will often reinforce another; what may only attract curiosity under normal conditions becomes a *signe victimaire* in times of acute stress (1978b:194–195; 1982:30–32). Girard emphasizes, however, that persecutors are not obsessed with eradicating difference. In keeping with the entire logic of the stereotyped crisis and the stereotyped crimes, fear is evoked by the specter of *non-différence* that emanates from those who do not differ as the

the conquered Christians to "keep the faith" during the centuries of Moslem occupation. Saint Eulogio was a ninth-century author of pious texts living in Al-Andalus (modern Andalusia). His major work, a *Liber apologeticus martyrum*, was designed to whip up anti-Islamic sentiment among the Mozarabic Christians of the south and strengthen the resolve of the Christian kings of the north. When the holy man's fervor aroused the ire of the collaborationist church hierarchy of Córdoba and led to his own martyrdom, his cult spread rapidly throughout the Peninsula (Sáinz Rodríguez 1980:341).

Spanish history offers repeated and instructive examples of the way in which consciousness of victimization reinforces a militant brand of Christianity. New opportunities for heroic martyrdom were provided by the Turkish domination of the Mediterranean in the seventeenth century and the subsequent activities of North African pirates and slave traders. Thousands of Spanish Christians were captured on the high seas and shipped off to Algeria or other countries to await ransom. An enormously popular oral/literary tradition grew out of these historical vicissitudes—*romances de cautivos*—cultivated assiduously by blind beggar poets well into the nineteenth century (Caro 1969:89–94; Marco 1977:II, 389–430). As Marco has pointed out, the frontiers between these novelesque ballads and diverse genres of Spanish religious folklore are often imperceptible (1977:II, 419). He himself divides the ballads into "religious" and "romantic" categories, with the miraculous intercession of a saint, Virgin, or Christ as the distinguishing motif of the first and amorous entanglements between captors and captives as the plot frame of the second (1977:II, 393–394). But martyrdom is the standard dénouement of both varieties.

Incitements to abandon their own God for Allah and the sexual overtures of the "Turk" or the Moorish princess comprise the functionally equivalent occasions of sin Christians face in these *romances de cautivos*. But in the finest tradition of the medieval martyrologies, Spanish men and women evince a fierce appetite for suffering that is more than a match for the sadistic tortures devised by their captors. A personage known as Blas of León, a former outlaw and swashbuckler-at-large, decides to die for Christ and manages to slay dozens of moros before he is caught and nailed to

members of the in-group do from one another (1982:36). Abnormal or nonstandard modes of differentiation threaten normal ones. 4) The fourth stereotype is the act of violence itself, depicted as the more-than-warranted slaughter or explusion of the contaminated and contaminating individual(s). It is not necessary for every persecution text to exhibit all four stereotypes; three and sometimes even two (1982:37) are enough for an objective "reader" to arrive at the conclusion that the violence was real, the original crisis was real, the crimes were not really committed, and their supposed perpetrators were innocent possessors of some difference that the community-at-large found menacing.

The first of Girard's four stereotypes is in harmony with the many studies that posit crisis as the necessary precondition for the flowering of vehement varieties of sociocentric defining symbolism (e.g., Cohn 1961, Kluckhohn 1966, La Barre 1972, Lisón 1983). The second and third reflect the important role played in the persecutory process by folklore—folk beliefs, to be exact, regarding the evil deeds of an isolated out-group and the mystical danger of things abnormal. The early Christians had been accused of sacrilege, black magic, incest, infanticide, and cannibalism (Lebreton and Zeiller 1975). The same accusations, along with well-poisoning, crucifix-flogging, and the vague but all-inclusive charge of "evil eye," triggered many a medieval lynching (Caro 1970b:65–70; Königshofen 1972; Trachtenberg 1983 [1943]:1–7). Barre Toelken speaks of recurrent or "multivalent" folk ideas that serve similar functions in any generic guise they happen to assume; the youngster-mutilated-by-feared-minority theme drifts from legend to rumor to song to novel to narrative ballad with surprising ease and still serves to whip up in-group resentment from Russia to Salt Lake City (1979: 176–179). The manner in which culprits have been identified through the ages is as standardized as the crimes attributed to them. Anomalous events and persons seem to share an *odeur* of mystical danger (Lewis 1976:108). "Look out for those marked by God" runs an old German proverb cited by Krappe in his classic discussion of the abnormal in folk belief (1929:204–211). Crisis intensifies this intolerance of the anomalous and the conviction that the hated minority group must somehow be in touch with malevolent supernatural powers. This is the phenomenon Trachtenberg studies in relation to medieval anti-Semitism. Plagues, social unrest, and the advance of Islam during the post-Crusade period contributed to Christendom's siege mentality and the result was an identification of the Jew with the devil. What Girard calls "victimage signs" were even interchanged between one and the other: Satan was often pictured with grotesquely overdone semitic features and certain Jews were forced to wear devil badges (Trachtenberg 1983:26 et passim). All of these fears, folk beliefs, and hasty conclusions combined to produce massacres whose pertinence for twentieth-century history is not open to dispute. Taken all together, the four stereotypes narrate how an in-group solved or tried to solve an identity crisis by force. Henceforth the in-group's absolutist criteria regarding acceptable ways to be different will not be exposed to the threatening relativism represented by other differentiating systems (Girard 1982:34–36). Like the miraculous legends of wartime, persecution texts manifest a fear-assuaging illusion against a background of violent crisis.

Girard provides a technique for the interpretation of folk legends that recount/transfigure a persecution from the viewpoint of those who carried it out or their sympathizers. These texts of disguised persecution can be distinguished from the saints' legends and martyrologies that contain hundreds of texts of undisguised persecution. The latter, to follow Girard's line of thought, feature a scapegoat *theme*; the former are influenced by the same scapegoating *mechanism* that structures the persecution itself without letting it be perceived as such by the perpetrators (1982:74–76). To refer to some narrative as a text of disguised persecution does not imply that the disguise was deliberately fabricated by the members of the violent in-group. Nor should what I term texts of undisguised persecution imply that such narratives do not hyperbolize and even fictionalize their subject matter. Both varieties confirm that self-justification is the first goal of sociocentric lore. We are not a panic-stricken mob of murderers but the valiant defenders of morality and the public good. Or, conversely, we are not a motley crew of sorcerers and cannibals but the privileged confessors of the one true God. "Oh, how great the glory of the ruler who should bring to light some Christian who had devoured a hundred infants!" as Tertullian sarcastically exclaimed (*Apologeticus*, 2.4; Guinagh and Dorjahn 1942:774).

Chapter 4

Martyrological Mythopoesis

That consciousness of victimization can even surpass pers naïveté as a generator of folklore is demonstrated by the ma dreds of legends that recount the words, deeds, suffering, a tyrdom of the early Christians and the huge body of Europ religious lore and festivals that has grown up around the laruelle 1975, Maldonado 1979). Attwater observes that

a high degree of authenticity and historical interest is a rather rare in the huge whole of earlier hagiographical literature; instead myth, folklore, legend, and romantic and "edifying" fiction. [196

The first people popularly recognized as saints were alway tyrs (Attwater 1965:8–9; Caro 1979:170–172), individuals s vinced of the moral superiority of their in-group's cult symb that they were willing to die for it. And when they did, th came magnetic badges of belonging for the surviving memb the in-group. The saints were the authentic "culture heroes" early Church; in glorifying them the early Christians exalted own difference and cemented their group identity. Success tually enabled them to stamp their point of view on Western ture in general.

Iberian martyrologies epitomize the transformations under by the Church during the decline and fall of the Roman Empire original humility of the followers of Christ evolves into ma self-righteousness. Spanish martyrs as presented by tradition cally confront their judges with sarcasm, threats, and insults (S Rodríguez 1980:308–317). The women who suffer tortures death are every bit as belligerent as their brothers. Saint Vict for example, who by all lights was a psychocultural fantasy of tenth century, invites her persecutor to do his worst, branding "filthy spirit" and "worm" (1980:309–312). After surviving tempts to bake, drown, and crush her—wherein exactly 1,540 gans are slain as a divinely sanctioned side effect—the sain heroine has her tongue excised; she promptly picks it up and hu it in the prefect's face, thereby striking him blind (1980:314–31 The cult of martyrs was a highly effective tool in the early Chr tianization of Hispania and the example of new martyrs help

post; he finally succumbs after three days of preaching the Gospels (Marco 1977:II, 415–416). The Spaniards do not always meet such a tragic but edifying fate; liberation is often secured with the supernatural assistance of a "specialist" in the field of enslaved Christians—the *Virgen del Carmen,* the *Virgen de Utrera,* or *San Antonio de Padua* (1977:II, 409–412, 417–420). In this way, persecution and the cult of saints reinforce each other through the final years of the nineteenth century; the blood of the last Hispanic martyrs waters the tree of popular culture and fuels the truculent fantasies of the blind bards and their listeners.

A martyr is a hero for his own community and a criminal for another. The history of Christianity proves that today's martyrs can even become tomorrow's martyrizers. I wish to call attention to what the chronicles and legends of disguised and undisguised persecution have in common. They both exhibit, in their respective "folk work" processes, a clear tendency to vindicate, to exaggerate, and to invent. If the crimes attributed to the *culprit* are horrendous and fully deserving of exemplary punishment, the *victim* is reputed to have suffered a long series of incredibly sadistic torments— "a single one of which no human body could survive" (Attwater 1965:12). Miraculous occurrences abound in texts of both undisguised and disguised persecution, for God is invariably on the side of the in-group. Each in its own way, the essentially creative narrations of disguised and undisguised persecution serve the logic of sociocentrism in times of crisis. The persecutors' naive defense or rationalization of their actions is as much in consonance with the need to idealize in-group identity as the fanciful martyrologies discussed earlier. In view of all these coincidences, it might be proper to distinguish two subclasses of one overriding persecutory mythopoesis.

It need not be assumed, however, that the two varieties operate within their own watertight compartments. Given the general ingenuousness and even obtuseness of these intense forms of sociocentric thought, it comes as no surprise to find that a single text can exhibit both persecutory and martyrological motifs. One of the Spanish *romances de cautivos* may serve as an example: Sailing to Rome with a newly fashioned icon of Christ, thirty Christians are assaulted by Moorish pirates and carried off in chains to Algiers. A

"Jewish shoemaker" purchases one of the captives for a slave and the icon for a footstool, inflicting cruel abuse on both; when the Christian speaks out against this sacrilege he is sent to the dungeon for three years. Friars finally arrive and offer to ransom captives and Christ; the Jew demands the icon's weight in silver. But when the icon is put up on the scales—miracle of miracles—it weighs a mere ounce and a half. The Jew is thereby foiled and the joyful Christians set sail for Rome in the company of their astute icon (Marco 1977:II, 417–419). This pious ballad combines the archetypal accusations of image desecration and usury and the archetypal representative of a feared minority with the miraculous redemption of the long-suffering true believers. Undisguised but novelesque persecution cohabits with persecutory lore in one traditional text.

The Wandering Jew represents a more familiar example of the same phenomenon: another miserable Jewish shoemaker who somehow manages to provoke Christ into a momentary betrayal of His entire philosophy (cf. Hasan-Rokem and Dundes 1986). The rigor of divine retribution perplexes the Wandering Jew's imaginary interlocutors in the unpolished verses of a blind beggar poet in nineteenth-century Spain:

Creimos fuera mentira	We thought it was false
Que un castigo tan severo	That such severe punishment
Pudiera Dios a un viviente	Could God to a mortal
Aplicar por tanto tiempo.	Apply for so much time.
¿Qué crimen pues cometisteis?	What crime did you commit?
¿Qué pecado tan horrendo	What sin so horrendous
Para que el Dios de bondad	That the God of kindness
Así os haya condenado	Has condemned you thus
A recorrer sin descanso	To traverse without rest
La redondez de la tierra?	The whole world round?
[Marco 1977:I, 309]	

As is well known, the hapless shoemaker's unpardonable sin was his refusal to allow Christ to rest on his doorstep, burdened as He was with the cross. It is possible to relate the tale to others that dwell upon the notion of a deathless life and treat it as either a curse or a boon (Baring-Gould 1967 [1866]:28–30). But such comparisons miss the essential point: the Wandering Jew is shown no mercy by Christ for having shown no mercy to Christ, a spiteful, eye-for-an-eye reaction wholly alien to the spirit of the Gospels. In its stern simplicity, the legend of the Wandering Jew bespeaks Christianity's inability to maintain (the real) Christ's main message—forgiveness for all men and women, without exception. If the Paschal scapegoat scapegoats too, singling out a Jew for eternal punishment, then pious Christians can only heed His example, while simultaneously luxuriating in the pity they feel for an individual incapable of same.

In sum: Girard demonstrates how a text can reveal itself to be the product of persecutory mythopoesis even when it contains no reference whatever to "victims" or "scapegoats" but only to "criminals," "demons," or "Antichrists." I have enlarged the concept of persecutory mythopoesis to include the texts produced from the self-righteous victim's point of view and which effect functionally equivalent fabrications. Finally, both perspectives meld when the presence of a visible scapegoat theme in the text (the martyr, the captive Christian, the desecrated icon) ironically works to justify the punishment or curse meted out to a scapegoat disguised as a villain (the Turk, the Wandering Jew, or, as we will see, the wicked witch).

Projection, Polarization, and Magico-Persecutory Thought

It is specifically the definition of magic in *La Pensée sauvage* that prompts Girard to speak of *la pensée magico-persecutrice*. Magic, says Lévi-Strauss, does not imply a disdain for logical causality but an intransigent demand for it (1966:18). Girard does not take this demand as evidence of healthy curiosity or of a harmless classificatory instinct, for magic reasoning can take over wherever and whenever the group urgently needs to determine the cause of its afflictions in order to take effective countermeasures. It is in the scapegoat that the primal community finds its prime mover, its polysemic first cause. Magico-persecutory thought is thus "true," says Girard, in that it is the sole hypothesis possible within a closed pressure cooker of crisis, rivalry, violence, and victimage, but obviously false when this system is transcended (1982 : 80–83).

Thus, Girard postulates a somewhat indirect relationship between magical thinking and mythopoesis: the excessive need for causality that dominates the thought patterns of persecutors leads them into committing acts of violence that either through concurrent hallucinations or posterior reflection and rationalization give rise to warped mythic and mythico-ritual "interpretations" of the crisis and its violent outcome (1982 : 51–54). Even without the intermediate agency of an act of violence, however, magico-persecutory thought can still influence the construction of myths, rites, and beliefs. For if it is defined as the desire to identify one uniquely culpable party and punish his transgressions, as a kind of absolutist intolerance of ambiguity, or indeed as a defense system against the evil magic of others (1982 : 80), then Girard's magico-persecutory thought is strikingly similar to the processes of "projection" and "polarization" that certain psychoanalysts have discovered in myths and fairy tales.

Otto Rank, for example, argued that projection lies behind the attribution of murderous impulses to the father in myths of heroes' births; he pointed out "the intimate relationship between the hero myth and the delusional structure of paranoics" (1959 : 94). Bruno Bettelheim has underlined the normal and even necessary role played by projection in psychic maturation, since only personalities firmly grounded upon choice between clear differences will be able to handle the ambiguities of real life (1975 : 9). Thus,

When all the child's wishful thinking gets embodied in a good fairy; all his destructive wishes in an evil witch; all his fears in a voracious wolf; . . . all his jealous anger in some animal that pecks out the eyes of his archrivals— then the child can finally begin to sort out his contradictory tendencies. Once this starts, the child will be less and less engulfed by unmanageable chaos. [1975 : 66]

This sorting-out process normally involves, as we will all recall, the physical elimination of the character who incarnates the child's fears and destructive wishes. In the end, the wicked stepmothers, ogres, witches, usurpers, orality-obsessed wolves, and anal-sadistic trolls will all "get what's coming to them." And this is all to the good, says Bettelheim:

Consolation requires that the right order of the world be restored; this means punishment of the evildoer, tantamount to the elimination of evil from the hero's world—and then nothing stands any longer in the way of the hero's living happily ever after.   [1975:144]

Bettelheim's sympathetic analysis of the wholesome effects wrought in young minds by fairy-tale "persecutions" is in sharp contrast to Girard's whole approach. One has but to study groups of children, affirms Girard, to understand persecutory mythopoesis, inasmuch as children constitute exceptionally frank exponents of victimizing behavior vis-à-vis newcomers, outsiders, and the physically defective (1978a:171). The magico-persecutory thought that informs fairy tales is anything but wholesome; the wicked witch is a walking conglomerate of abnormal traits or victimage signs—she is hideous, she limps, she cackles, she is physically deformed and morally monstrous (1982:73).

To ask whether fairy tales should comprise a special category of persecution texts is not an idle question, bearing as it does on the issues of projection, polarization, and the venting of destructive wishes. Perhaps the subject is best considered in the light of another way in which projection can influence folkloric creativity without the intervening act of violence Girard posits. A standard textbook of psychoanalysis states that

the crimes and vices which we attribute to our enemies in times of war, the prejudices which we bear against strangers, against foreigners, or against those whose skins differ in color from our own, and many of our superstitious and religious beliefs are often wholly or in part the result of an unconscious projection of wishes and impulses of our own.   [Brenner 1974:92]

Here we have a compelling formula for the folklore and folk ideas about out-groups that in-groups employ to consolidate their identities. As I attempted to establish earlier, this "exoteric" lore often contributes to the exacerbation of social conflict that leads to bloodshed, especially the intra-community bloodshed of persecution. The second and third of Girard's own stereotypes testify to the important role played in the persecutory episode by folk beliefs (as seen in the archetypal crimes and victimage signs of the hated minority). Girard could hardly deny the existence of projection or a mechanism similar to it. Where he would most likely part company with the psychoanalysts is in the ultimate origin attributed to such a mechanism. The latter emphasize the appearance and psychic functioning of projection in the early years of life; Brenner cites three classic psychoanalytical studies that suggest

that the model for the psychological mechanism of separating some of one's thoughts or wishes from one's own mental life and projecting them into the outer world is the physical experience of defecation, which is familiar to the child from earliest infancy.   [1974:93]

Likewise, the "split images" and polarizations that Rank and Bettelheim find in myth or fairy tales are always employed to sort out conflicting drives within an individual psyche. But Girard's psychology is based entirely upon social mimesis. He disects mythic narratives as documents of social contradictions and conflicts, not internal psychic ones. His attention is drawn to what he calls *mimétisme primaire*, mimetic rivalry, and the mimetic propagation of hostilities and hallucinations during times of crisis. It must be pointed out, however, that this latter phenomenon has not been ignored by psychoanalytically minded researchers. La Barre's treatment of the subject (1972:53–57, 366–367) is evidence of a basic affinity between classic insights of Freudian psychology and Girard's social psychology of mimesis—divided as they are over the exact size of the group most relevant to human behavior (family or mob).

Girard would not negate the importance of polarization in mythic thought any more than he would negate the process of binary conflict mediation Lévi-Strauss has uncovered; but he would trace all these forms of symbolic differentiation in mythic thought to the anxieties of a group menaced by the "fearful symmetry of mimetic rivalry" (1978b:164)—not the anxieties of a child contemplating his feces or a Chaco Indian contemplating honey and ashes. Girard means to center the issue in the vital terrain of human groups whose very survival depends on their ability to *be* groups (i.e., discrete machines that project and differentiate).

Dualism of one kind or another is bound to show up in myths and tales—at the level of content or at the level of structure. Fischer affirms that conflicts or polarities will still be voiced or mediated even when there are no simplistic, clear-cut distinctions made between "good guys" and "bad guys" (1963:255). Girard makes the Lévi-Straussian meditation on difference and non-difference his own and tries to carry it one step further. Or one step back, rather, since he seeks to account for the very possibility of Lévi-Strauss's categories; he posits something prior to their infinite manipulation of symbols in kinship and mythological systems. Non-difference is not a mere logical ploy, but the prototypical crisis that precipitated the deployment of "civilization as we know it."

Caro Baroja and the Archetypes of Accusation

Spain has become a privileged source of information about the interaction of folklore and persecutory archetypes, thanks to a half-century of continuous research by Julio Caro Baroja. Caro has analyzed witch hunts from the thirteenth through the nineteenth centuries and has postulated that many so-called witches were the victims of what might best be described as an infantile magico-persecutory projective mechanism. Sifting through centuries-old records kept by the Inquisition, Caro found that the star witnesses in witchcraft trials had often been children. In the trial of several women in Fuenterrabía (Guipúzcoa), for example, in May of 1611, a number of children from eight to fourteen years of age swore that these women had magically summoned them in the dead of night to participate in *aquelarres* (Basque for black sabbaths) where they were lashed, branded, sexually abused, forced to dance naked, curse God, spit upon crucifixes, and so forth. Caro interprets his data in the light of "mythomania," a word coined by an early twentieth-century French psychologist to describe the more-or-less pathological tendency of certain children and adolescents to fabricate crimes, attribute them to some innocent adult, and eventually come to believe the false accusations themselves (Caro 1961:310–313; 1947: 200–204). Like Girard with his persecution texts, Caro is struck by certain details in the lies that consistently recur over time, and reasons that a similar mythomania must have compelled some young people living in backward areas of Europe to invent and propagate their tales of witches.

In the testimony of children given during witchcraft trials, episodes of the most scandalous obscenity are never lacking. It is not always easy to determine how much was due to judicial or familial suggestion. But sometimes this is clearly the case, as in the trial of the witches of Fuenterrabía. [1961:312]

The chief witness in that case had been an eleven-year-old girl whose own pathology most likely mirrored the larger pathology of her social milieu. Girard may be right in suggesting that the behavior of children provides insight into persecutory mythopoesis—not because they are especially vulnerable to pathological impulses, but rather because they are so responsive to their environment. Mimetic creatures par excellence, they will easily reproduce and thereby "confirm" the fears and fantasies of the community at large. What is at stake in tales and tale-bearing is not ethics but socialization. Bettelheim affirms that children crave assurance that they can succeed at growing up, and stresses the vital role played in this process by entertaining fantasies implicitly approved by adults (1975:10–28). Chronic or acute crises thrust human groups into a mimetic labyrinth where suggestion leads to inventions that are believed and fuel further suggestion. Here is one more good reason for avoiding a simplistic dichotomy of manipulators and manipulated when studying the fomentation of scapegoating violence. The essential question is not "Who told the lie?" but "Why was the lie believed?" (cf. Girard 1982:61, 130)

Belief in magic was almost universal during the Middle Ages and Renaissance. People who knew the "magic arts," the right substances and the right formulas, were in demand. The icons and relics of saints were often imbued with what can only be considered magic properties as well, but the community's divine protector was not to be approached for individual requirements of an erotic nature—for which there were "real life" specialists in most communities (Caro 1974a:229–236). At the same time, there really were socially maladjusted women, without family or connections, dishonored and poverty-stricken, who came to console themselves with certain varieties of solanaceous plants (belladonna, henbane, mandrake) and entertain delusions of night flight and secret powers (Caro 1961:314–315). Already despised or feared by adults—when not sought out for ulterior motives—such women would comprise a natural target for the scapegoating, projective minds of the young. Caro himself does not point a finger:

This business of witchcraft ought to produce pity more than anything else; pity for the persecuted, who wished to do evil things, although they didn't, and who lived tragic and frustrated lives for the most part. Pity, too, for the persecutors, because they considered themselves threatened by numberless dangers, and only for this did they react with brutality. [1961:318]

The frightened villagers' "delusions of persecution," in other words, had led them to persecute.

The negative potential of mimetic suggestibility is not the only Girardian idea that Caro's research can corroborate. In a number of studies that deal with archetypal representations in history and folklore, Caro delves into the stereotyped denunciations that have surfaced over and over again in episodes of collective violence. The alleged crimes of witches constitute a prime example: from ancient Rome to nineteenth-century Zaragoza, people have tended to be taken in by the same spurious rumors of potions and hexes and to react in the same forceful ways (1974a:185–295; 1974b: 215–258).

Like other archetypes or multivalent folk ideas that do not necessarily relate to persecutory thoughts or deeds, the "witch" accusation persists over time and gets adopted and adapted in a hundred different ways according to local circumstances. Unlike Girard, Caro is as interested in the minute study of these local adaptations as he is in the general mythopoeic model. Both phenomena respond to a dynamic of "vulgarization" wherein real people or events become legendary and legendary figures or events become concretized (1979:94–100). The first possibility is exemplified by an early nineteenth-century Spanish seamstress who became the captain of a marauding band of *bandoleros* in the Sierra Morena and was finally executed; her exploits served as the basis for a number of local legends influenced by the "Serrana de la Vera" archetype (1969:390). Torralba, for so she was called, was said to have been a tall, beautiful blonde who had a habit of seducing and castrating young men. But the second possibility is even more curious, for sometimes a legendary personage "materializes" in a real, flesh-and-blood impostor or lunatic: any number of sixteenth-century individuals claimed to be the long-lost King Sebastian of Portugal until imprisonment and torture changed their minds (1979:135–140). Caro suggests that some strange mimetic suggestibility seems to be at work once again in such cases (1979:140).

That mob violence is similarly archetypal in nature is borne out by an abundance of historical data. *Bulos,* or stereotyped rumors, constitute a veritable Ariadne's clew for Caro in his studies of witchcraft, anti-Semitism, and anti-clericalism in Spain. In all three cases, *bulos* serve to detonate episodes of real violence when popular persecutory delusions have been exacerbated by some sort of catastrophe.

Following his usual exhaustive examination of the sources, Caro concludes that medieval Jews were despised for religious motives (deicide), economic motives (avarice and usury), psychological reasons (the Jew's intelligence and/or arrogance), and physical differences perceived to be disagreeable (1978 [1962]:I, 104). These archetypal notions can be found glossed in erudite and libelous tracts or succinctly expressed in proverbs. But standardized folkloric slurs were mild compared to the standardized rumors that triggered ghastly massacres all over Europe for centuries; time and again the Jews of a given locality were "discovered" to be master magicians, nefarious poisoners, ritual murderers, and so forth (Trachtenberg 1983:97–155). In most cases, says Caro, the latent "mystico-terrorific tendency" of the people was stirred into action by popular preachers and itinerant friars that the official Church was hard put to control (1978:I, 114–118). Suggestible children were behind other incidents, inevitably! Madrid rose up in righteous anger in 1629 when a group of Portuguese Jews decided to flog an icon of Christ they kept in their house on Infantas Street; the icon had even spoken up to demand the reason for such mistreatment. The heinous sacrilege had been "revealed" by certain youths who attended school with the sons of the Jews. While the hapless foreigners awaited the fires of an *auto de fe* (finally celebrated with unusual solemnity in 1632), the boys and girls of the city "went around singing couplets against the accused" (Caro 1970b:65–66). Not only did popular poetry celebrate the affair of the so-called Christ of Patience; Lope de Vega dedicated an eglogue to the theme and a number of anti-Semitic tracts were brought out.

Two confraternities were soon founded to keep the memory of the miracle alive (1970b:67–70). If so many cultural expressions and institutions could stem from one single magico-persecutory episode, small wonder that the atrocities of the wicked Jews remained a staple of blind beggar ballads in Spain until the demise of the genre itself in the first years of the twentieth century (Caro 1978: II, 456; Marco 1977:I, 310).

The history of Spanish anti-clericalism replicates this familiar dynamic of folklore, crisis, rumor, and persecution. Irreverent humor and folk satire of fat, licentious priests and monks had been around for centuries, but the decomposition of the Ancien Régime in Spain and the clergy's support of the Carlist movement, along with other anarchic disorders of the early nineteenth century, turned the exoteric lore into political programs—and pogroms. The brutal attempts on the part of reactionary Absolutism to purge Spain of liberal and constitutional ideals only served to produce a host of popular martyrs, of whom Mariana Pineda is the most famous representative. Once again, Spanish history structured itself as *mythomachia*.

In the process of creating a Liberal mythology, with its gods, demigods, and evil spirits, with many given over to the hostile interpretation of the Church's every activity, the moment came when a large part of the populace attributed to it and to its ministers the same kind of secret codes and malignant acts that the preachers and friars of another epoch had attributed to heretics and Jews, or to Freemasons in more modern times. [Caro 1980:147]

Then came the cholera epidemic in midsummer of 1834. Historians disagree as to whether the *bulo* that the Jesuits had poisoned the water originated with some secret society or was the "spontaneous combustion" of Madrid's frightened masses. But they do agree that at least seventy-five Jesuits, Franciscans, Dominicans, and personnel of other orders were slaughtered on 17 July 1834 (Caro 1980:150–153). Other crises were to produce similar or even more virulent massacres in 1835, 1909, 1931, and 1936 (Thomas 1961:165–179; Caro 1980:154–155)—each followed, inevitably, by a new round of martyrological mythopoesis on the part of the aggrieved or their allies.

CONCLUSION

Persecution texts do not constitute the end of Girard's research but only a means, an easily verified platform for a not so easily verified and even controversial hypothesis. Briefly put, Girard attempts to derive myths, rites, taboos, and the concept of the sacred itself from a "victimage mechanism" he considers to be analogous to persecution. How much explanatory power pertains to this thesis remains to be seen, but it unquestionably represents a major development in post-structuralist anthropology.

Whatever role persecution might have played in the origins of sacred mythology, its role in the genesis of folklore is patent. Caro Baroja has demonstrated that folk accusations and the folk terrorism they can provoke conform to an orderly pattern across the ages. The exoteric jokes and insults with which members of one socioeconomic group distinguish themselves from another comprise the general precondition for persecution. Crisis constitutes another necessary but insufficient ingredient. *Bulos* actualize the sociocentric lore in a fitting historical moment and the result is violence.

Historically, people have always found it easier to say "we are persecuted" than "we persecute." The names change, the villains change, yesterday's accusers become today's scapegoats. The bitter memory of past martyrdom cries out for new martyrizing. By no means should it be inferred that the process confines itself to Spain or to any other place in particular, nor that magico-persecutory projection is a thing of the past, still less that the solution lies in taking firm action against "scapegoaters." Violent deeds typically camouflage themselves as moral prerogatives. In the final analysis, the study of folklore serves to unmask the mechanics of our self-deception.

5

Crime and Punishment in Folk Religion

Like folk religion everywhere, folk religion in Spain can be approached as a more-or-less coherent system of rewards and penalties for moral and immoral behaviors. Without devaluing the wholesome pleasure of hearing a good story told well, religious folk legends can be seen fulfilling a normative function: exemplary piety is rewarded, as in the miracles of saints and their icons, and impiety is exemplarily punished, as shown in historical episodes of scapegoating and their texts. In the latter case, popular justice simply mimics the divine variety.

In Spanish folk religion, positive and negative modes of reinforcement are clearly personified. God has traditionally been in charge of the chastisement of criminals while clemency and forgiveness have been the almost exclusive domain of María. Sometimes the Virgin consoles the victim of said criminals; at other times she intercedes for criminals who somehow maintained her cult in spite of their disorderly lives; at still other times, her opportune intervention keeps the crimes from being committed in the first place (Caro 1969:123–126; Marco 1977:II, 491–500). But not even María can defuse God's wrath when it comes to certain crimes, specifically sacrilege, incest, and parricide.

Yet with this we have hardly covered the scope of traditional moral reinforcement. For what is to be done with all the people who sin grievously but regret it later? Folk religious thought cannot always resort to a convenient scapegoat; some of the time, if not most of the time, an individual must recognize that he or she alone is to blame. Unlike the magico-persecutory search for an outside culprit, guilt feelings locate the culprit in one's own person. All the same, few people are willing to admit that they deserve the exemplary punishment meted out to the "real" evildoers. Accordingly, punishment will be reserved for those sinners/criminals who do not repent; for those who are willing to do so, penance is the proper medicine. The pious can purge sins committed because they are disposed to inflict a degree of punishment upon themselves; the impious are stubborn and arrogant beings who are "asking for" definitive correction. Trachtenberg thinks that the Jew came to be linked with the devil as the only possible explanation for his "stubborn" refusal to acknowledge what God had revealed to all men (1983:17–19). Small wonder, then, that the "demonic Jew" was such a logical target for divine/popular vengeance.

Much of the exemplarity of divine punishment derives from its immediacy; the God of popular legends does not like to wait until the criminals have died to apply his wrath. In one of the blind beggar ballads cited by Caro, no sooner does a young gentleman murder his father than he undergoes a terrible metamorphosis,

pues en medio de la sala	for in the middle of the room
liado todo su cuerpo	twisted lay his entire body
de una espantosa culebra,	into a frightful serpent,
todo cubierto de pelo	all covered with hair
con los dos pies de caballo,	with two horse's hooves,
las manos de león fiero,	the paws of a fierce lion,
la cabeza de dragón,	the head of a dragon,
las orejas de jumento,	the ears of a jackass,
solo le quedaba el pecho	only his breast remained
de hombre . . .	that of a man . . .
[1969:122]	

Not only does the punishment fit the crime, it *is* the crime in this ingenuous Spanish legend, if one follows Girard in associating monsters with *crimes indifférenciateurs* like parricide (1972:237–248; 1982:51–54).

Incest or the murder of close relatives have preoccupied the popular and the cultured mind alike for many centuries. Both the Greek tragedian of fifth-century Athens and the blind bard of nineteenth-century Spain—mutatis mutandis—are obsessed with sexual-familial crimes and their punishment or expiation. Both seem to have provided aesthetic pleasure and cathartic relief to their respective publics (Caro 1969:146–147). Caro is particularly drawn to the Oedipal themes in a number of fascinating Spanish legends that took shape in the darker moments of the Middle Ages and have since occupied a privileged place in the moral *Weltanschauung* of folk Spain. The legends are as specific about names and places as they are vague about dates, in keeping with the socio-centric (rather than chronocentric) character of folklore in general. A brief survey of these stories and the theoretical problems they present will lead us closer to a viable model of magico-persecutory creativity in Spain and elsewhere.

Archetypal Sins, Legendary Expiations

A young nobleman of Navarre named Teodosio (or Juan García) is obliged to leave his young wife in his manor at Goñi to serve his king in a struggle against the Moors; after a prolonged absence he returns unannounced, to be met by the devil disguised as a holy hermit (or shepherd), who informs him that his spouse is just then committing adultery with a servant. Rushing home in a fury to find a man and a woman in his bed, Teodosio draws his sword and slays them on the spot—man of honor that he is. Satisfaction turns to consternation when he meets his wife returning home from Mass, and consternation to horror when she reveals that his own father and mother were the innocent occupants of the bedchamber. Teodosio journeys to Rome to throw himself at the feet of the Pope, who absolves and assigns penance: Teodosio is to wander the face of the earth with a collar and chains until they wear out or break of their own accord. Seven years later, his solitary wanderings have brought him back to his native Navarre where he stumbles upon a dragon sleeping in a cave on Mount Aralar. Just as the monster begins to gobble Teodosio's chain, Saint Michael the Archangel appears to dispatch the dragon and inform the penitent that he need wander no more. Don Teodosio is happily reunited with his wife but leaves her again to build a church to Saint Michael on the site of his miraculous apparition (Caro 1974b:155–181).

Another Christian legend of much wider diffusion than this repeats the involuntary double parricide motif and replaces the element of temptation with that of prophecy. A deer he has just hunted down prophesies to Julian that he will slay his parents; naturally, all further precautions are useless, the deed is done, and the "glorious parricide" (for so he is called in Lope de Vega's play) expiates his crime through the construction of hospitals and houses for the poor (Attwater 1965:206–207; Caro 1974b:185–188, 211–214). Many other saints have since been "contaminated" by the Hospitaller's crimes and self-imposed penance alike (Attwater 1965:207).

The apocryphal legend of Judas Iscariot comes the closest to the Oedipal pattern, for the tradition that extends from Russia to Ireland has him unwittingly kill his father and marry his mother before joining up with and betraying Christ (cf. Edmunds 1985:61–67 et passim). In the Irish version, an itinerant scholar makes the appropriate prophecy to Judas' mother on the day of his birth, reinforced by the discovery of a birthmark shaped like a black cross between the baby's shoulder-blades (O'Sullivan 1974:68). Watch out for those marked by God!

But a certain pious legend placed in circulation by the blind bards of Spain pulls out all the stops. A prince of Hungary named Hisano rapes his own daughter; she thereby begets a baby who is abandoned and subsequently reared by Prince Albano of the same nation. When he grows into manhood, Albano's adopted son (also named Albano) falls in love with a portrait of the daughter of Hisano. They are married. Just before he dies, the elder Albano reveals to the younger that he was really adopted and produces a pair of twenty-year-old diapers as proof, whereupon the Princess faints. The younger Albano and his wife/mother decide to go to Rome to seek forgiveness of the Pope, and even convince Prince Hisano to accompany them. As is his wont, the Pope commands the trio of penitents to wander the face of the earth for seven years

por entre montes y breñas,	among mountains and crags,
sin que vistiesen camisa,	without clothing yourselves,
ni sentasen a la mesa,	or sitting at tables,
ni se quitasen las barbas,	or shaving your beards,

y que hagan abstinencias,	and may you fast,
se pongan fuertes cilicios,	and wear harsh sackcloth,
que coman silvestres yerbas	may you eat wild grasses
y que lloren sus pecados . . .	and bewail your sins . . .
[Caro 1969:129–130]	

Seven years later, just when their sins are nearing expiation, the devil tempts Hisano and he repeats the same incestuous crime he had committed so many years previously. Albano kills father and mother, quite voluntarily, and sets out immediately to throw himself at the feet of the Pope. This time his penance is for life. He becomes a hermit and builds a shrine at the scene of his crimes where he prays for his parents' souls in front of their skulls. Seven years pass and Albano dies a saintly death (Caro 1969:129–130; 1974b: 190–192).

Caro assembles the last three legends as part of his study of Don Teodosio de Goñi and compares them all to the myth of Oedipus. The same themes of parricide, incest, and expiation appear throughout. The role played by fate in the Greek legends seems to be replaced by temptation in the Christian ones, with the exception of the apocryphal crimes of Judas. Both Cadmus and Saint Michael are dragon-slayers, etc. (1974b:192–198). But with the major and minor details of the enigma delineated, Caro desists. Always the cautious scholar, his own conclusions are modest compared to the fascinating possibilities of the material and the prodigious bibliographical pains he has taken to unearth it.

Girard cannot compete with Caro in terms of erudition—very few scholars could—but he does have at least one idea that might help to fathom the curious corpus of legends presented above. For by way of advancing his argument that persecution texts constitute the key to world mythology, Girard recurs to Oedipus. As is well known, the "myth" of Oedipus is in reality a composite picture drawn from the writings of several Greek authors and from several problematic fragments of a lost epic known as the *Thebaïd* (Tripp: 1970:422–423); Girard, like many theorists of myth before him, works primarily with the story as it is presented in the famous dramas of Sophocles. Having dealt at length with the subject in *Violence and the Sacred* (1972:104–134), Girard comes straight to the point in *Le Bouc émissaire:* the four stereotypes that shape the oral or written texts of naive persecutors are all spectacularly present in *Oedipus the King* (1982:38–41). In the plague that ravages Thebes we have the indifferentiating social crisis that dissolves personal relations into mimetic strife. In the accusations of parricide and incest we find the stereotype of indifferentiating crimes. Oedipus, the lame outcast/king, parvenu and former exposed infant, is a walking (or limping) conglomerate of victimage signs. It can even be observed, following Krappe (1929:209–210), that Oedipus' self-blinding adds one more to the list. Oedipus is the ultimate margin, the nonclassifiable physical and moral monster that destabilizes all identities; his mother is his wife and his children are his brothers. He is, says Girard, "l'assassin de la différence" (1972:115–116). His expulsion from the city constitutes the final stereotyped persecutory representation and logical resolution of the entire process.

Unlike other theorists of myth, Girard does not base his hermeneutic system on Oedipus nor does he confuse the myth with the play; on the contrary, he recognizes that Sophocles' intervention is what makes the tale so useful for his essentially didactic purposes. Girard wishes to show that the same elements that structure and disguise the ungentle events of persecution adopt a similar disguise in one of the great sacrosanct icons of Western Humanism. Girard wants to prove that our reaction to texts depends all too often on their "commercial packaging" (1982:46).

The idea that the Oedipal drama can be read like a persecution is an exciting one. But Girard is at pains to emphasize that his is not yet another symbolic interpretation of Oedipus. The plague, the accusations, and the lame culprit do not "stand for" the persecutory stereotypes in an allegoric or metaphoric manner. A given thematic element may be classified in terms of one stereotype or another but the stereotypes are only representations themselves, collective and necessarily warped manifestations of an underlying control system. Girard is not, therefore, a late French ramification of *The Golden Bough* with its pursuit of the thematic scapegoat of legend or ritual. Rather, he is on the trail of a behind-the-scenes *anathème* (1972:128) or scapegoating mechanism—the hypothetical motor that drives not just Oedipus but myths everywhere. Girard theorizes that successive elaborations of early myths are governed by a desire to erase the traces of collective violence. Lévi-Strauss's mode of structuralist analysis is too "rudimentary"

(Girard 1982 : 106) to perceive this cover-up process, which works over vast periods of time and is motivated by a feeling of malaise that mathematically minded ethnologists must recognize if they ever hope to understand even the strictly transformational aspects of myth (1982 : 107–108). During the first stages of the process, the mythic representations of collective violence are gradually replaced by representations of individual violence. A new phase begins with the so-called birth of philosophy and with Plato's explicit project of effacing even these "traces of the traces" (1982 : 111–113). An intolerance of the ambiguity that lies at the heart of the primitive sacred brings about a progressive idealization of the gods and heroes and the "poetic minimization of their guilt" (1982 : 117), as evidenced by Aristotle's formulation of hamartia.

Other scholars have essayed theoretical descriptions of the "phases" of mythic development and how they relate to historical/cultural evolution in general. Cook, for example, coincides with Girard in arguing that "the vast and algorithmic circular definitions of Lévi-Strauss" do not come first in the evolution of mythology (1980 : 10). Further, nonbinary phases are generated, says Cook, by ever greater degrees of consciousness regarding the mythic process and its interactions with language (1980 : 1–66). Here Girard asserts the contrary: not ever greater consciousness but ever more effective cover-up governs myth's evolution. This enables us to account for those writers and poets of Greece and Rome whom Harry Levin has called "Pickwickian," since "so far as they could, they moralized or rationalized or allegorized the embarrassing misbehavior of their Olympians" (Levin 1960 : 105–106).

So far, so plausible. But further evolution is portrayed by Girard in terms of a rather mechanical decomposition: when equivocal archaic myths eventually give way to myths where good and evil are clearly separated, a monster will typically inherit the three stereotypes of crisis, crimes, and victimage signs, and the definitive act of violence becomes the salutary prerogative of a hero (1982 : 118). A great many legendary figures are thereby accounted for, except, unfortunately, the ones we are most concerned with—Saint Julian, Don Teodosio de Goñi, San Albano, et al. Here we have no poetic or Pickwickian minimization of guilt but double and triple doses of it. The protagonists are simultaneously saintly heroes and moral monsters. Their legends would seem to reverse Girard's hypothesis of a unidirectional mythic cover-up by explicitly restoring indifferentiating violence to the sacred. But that is not all. The tragic knowledge of guilt introjected by our Oedipal saints would seem to reverse the "normal" projective course of magico-persecutory thought.

From Guilt to Grace

Taken together, the Oedipal legends of Christian Europe and their truculent Spanish adaptations reveal both the advantages and the shortcomings of Girard's rereading of the legend of Oedipus. First the advantages. Caro did not see the connection between his *bulos* and the Oedipal crimes attributed to Don Teodosio and his counterparts, nor did he intuit the persecutory structure of their penitence. The saintly monsters set off to atone for their crimes as solitary outcasts. Expulsion from society is the necessary condition of their own *via purgativa*. Furthermore, the punishments they undergo not only fit their crimes, they epitomize them. Consider the rebarbative history of San Albano, with its double incest, double penitence, and something more complicated than double parricide—for in killing his mother and father Albano eliminates his sister, his adulteress wife, and his grandfather. Such are the confusions and contradictions wrought by indifferentiating crimes. And they are replicated in the acts of atonement prescribed by the Pope, for the sinners are sent off to live like animals in an undifferentiated state of nature, eating grass, sleeping on rocks, going about nude, and so forth. The element of fate that attends to the Oedipus myth has a functional, if not ideological, equivalent in the intervention of the devil. How was Teodosio to know that the holy hermit who greeted him on the road to Goñi was not what he seemed? Further, the Girardian notion of victimage signs is particularly relevant to the Oedipal Judas—easily recognized by the black, cross-shaped birthmark on his back. The folk attribution of parricide and incest to a traitorous arch-villain like Judas tends to bear out Girard's discovery of a persecutory pattern in the legend of Oedipus. In sum, it would seem that all these legends are as susceptible as persecution texts of being "deconstructed" into their component stereotypes.

But there is still a major difference to be accounted for. The victims of persecutions do not exercise their right to atone for their crimes, if indeed they are even granted such a right. Instead, real scapegoats in scapegoating texts are generally represented as incapable of regret. Their very impiety grants the pious a sort of "license to kill"—analogous to the right of God himself to mete out capital punishment to the obdurate. But Oedipus, Judas, Saint Julian, and all the others judge and condemn themselves or willingly submit to the Pope's harsh punishments. Like Oedipus, the hapless Christian noblemen and noblewomen are fully capable of the horror and disgust that the discovery of their guilt elicits. How are we to account for this? How does one cover the structural or chronological gap between persecution and guilt feelings?

That *Oedipus Rex* presents one individual's painful assumption of guilt is clear from the text alone; the view that it also exemplifies the psychological process itself was forthrightly advanced many years ago by the "existential" psychoanalysts. As rendered by Rollo May,

Oedipus calls the old blind seer, Tiresias, and thereupon proceeds a gripping and powerful unfolding step by step of Oedipus' self-knowledge, an unfolding replete with rage, anger at the truth and those who are its bearers, and all other aspects of man's most profound struggle with recognition of his own reality. . . . The whole gamut of psychoanalytic reactions like "resistance" and "projection" are exhibited by Oedipus as the closer he gets to the truth, the more violently he fights against it. [May 1960:36–37]

Once the ugly unconscious urges have been dredged up, new ethical possibilities come into view. To better understand this "progressive" function, we must go to the play Freud ignored, *Oedipus at Colonus.* By now the aging Oedipus has "come to terms with his guilt" and thereby has acquired the power

to impart grace. . . . But there is also a clear symbolic element to make the point of his grace unmistakable: the oracle has revealed that his body after death will ensure victory to the land and the ruler which possess him. [May 1960:41–43; emphasis in original]

Other scholars with no symbolic reading to assert have not failed to notice the grace motif. "Before our eyes," observe Cook and

Dolin, "the old, blind outcast is transformed into a protective spirit, a quasi-divine power to be revered and cherished" (1972: 151). For Edmunds, "Oedipus miraculously enters the earth at the time of his death, and as a cult hero he becomes a chthonic power" (1985:38). That the protagonist of Sophocles' last play is a new man (or a new god) has not been lost on Girard, either, but the explanation he offers entirely eliminates the need for May's attribution of ethical self-awareness to Oedipus:

Religious thought is necessarily induced to see in the *victime émissaire*, that is to say, simply, in the last victim, the one who suffers violence without provoking new reprisals, a supernatural creature that sows violence only to reap peace, a fearful and mysterious stranger that makes men ill to cure them afterwards. . . . The beneficial Oedipus that follows the expulsion emerges from the malefic Oedipus of before but without nullifying him. [Girard 1972:131–132]

Old blind Oedipus can impart grace because he is the sacralized victim, the source of disorder purged and reified into the fount of order and blessings, and not because he has "come to terms with his guilt."

Edmunds has rejected Oedipus' alleged assumption of guilt from a different perspective and has censured

a common tendency amongst scholars to interpret Oedipus at Colonus in terms of the inner Oedipus, of qualities that he has attained through suffering, endurance, and deeper wisdom. But as soon as the ancient legend is studied with reference to folklore analogues, the problem of the end of Oedipus's life in relation to his earlier crimes is necessarily recast in terms of the story pattern, and the goal becomes one of explaining this relationship, not as a development of the hero's inner self, but as a unified action forming a definable kind of biography or pattern of life. [1985:6]

In order to reconstruct this biography, Edmunds carefully assembles both the ancient fragments of the Oedipus legend and the medieval and modern analogues (1985:47–224). As it turns out, however, notable analogues like Pope Gregory, King Armenios, and Saint Andrew do indeed attain greater wisdom and self-awareness through suffering and penitence, just like Don Teodosio de Goñi and San Albano. But Edmunds is not moved to alter his basic pattern of Oedipal life; the motif of penance is simply "a chthonic phase in the hero's exaltation" and the element of self-awareness is nothing more than "a capacity of the tradition itself for self-reflection" (1985 : 38–39).

There is much to be said for Edmunds' formalist approach. On the face of it there is little to keep us from assimilating the medieval legends to the archaic one—or vice-versa, for that matter. For when Oedipus is described as a mysterious benefactor, a bestower of grace or "a quasi-divine power to be revered and cherished," he begins to sound very much like a saint. His "relics" are even the hotly disputed object of intercommunity contention, a theme found over and over in saints' legends. To follow this line of thought would not imply a willful devaluation of Christianity's moral innovations, only the recognition that historical Christianity did not change certain key elements of "pagan " (i.e., rural) morality. The local cults of saints that bloom all over Europe in the first Christian millennium are essentially continuous with the pre-Christian cults of local divinities or guardian spirits. Evangelical notions of pacifism, kindness towards enemies, and so forth do not interfere with such local devotions any more than Plato's Ideas interfered with grave cults in rural Greece. Nevertheless, in stressing the continuity of folk religion or folk narrative, we are left incapable of accounting for the Oedipal saints' intense introjection of guilt feelings.

A promising explanation for the undeniable internal evolution of the Oedipal pattern can be derived from the work of Tobin Siebers. Siebers argues that once accusations like the ones Oedipus fell victim to have become social categories, they subsequently become available to neurotic individuals for *self*-accusation (1983 : 138–139). Siebers finds an archetypal model in Freud's *Leichenvogel*, alias the Rat Man, compelled to carry out protective rituals when "he discovers in himself a great criminal whom the great man in him must vanquish" (1983 : 121).

The Rat Man, however, experiences this oscillation of sacred extremes with startling rapidity. For him, good and evil share a common instant and spring from the same source: his own uncanniness. Herein lies the essential difference between the neurotic and primitive universe. The primitive community preserves its own sense of benevolence by situating the uncanny in others; its behavior obeys and reinforces its own collective representations. The neurotic, also determined by collective representations, rests at the center of the system. Like the fascinator, he embodies those features that the society isolates and expels in order to achieve order. [1983:127]

The Oedipal saints of Spain and elsewhere could profitably be seen in this light, true neurotic individuals of their time who interiorize the most dreadful crimes and thereby take a load off their societies. It would have been just as legitimate, therefore, and perhaps more efficient, if Freud had discovered a "San Albano complex" in his patients, inasmuch as that Spanish family romance artfully concentrates father-daughter and mother-son incest and murder in one plot line.

But we are still a step away from a satisfactory solution. Girard and Edmunds emphasize magical or chthonic grace at the expense of guilt, while Siebers accounts for the origins of self-torture at the expense of grace. In the numinous primitive/neurotic world inhabited by our Oedipal saints, however, you cannot have one without the other. Somewhere along the line, the magico-persecutory logic of expulsion from society turns into the expiation of the sin *and* the recovery of the sinner. In the words of Paul Ricouer, "order cannot be reaffirmed outside of the guilty person without being reaffirmed within him too" (1969:44). What begins in horror and the dread of disintegration, or indifferentiation, can eventually lead not only to the identification and removal of the defiling agent but to his reabsorption into the right order of the world. The evidence may not warrant the acute ethical subjectivity that May diagnoses in the aging Oedipus, but the existential psychoanalyst was not far off the track. It would surely be a mistake to think that cultures before Christ knew nothing of the internal assignation of blame (cf. Ricouer 1969:33–43).

None of this means that a notion as useful as magico-persecutory thought must be dropped, but only amended to include both "regressive" and "progressive" modes of moral reinforcement. Magico-persecutory thought might henceforth be defined as 1) the projective mechanism that induces persecutory urges and actions, and 2) the introjection of persecutory feelings (guilt) initially aroused by one's own retrograde desires or deeds. Both varieties are "magic" in their resolute obsession with locating causes and identifying culprits; but where the first sparks intergroup and intra-group violence, the second begets penitence and piety. Should a hierarchical relationship be posited between the two? Are penitential behaviors more "mature" than persecutory ones? Or do both betray a stunted ethical growth in their exclusive dependence upon supernatural sanctions to guarantee social order and their concomitant vision of God as an inflexible and authoritarian judge? These are loaded questions indeed.

What is clearly unacceptable, however, is the idea that "tradition itself is capable of self-reflection" (Edmunds 1985:39). Stories do not tell themselves, they are told by people, and people have needs that go beyond storytelling for its own sake. Of course pious legends have a structure that can be analyzed in terms of romance conventions, motifs of descent and ascent, and so on (cf. Frye 1976: 148–149); but they also have a *function*. Consolation, primarily. Traditional moral reinforcement, B.C. and A.D., is set up to deal with those who repent and those who do not—given the timeless human tendency to err. Primary fantasy temptations require the cathartic outlet and normative dénouement that folk legends of all ages provide. No matter how wicked you think you are, Oedipus (or Teodosio or Julian or Albano) was even worse and he was still able to make amends after all. In the life-and-crimes of the archetypal saintly parricide, guilt leads to penitence, penitence to purgation, and purgation to Ricouer's restoration of personal worth (1969:44).

A final demonstration of the gains consolidated and their special relevance to Spain is in order. As it happens, there is one more fascinating Spanish legend, wholly autochthonous and of unusual longevity, that portrays how one man's sex crime triggers nothing less than a war that destroys an entire culture and is finally expiated by his own penitential self-destruction. A brief analysis of this striking story will verify the explanatory power of the refined version of magico-persecutory thought that I propound above and simultaneously recapitulate the importance of sociocentrism, crisis, and violence to folkloric creativity in Spain.

The Legend of the Loss of Spain

As Menéndez Pidal pointed out in 1925, the legend of King Rodrigo possesses a number of features that set it apart from the other "historical-epical" legends of Spain: it is by far the most archaic, having its origins in the catastrophic collapse of Visigothic society in the eighth century; it is the only one to have been produced and transmitted with the close "collaboration" of Christians and Moslems; it has appeared in a greater variety of generic guises than any other legend, including chronicle, ballad, chivalric romance, learned poetry, historical novel and drama; and it has become imbued with religious values to an unparalleled extent during its twelve centuries of continuous existence (1925 : I, x—xxi). This unique tradition comprises a number of contradictory elements. Rodrigo is seen as either the very model of Christian kingship or a degenerate violator of religious and sexual mores. Florinda (or many other names) is either a pure and innocent virgin, victim of Rodrigo's lust, or a wily seductress who bewitches him. Julián, her father (sometimes husband), is alternately pictured as either a despicable traitor to his faith and homeland or a righteously indignant defender of his honor. Apart from these polar variations in how the main actors are personified across the ages, the result is always the same: Rodrigo's sin brings about the Moorish subjugation of Spain and must be purged in the end by "a ghastly penance of grandiose and barbarous symbolism" decreed by God himself (1925 : I, xii).

The mythogenetic motor is thus the collapse of Gothic hegemony and the painful determination of *who* and *why*. But the social contradictions among the conquered Christians prevented general agreement on the historical facts of the matter—just as Fischer's discussion of conflicting tale traditions might have led us to expect (1963 : 252); hence there were two "competing" scapegoats at first. The lower-class, mainly Hispano-Roman majority was quick to fix blame upon the Gothic King Witiza. The minority of upper-class Mozarabes of Gothic origin who were sympathetic to Witiza and fairly comfortable under Moorish domination gradually countered with their own scapegoat, Rodrigo. This is the version that found favor with the official Arab chronicles, while the other remained in oral tradition and gradually percolated up to the Christian "refugees" of northern Spain (Menéndez Pidal 1925 : I, xxxvi—xliii; Smith 1964 : 51—52). For the invading Moors, meanwhile, the whole affair came to be regarded as a kind of miraculous legend of holy warfare that proved that Allah was on their side. They eventually added new motifs derived from Middle Eastern folktales or the Islamic tradition of sacro-martial miracles known as the *Fotuhat*, as exemplified by the stereotyped accusation of the violated palace, sepulcher, or taboo that was added to Rodrigo's trespasses (Menéndez Pidal 1925 : I, xliv–xlvi). But the seduction of Julián's daughter (or wife) remained the major precipitating scandal. The authority of the Arab chronicles was great enough to establish Rodrigo as the sole culprit for all sides involved after a few hundred years had elapsed.

What began as crisis-induced creativity and sociocentric logomachy eventually became one of the great cultural motifs of Medieval and Renaissance Spain and remained popular even in the nineteenth century. This is not the place to engage in a detailed exposition of the multitudinous literary and folkloric adaptations of the legend of the last Goth; Menéndez Pidal needed three volumes for that endeavor. Suffice it to say that over the course of twelve centuries Rodrigo and the other characters have been treated in a great variety of styles without changing the basic passional structure of the drama and its gripping backdrop of catastrophe. Menéndez Pidal himself stressed the importance of the entire Rodrigo tradition over and above its form at a given historical moment and affirmed that the contributions of individual creators could only be properly assessed if the nature of the tradition as "living organism" came to be understood (1925 : I, xiv–xv; III, cxv–cxvii). Though such biological metaphors can no longer be taken seriously (Handler and Linnekin 1984 : 277–279), the concepts I have developed thus far can vindicate the holistic view of the Rodrigo cycle that Menéndez Pidal had in mind.

Briefly stated, the "living organism" of the Rodrigo legend gradually generated the themes of guilt and redemption from inside the original scapegoating "skeleton." As the memory of the great crisis subsided, along with the hostile or opportunistic allotment of blame it had engendered, later generations would

1) continuously rework or "recontextualize" the tradition as an expression of cultural identity—a familiar process, and
2) develop the pious and normative potential that inheres to *all* legends that begin in magico-persecutory mythopoesis.

Rodrigo's penitence does not become traditional until some six centuries after the original catastrophe. Like the outcast-saints of the legends discussed earlier, the king wanders alone and miserable among the crags, until he reaches a shrine attended by a hermit. Rodrigo begs the holy man to prescribe some penance that will fit his horrendous crimes and the latter refers the matter to higher authority.

Fuele luego revelado	It was later manifested
de parte de Dios un día	by God one day unto him
que le meta en una tumba	that he get into a tomb
con una culebra viva	with a live snake
y esto tome en penitencia	and accept it as penance
por el mal que hecho había.	for the evil he had done.
[Díaz Roig 1981:117]	

Rodrigo joyfully accedes to this divinely sanctioned punishment, but three days pass and the serpent does nothing. The holy hermit weeps, prays harder still, and later returns to find Rodrigo moaning.

Dios es en la ayuda mía,	God is come to help me,
respondió el buen rey Rodrigo,	good King Rodrigo answered,
la culebra me comía;	the snake is eating me;
cómeme ya por la parte	now he is eating the part
que todo lo merecía,	that most deserves it,
por donde fue el principio	that which was the origin
de la mi muy gran desdicha.	of my great misfortune.
El ermitaño lo esfuerza,	The hermit encourages him,
el buen rey allí moría.	the good king was dying.
Aquí acabó el rey Rodrigo,	King Rodrigo perished here,
al cielo derecho se iba.	he went straight to heaven.
[Díaz Roig 1981:117]	

In twentieth-century versions of the legend collected in rural Spain, the punishment remains the same but the crime has been changed—to incest (Gutiérrez Esteve 1981:III, 44–50). This is a telling coincidence of "traditionalization" and "Oedipalization," one that underlines the kinship of Rodrigo, Teodosio, San Albano, et al.

Perhaps we can now formulate a general "law" of magico-persecutory thought that would cover both its initial potential for violence and its subsequent fictionalization: the projective you-are-guilty paradigm shifts towards the introjective I-am-guilty paradigm as the extreme stress that provoked the first subsides. Or to put it another way, the "sacrificial" mechanisms that afford a threatened in-group its last line of defense are supplanted by the "confessional" mechanisms that regulate traditional societies in times of relative peace. What keeps this whole scheme from being evolutionary is the ever-present possibility of a return to sacrificial or expulsive procedures in times of renewed stress, when self-defense reasserts its logical/chronological hegemony over self-knowledge.

The legend of Rodrigo has been analyzed by Bruce Beatie in his attempt to prove the superiority of Russian structural morphology over Menéndez Pidal's *neotradicionalismo* (Beatie 1976). In essence, Beatie seeks to establish a new way of accounting for the traditionality of the Rodrigo cycle based on the systematic application of Proppian tale "functions"—even though he recognizes that Propp developed his theory to account for the structure of fairy tales, not tragic narrative ballads (1976:47). In attempting to overcome this difficulty, Beatie assimilates fairy tales to the genre of romance and alters the meaning of a number of crucial functions:

I suspect, judging from this analysis of the Rodrigo cycle as well as from other observations, that the *functional* difference between a romantic and a tragic narrative occurs only in the second half, and that it is not a matter of different function, but of *transvalued* functions: the "reward" is death, not a wedding; the "recognition" becomes self-perception, the "exposure" becomes confession, and the "punishment" becomes penance: in short, in a tragic narrative the roles of hero, false hero, and villain become melded. . . . The tradition clearly cannot decide whether Rodrigo is a villain or hero, and as a result motivations in the rest of the tale are ambiguous. [1976:47–48; emphases in original]

Beatie's attempt to salvage Proppian narremes leads him to describe the Rodrigo cycle in the same way that Edmunds describes the analogues of Oedipus. Heroic culprits, punishment as penance—these are indeed the observable ambiguities of the tradition, along with the others listed by Menéndez Pidal. But if we are to have any hope of making sense of them, narrative functions must be subordinated to sociopsychological ones. Again, stories do not tell themselves. When one approaches pious legends in terms of magico-persecutory thought and stays on to witness the end of "infantile" projection and the always painful but ultimately consoling acknowledgment of one's own failings, then apparent ambiguities can be swiftly resolved against the gestalt of traditional moral reinforcement.

The ongoing "invention of tradition" that characterizes folklore in general can be collated with moral progress in the Spanish legends I have dealt with. It is legitimate to speak of textual and moral evolution as long as it is stipulated that any gains won are provisional and can be lost in new crises and new crisis-induced fabulation. These are the parameters in which traditional supernatural sanctions move, in one direction or the other, across the ages. Evidence would seem to confirm that historical Christianity "backed down" from the sublime anti-mythic and anti-persecutory insights of the Gospels, as Girard maintains (1978a: 266–373); but even inside the general constraints of popular piety, healing catharsis and moral progress sui generis are still possible.

6

Popular Justice Justified

Sociocentrism is the living matrix of vast segments of Spanish culture, including folk beliefs and folk humor, popular piety, traditional concepts of honor and shame, legends, rites, and fiestas. It has been established that consciousness of opposition is intrinsic to sociocentrism and its cultural vehicles: one group defines itself in relation to others in a system of comparison, interaction, and confrontation. It is a relatively straightforward matter to follow up the logic of intra-community logomachy through the evocation of an enemy horizon and the resultant intercommunity mythomachy, insult-trading, ingenuous exaltation of the local patron saint, festal feuding, and so forth. None of this is particularly problematic from a theoretical point of view. What complicates the picture is the phenomenon of persecution. Persecution is not interested in the maintenance of reciprocal or mutually cooperative hostilities—it wants to destroy the opposition. It will hear nothing of half-way solutions. Persecution is a more desperate answer to identity crisis; it seems to respond to more primary sociopsychological mechanisms; it seems to have more to do with what consolidates groups and makes them successful ecological competitors in the first place. At the same time, it is more "magical" in its resolute urge to search out and punish. . . .

The vicissitudes of history and geography have made Spain an ideal "laboratory" for observing the cultural consequences of war and persecution, but this hardly means that her towns and cities are perennially engaged in guerrilla warfare or that they are chiefly composed of marauding lynch mobs. It may be, indeed, that one of the great adaptive mechanisms of Spanish culture lies in the ritual canalization of collective violence. To paraphrase a Spanish proverb, the blood hardly ever reaches the river. This is no mean achievement, after all, and one for which folklore can take its share of the credit.

In the sphere of "symmetrical" sociocentrism, violence is kept in bounds by festive confrontations between two or more similar-sized groups or segments of the same group, whereas the asymmetric sphere of sociocentrism maintains itself through the festive elimination of a traditional culprit. Ritualized rivalry and scapegoating do not occupy watertight compartments: they can coexist in the same festal environment and the first can even slide into the second, as evidenced by a handful of *moros y cristianos* celebrations that culminate in the shooting of the "traitorous Moor" (González Casarrubios 1985 : 158). Both major categories of ritual violence are equally dependent upon religious symbolism. Both give rise to diverse forms of folklore that never fail to fortify a community's sense of identity and satisfy its aesthetic urge.

Nevertheless, in light of my review of persecutory mythopoesis, magico-persecutory thought, and the legends of remorse-ridden Oedipal saints, it might well be suspected that, in comparison with the reciprocity of festal feuding, the one-sidedness of festal scapegoating will prove to have profounder links with traditional moral reinforcement, greater psychological subtlety, more room for the free play of fantasies and guilt feelings alike, and the capacity for a more intense or thoroughgoing catharsis. The central obsession of historical Christianity and the most solemn fiestas of Spain— those pertaining to the Passion and Resurrection of Jesus—may be related in some intimate way to the asymmetric canalization of collective violence, to say nothing of the raucous disorders of Carnival and the orderly bloodshed of the bullfight. Everything suggests, therefore, that a closer look at festal scapegoating will enable us to lay hands on some vital keys to Spanish popular piety and popular culture.

It must be pointed out that to use the word "scapegoating" is to impose an a priori anthropological interpretation upon the phenomena in question. Asymmetric sociocentrism does not and cannot picture itself in such terms; the ritual violence it practices is never understood as a question of victimization but as one of *justicia popular*. Any enemy of God's is an enemy of mine—so goes the groupthink of popular justice. And since the enemy always makes the first move, he only brings upon himself the group's violent punishment of his perfidy; popular justice is another name for legitimate self-defense. This simple but foolproof rationale lies at the heart of folk Spain's major simulacrum of popular justice: the festive destruction in effigy of that archetypal enemy of God and his people, Judas Iscariot. This custom constitutes the expedient point of departure for the exploration of others that rely on real, flesh-and-blood victims (bovids, cocks, swine, etc.).

Burning Judas

Easter Sunday is the day commonly set aside for the execution of Judas, following his "resurrection" in the form of a simple wire framework stuffed with fireworks and flammable material. The phase of construction is as fundamental to the overall significance of the ritual as the subsequent phases of display and destruction, and is normally the privilege of either the young women of the village or the young men of military age (*quintos*). What the well-dressed effigy will wear is the main concern of its makers. Clothing can be donated but is preferably stolen from the clotheslines of careless neighbors during Lent. In most places the neighbors are granted the right to ransom their laundry before it is burned along with the effigy (González Casarrubios 1985 : 58). Stealing the effigy of a neighboring town has been a time-honored practice as well, one that has given rise to traditional *coplas* like

En Pinilla nació el Judas,	The Judas was born in Pinilla,
por Vallorente pasó,	passed through Vallorente,
y por su mala cabeza,	and for his foolhardiness,
en Peralejos murió.	he perished in Peralejos.
[García Sanz 1948 : 620]	

In the province of Logroño, the people of Nalda have traditionally claimed that Judas himself hailed from Viguera, a rival town within earshot of Nalda (Caro 1957 : 277).

Once constructed, the Judas must be displayed in a suitable manner—impaled on a pole in the town plaza or hung from a church
tower, a tree, or the balcony of city hall. García Sanz relates that, in
contrast to Carrascosilla de Huete (Cuenca) or Menasalba (Toledo),
no town in the province of Guadalajara beats its Judas with canes
or parades it around on a burro (1948 : 619–620). Obscene placards
are often hung around the effigy's neck, or it is tossed on a blanket,
smeared with excrement, insulted, stoned, and so on (González
Casarrubios 1985 : 57–58). In Peñalba de la Sierra (Guadalajara), a
pair of male and female effigies known as *El Judas* and *La Judas* are
suspended between the two giant elms of the plaza to the tune of

Judas Iscariote,
que mató a su padre
con un garrote,
y a su madre,
con una espada.
Calle usted, padre;
calle usted, madre;
que no ha sido nada.
[González Casarrubios 1985 : 58]

Judas Iscariot,
who killed his father
with a cane,
and his mother,
with a sword.
Hush, father;
Hush, mother;
it didn't hurt a bit.

The *dromenon* of the effigy's destruction is also accompanied
by some *legomenon* wherever it takes place—proverbs, satirical
verses, ribald songs, and especially the *testamentos* that constitute
the major vehicle of popular censure in Spain (García de Diego
1953, 1960:298–301). It would seem that neither the rituals nor
the folklore they generate could be labeled "persecution texts" in
the sense of distorted accounts of real acts of collective violence
(Girard 1982 : 18); the New Testament Judas did not perish at the
hands of a mob and he never set foot in Spain. But the matter would
change if "Judas" were taken to represent "Jew." There is at least
one Spanish fiesta, the famous *Pero-Palo* of Villanueva de la Vera
(Cáceres), that may well be derived from a real medieval massacre
or expulsion of Jews.

Like the Judases shotgunned and burned all over Spain, the Pero-
Palo is an effigy whose fabrication is carried out by local *mozos* and
mozas with materials at hand. But the rite possesses a number of
features that set it apart: its duration (Sunday, Monday, and Tuesday of Carnival), the great variety of subrituals and superstitions it

gives rise to, its staged reenactment of a judicial proceeding, and
the copious nature of the folk poetry that explains why the Pero-
Palo deserves death:

El Pero-Palo nosotros
queremos para quemarle,
que son Judas que hacemos
afrenta de su linaje.
Esos de los gorros negros,
azules y colorados,
no son de la buena gente,
que a Cristo crucificaron . . .
Ese que llaman Revive,
por su nombre Pedro Pablo,
le ha salido la sentencia
que tiene que ser quemado . . .
Judíos poneis al punto
que viene la Inquisición
que ha salido de Llerena
que nuestro Rey lo mandó.
Si se acabara la casta
mejor para el mundo fuera;
mejor fuera para Dios
si de esa casta no hubiera . . .
Que se junte mucha leña
y se haga un joguerón
y allí se vaya echando
los de la mala intención.
Judíos, mi Padre es Cristo,
vosotros me la matásteis;
cada día que amanece
veo quien mató a mi Padre.
El año de ochenta y uno
nos dieron la jugarreta
entre judíos e intrusos
y gente de mala jeta. . . .
[Ramón y Fernández 1950:92−94]

We want the Pero-Palo
to burn him up,
it is Judas that we make
shame of his lineage.
Those with the black,
blue, and red caps,
are not good people,
for they crucified Christ . . .
He who is called Revive,
Pedro Pablo by name,
the verdict has been declared
that he must be burnt . . .
Jews, watch out
the Inquisition is coming
It has departed Llerena
as ordered by our King.
If the caste were eradicated
it would be better for all;
it would be better for God
if there were no such caste . . .
May lots of wood be gathered
and a bonfire be built
and into the fire be thrown
those with evil intentions.
Jews, my Father is Christ,
you killed him on me;
with every day that dawns
I see who killed my Father.
Back in eighty-one
we were double-crossed
by Jews and intruders
and ugly-looking people. . . .

Fifty or sixty stanzas of varying rhyme and meter combine ram-
bling invectives with accounts of hostile confrontations with Llerena and other neighboring towns (reputed to be full of evil-minded
Jews). The three day celebration culminates in the mock trial of
Pero-Palo, impersonated by a man draped in a sheet and mounted
on the oldest and most wretched burro in town. One of the judges

eventually rises to read the sentence—"condemned to death by the Popular Tribunal for crimes of high treason." Donkey and rider are then paraded through the streets of Villanueva amidst great fanfare. In the afternoon the effigy is carried around in a mock procession by young women dressed in the regional attire of Cáceres, who pause every now and then to spin Pero-Palo around on the pole that supports him; this maneuver is known as the *judiada*. Other women pretend to weep upon hearing that Pero-Palo may be pardoned for his crimes. Other segments of the population intervene in ritual jests too numerous to relate until the final moment of the representation, when the effigy is blown to bits by a "firing squad" (Ramón y Fernández 1950:87–92; Gutiérrez Macías 1960:355–356). From his study of the folk poetry and the history of the area, Ramón y Fernández concludes that the fiesta of the Pero-Palo commemorates some violent incident provoked centuries ago, perhaps as early as the fourteenth century, by Jewish "irreverences with regard to our religion" (1950:95). Yet the only "solid" evidence we have is the fiesta itself, and its endless stream-of-consciousness diatribes.

The temptation to associate the hundreds of ritual burnings of Judas with the Spanish Inquisition's fiery *autos de fe* is a difficult one to resist. More so when we learn that the *autos* were often held to "celebrate" royal coronations, weddings, military victories, etc., and that they were taken as occasions of festal revelry for nobles and commoners alike (Bennassar 1985:146–147). An *auto de fe* was not an act of popular justice, but a justly popular exercise in institutional exorcism that stimulated the masses in much the same manner as the festive "hanging days" of England (Sueiro 1974:324–326). At least one prestigious Spanish folklorist has considered the folk executions of Judas to be so much mimesis of the *autos de fe* of yesteryear (García de Diego 1953:63).

But from here to a *gesunkenes Kulturgut* hunt for other automatistic survivals is but a step. Do the people of hundreds of villages across Spain only burn Judas because their great-great-grandfathers did, or can such behaviors be found to make sense now, functional or psychological sense for the groups involved? In every act of popular justice there is an implicit process of "diagnosis" (the enemy of the people is identified) and "cure" (he is eliminated). This suggests that the festive destruction of Judas ought to be seen against the general background of all the non-festal folk procedures for the location and expulsion of evil in any guise; these in turn can be shown to rest upon the web of conflicts and alliances that structures life in rural communities.

The Diagnosis and Treatment of Envy

Now we come face to face with the deepest layer of sociocentrism and with an enemy horizon that is operative *inside* the boundaries of the community. For there are neighboring towns and neighbors within towns, separate households that compete for scarce resources in a fairly static agrarian economy and produce what might be considered the most primary kinds of folk fears and folk remedies, as well as standard ritual means of prevention like the ones Lisón has found in northwestern Spain:

The local universe is visualized in terms of inside and outside; the first is known and the second is unknown; in the former one lives and prevails, while the latter is a source of uncertainty and must be purified. . . . Rituals surrounding the house repeatedly confirm this polarization. Numerous rites of defense and separation from the environment evoke the image of a medieval castle protected by ramparts. . . . This ritual obsession with purifying entries and protecting exits—the limits—highlights the household's unicity, its separation from and opposition to the little local universe that surrounds it: the village, that is, other households and people. [1974: 102–103]

No matter how carefully it is carried out, however, this ritual prophylaxis cannot always stave off the numerous occasions for injury or wickedness that inhere to the very order of things.

The perennial scarcity of land and resources makes suspicion endemic in many parts of rural Spain—suspicion not of strangers, in this case, but of those one knows all too well: the neighbors. The mistrust of fellow ecological competitors conditions the symbolico-moral outlook of each. Anything that goes wrong for no apparent reason is routinely attributed to the hidden envy of some neighbor, though one can never be sure which. The traditional war between the sexes furnishes an especially fertile soil for the flowering of such paranoid thoughts and speculations (Cátedra Tomás 1976: 36–42). Lisón describes village society as the interaction of "vectors of hostility" (1974:112), an appropriate metaphor since envy is reified into a metaphysical force field whose destructive rays can strike anywhere. Envy, says Risco, "is not a sentiment but an action" (1961:69). Envy is a broad, general, impersonal, free-floating ill will that always recurs to the same device to produce its pernicious and even lethal effects: evil eye. The chief target of evil eye, as might be imagined, is the *casa*, including the people who live in it, their livestock, and their crops. When the fortunes of the household take a sudden turn for the worse, one knows that it is being envied, actively envied, and diverse rituals are called upon to "disinfect" it. Significantly, envy's evil eye is especially prone to attack during moments of crucial importance to the long-term integrity of the household—the birth of a son, the marriage of a daughter, or the sale of a cow. Since the cow is the economic motor of the *casa* (Lisón 1974:119), the most sightly heads are kept out of sight, for to see is to envy. Pigs, mules, and oxen are no less vulnerable, and endless rites have been created to protect these animals. *Mal de ojo* (evil eye) is considered to be responsible for different types of contagious diseases or infestations, bad luck, clumsiness, fires, insanity, crop damage, and sexual dysfunction (Risco 1961:72–78; Cátedra Tomás 1976:22–25). Folk medicine in Spain is largely composed of magical methods of defense, diagnosis, and cure of evil eye. Of the eighteen *curanderos* or folk healers currently practicing in the province of Ciudad Real, for example, nine are generalists, one fixes broken bones, and the other eight are specialists in the elimination of *mal de ojo* (Ramírez Rodrigo 1985:356–357). Where the generalists depend on their intimate knowledge of herbs and natural remedies, the specialists derive their curative powers from God.

It must be emphasized that we are dealing with a hermeneutic system devised by the people themselves, one that accords with the rivalry-ridden structure of an economically static rural society. Standing outside the system, it is easy to say, as Castillo de Lucas does, that the villagers are engulfed in the most benighted and erroneous sorts of superstition (1968:132–135). But this is to overlook the adaptive nature of folk beliefs and their real, functional benefits for the people involved. The system itself paradoxically promotes social harmony in the very midst of social strife in at least three major ways: First of all, a cleansing kind of projection is carried out when envy is conceived of in quasi-metaphysical terms. A group of neighbors who quarrel and compete but who need each other all the same effectively transform malice into an impersonal force, identify it with the very nature of the cosmos, and thereby relieve each other of much of the blame. Secondly, one does not have to be a doctrinaire Freudian to posit that the suspicion or hostile intent one neighbor may harbor for another can by a circuitous process arouse feelings of guilt, guilt defined as an inner fear of vengeance or punishment for wrongdoing. How this brand of magico-persecutory thought functions in a folk milieu is described by Lisón in his study of Galician *envidia*. The process, as usual, begins with diagnosis; some mishap has overtaken a given individual and he immediately traces it to envy. Lisón reconstructs the subsequent reasoning: "Is it only one envier or are there several? If there are several, why do they all plot against me at once?" (1974:120). In the auto-interrogation session that follows, the individual reviews his recent conduct toward his neighbors and often finds himself to be fully deserving of the misfortune he has incurred:

Indeed, last Sunday at the tavern I was too harsh in speaking with Antonio; I still haven't forgiven Amaro for letting his cows enter my pasture; one night I used Rosalindo's water without permission; what's more, yesterday Agueda came by asking for a jar of milk and I told her we didn't have any. [1974:121]

Ironically, pangs of conscience born in the ongoing community game of intrigue and mistrust ultimately make a villager more conscious of his or her neighborly duties. Where Llompart affirms that religion is what gives the Spaniard his social conscience (1968: 231), Lisón traces it to the dynamics of envy! Avarice, gossip, and unseemly ostentation are kept within bounds in much the same way (Cátedra Tomás 1976:12−15; Gilmore 1987:166−170).

Finally, the projective and introjective varieties of magico-persecutory thought that prevail in Spain's folk enclaves establish orderly procedures for the expulsion of ill will that may even increase in efficacy at more inclusive levels of sociocentrism. At the most basic level, the people who derive their identity from a certain family or *casa* employ magic rites to defend themselves, their buildings, and their animals. If evil eye strikes, it will be ritually purged—a "therapeutic" measure always understood by the people involved to be simple self-defense. Moving outward one level, the independent households of a community band together to protect themselves from an extra-local brand of evil that is symbolized, more often than not, by the figure of the witch. All the vectors of hostility that crisscross the community converge on this fearsome creature. Preventative and curative aspects of folk rites often coincide in great festivals of purification like Saint John's Eve, when witches are mystically driven out or warned away with bonfires that simultaneously heal the victims of their malice (Bobadilla Conesa 1981). The mimetic strife that originates in the very structure of village society is temporarily dissolved in miraculous and cathartic *communitas*.

From Popular Justice to Popular Censure

How do the festal bonfires of folk Spain relate to the festive burnings of Judas in effigy? That both represent fiery forms of disinfection is clear enough. Another element of continuity can be found in the archetypal persecutory accusation of evil eye. Jews have been as susceptible to this charge as witches over the centuries, and with far more disastrous consequences. The first mass attack upon the Jews as sorcerers, in twelfth-century England, was triggered by Richard the First's refusal to allow a delegation of Jews to "observe" his coronation (Trachtenberg 1983:70–71). The evil eye is still known as *Judenblick* in certain areas of rural Europe (1983: 232). The fact that Judas is not specifically charged with *mal de ojo* in Spain does not necessarily liberate him from "guilt by association" with the alleged magical malevolence of his race; as far as Spanish villagers are concerned, says Lisón, it is not necessary to be a witch or a sorcerer nor to possess evil eye in order to cause harm: to harbor "ill will" is enough (1974:115). The Jews who are associated with Pero-Palo in Villanueva de la Vera's festive lynching are repeatedly referred to as *los de la mala intención*—those with evil intentions—(Ramón y Fernández 1950:92–94), a veritable catchall crime that serves to remind us that persecution typically begins with an in-group's "delusions of persecution."

It can be conjectured that Pero-Palo and other Judases are put to the torch for blighting glance, crimes of high treason, parricide, and any other loathsome machination that the community projects onto its appropriate traditional targets and expurgates. What is "superstitious" folk medicine at the household level becomes *justicia popular* at the community level. Sacrificial efficacy is a function of consensus and the combined power of multiple vectors of hostility focused in a single direction. But it would be a mistake to assume that the inhabitants of Spanish towns and villages are unaware of the potential for violence that accrues to their rivalrous personal relations or are ignorant of asymmetric ritual's genuine functionality. For example, the bonfires lit by the people of Salas de los Infantes (Burgos) in late November are not to warn away witches but to symbolically do away with all the quarrels, jealousies, and disagreements that have disturbed the domestic peace throughout the year—so say the people themselves (Blanco 1983:135). The fires are kept burning for three days during the fiesta of Saint Cecilia while the two thousand neighbors rekindle their sense of solidarity on the threshold of the long Castilian winter. The fiesta of Saint Joseph in Valencia represents a more famous example of such conscious purificatory pyromania. There, an army of craftsmen works all year long to construct the enormous *ninots* or *fallas* that satirize local, national, and international iniquities; on the night of March 19th they are all set ablaze at once with stunning results. The social life of the city is largely composed of the contests, dances, excursions, benefits, parties, and work sessions that every neighborhood organizes to fund its *falla* and other festal activities (San Valero Aparisi 1969:215–218; Sanmartín Arce 1982:51–53). *Las Fallas* provide a splendid example of how the "absolutist" attitude of asymmetric ritual expulsion can propel a "relativist" system of symmetrical sociocentrism, since every neighborhood's *ninot* symbolically defines its identity in keen competition with the others. As with the brilliant urban versions of *moros y cristianos*, cooperative rivalry eventually serves to cement the prestige of the entire city.

But the most widespread and beneficial forms of popular satire are to be found not in urban but in rural Spain, where the strife and conflicts of daily life are dissipated not only with fire but with something akin to confession.

Collective justice is the motive behind numerous ceremonies that take place in our towns in which the neighbors are publicly censured and their faults proclaimed, in which no one has the right to take offense, and in which the guilty party accepts the punishment of public shame and the laughter of his fellows.   [García de Diego 1960:295]

Popular censure can take a great many verbal or ritual forms and appear in a wide variety of festal contexts. In his lengthy analysis of wintertime folk masquerades in Castile, Caro Baroja concludes that a principal function of these carnivalesque rituals is the renewal of group identity through the deliberate airing of intra-community grievances and malicious gossip (1963:288–289). The evils attaining to neighborly coexistence can best be expelled, it seems, by stripping away the secrecy that normally cloaks such evils, by making public, in a ritual framework, all of the private scandals that undermine community solidarity. This confessional purgation is usually accompanied by simulated combats between "good" and "evil" personages and the eventual triumph of the former. The communal secrecy of masks permits divisive secrecy to be unmasked—satirized, neutralized, and laughed away. Though agricultural concerns and implements (especially the plough) loom large in these rustic rites, far more is at stake than the rebirth of Frazer's or Mannhardt's vegetation spirit (Caro 1963:290–293).

The *romería* is another festal genre that lends itself to the humorous purging of collective sins. During the annual festivities in honor of the Virgen de las Nieves held at her sanctuary to the north of Espinosa (Burgos), ten masked figures execute archaic dances that represent the struggle between good and bad and then recite verses and "sermons" that

are listened to with hilarity by the whole assemblage, although the people of Espinosa are the only ones who really understand the jokes, since the themes treated always refer to very domestic situations that they alone know about.   [Blanco 1983:96]

Esoteric humor thus ratifies an individual's sense of belonging to the in-crowd, even when he or she is the butt of the joke.

The principal vehicle of popular censure has been the testament, a type of popular literature modeled after the legal document in which some animal or historical personage symbolically distributes the different parts of his body for purposes of satire—"I bequeath my tongue to _____ (some gossip or charlatan), my muscles to _____ (some notorious sissy), my ears to _____ (some deaf person)," etc. By way of advancing her argument that this jocular genre derives from the religious sacrifice of animals in ancient Rome, García de Diego recurs to the festive beheadings of hens and roosters that remain popular throughout rural Spain and are often accompanied by songs that allude to the hapless bird's bequest (1953: 28–34). In many villages the custom forms part of Carnival and is frequently the prerogative of the young women, who bury the cock up to its neck, blindfold each other, and set to work with staffs; their victim comprises the main course of the communal feast that follows (González Casarrubios 1985: 35–36).

Rooster-running, for so it is called, has a special significance when carried out by soon-to-be-conscripted young men. In most places it functions as a vertitable rite of passage, one which calls forth its own subvariety of popular censure. While their godmothers pamper and fatten the sacrificial fowl for months on end, the *quintos* busy themselves with the preparation of their "relations." These are humorous autobiographical speeches in verse in which the young man makes a clean breast of the different pranks he has been involved in over the years as well as all the negative facets of his personality. In Guarrate (Zamora), the *quintos* seek out local "bards" to assist them in the preparation of their relations (Blanco 1983: 17–18). Mounted on horseback in full uniform, each young man recites his comic confession to the rooster dangling head-down from a rope slung across the plaza. Outsiders are usually hard-pressed to follow the relation, Blanco relates, for its many oblique references to incidents familiar to the insiders alone (1983: 19). Upon concluding, the *quinto* draws his saber and condemns the rooster (and his past disgraces) to an ignominious death. At least one anthropologist has described this rite as symbolic self-castration in the service of community stability (Delgado Ruiz

1986 : 144−147); others are content to dismiss the whole affair as pure barbarism (Martínez 1986 : 16).

As it turns out, one of the most popular exponents of the parodic folk genre of testaments has been the Testament of Judas, and, not surprisingly, the festive cremation of Judas in effigy has been the traditional occasion for its recital. That the ritual destruction of Judas is taken advantage of for purposes of popular censure constitutes striking confirmation of their kinship. The people of a given village purposefully associate their mistrust, petty jealousies, and strife-ridden social relations with the exemplary punishment meted out to their common enemy. The collation of *justicia popular* with *censura popular* reinforces the positive bonds and mores that enable small communities to survive and confirms that rites like the burning of Judas "survive" because they respond to current, ongoing social and emotional needs. True enough, a person does not usually step forward to declare his guilt as in the rites of rooster decapitation; but in certain circumstances people do not mind being accused or mocked, provided their own identity is intimately bound up with that of the mockers. The fact that a neighbor will actually feel slighted or left out if his name is not included in the festive fault-finding (García de Diego 1960 : 295) dramatically demonstrates that the ordinary rules of honor and shame have been temporarily suspended in favor of something more satisfying. We are all alike after all (a group seems to say), even in our sins; let us get them out into the open and defuse them, or burn them up along with the Judas.

It is at the village level that magico-persecutory ways of thinking most patently reveal their diagnostic demands, defensive posture, and sacrificial efficacy—sacrificial in the Girardian sense of an inner potential for violence projected outwards, reified, and sanctified. A village achieves unity by ritually evoking the specter of its enemy horizon and by creating a unified focus for the vectors of hostility that charge the local force-field of ill will. But the villagers are not as enthralled in purblind *méconnaissance* as we might have been led to expect. The Spanish ethnographic data confirm once again that projective mechanisms of group solidarity provide a matrix for introjective or confessional ones. Once again we see the canny coexistence and even symbiosis of ritual means of self-defense and ritual support of self-knowledge.

7

Spanish Catholicism on Trial

Religious folklore can reflect persecutory thoughts or deeds in two ways, depending upon the viewpoint of the group that propagates the lore. From the perspective of a victimizing group, we obtain legends, tales, and rituals that camouflage victims as culprits and persecutions as acts of collective or divine justice. From the perspective of a persecuted group, victims are innocent and the violence done to them will be remembered as the unprovoked savagery of tyrants or mobs. Though the second view is undeniably closer to the facts of the matter, medieval martyrologies prove that it too is susceptible to the sociocentric manipulations and fabrications that serve to reassure the community, shore up its worldview, reinforce its moral standards, and even gratify its aesthetic sense.

Spanish folk legends and folk rituals demonstrate that, in practice, the perpetrators of popular justice typically portray themselves as the innocent victims or the defenders of the innocent victims of some evildoer. The group sees itself not as the aggressor but as the redresser. This simple but expedient rationale supplies the ethical scaffolding for rites like the burning of Judas in effigy or the expulsion of witches, and is not impertinent to the festive beheading of the cock or the sacrifice of bovids. Animals are not criminals, of course, but the rooster's apparent lasciviousness and the bull's violent charges effectively prevent them from being perceived as scapegoats.

Representations of popular justice are always light hearted and even comic affairs, unlike popular representations of injustice that dwell upon the tragic and sorrowful aspects of a victim's demise. History has made of Spain an ideal "laboratory" for the observation of both. Yet no attempt has been made thus far to collate its disguised persecutory culture with the undisguised kind or to relate festive rites of victimization with mournful ones. Is one category of persecutory mythopoesis more instrumental than the other to an understanding of Spain's popular religiosity? Or could one even exist without the other?

The script that structures the popular theatre of Holy Week is loosely based on the narrative of the Gospels but owes much more to the devotion to the crucified Christ that was fomented first by the Franciscans of the fifteenth century and afterwards by the Church of the Counter-Reformation (Christian 1976:66–70). It is more than likely that this devotion to the Passion reflects an erroneous or "sacrificial" reading of Christ's career of the sort described by Girard (1978a:324–329). To be sure, Girard is hardly the first to call attention to the gulf that separates the Evangelical Passion from the one developed by historical Christianity.

There are not a few modern intellectuals who genuinely believe that Christianity, centering as it does in the Cross, has exerted its power by an appeal to, and indeed a secret stimulus to, man's hidden obsession with suffering and even blood-lust. They point to the popular piety and art forms of the centuries—crucifixes, paintings, and sculpture representing specifically the tortured Christ, as well as the hymns, poems, and homilies dwelling in an ambiguous way upon the blood of Christ. It is not surprising that such observers find it difficult to draw the line between the healthy and the morbid. Psychology appears to speak all too relevantly of masochism and sadism. Social psychology speaks of repressions and ritual compensations and of ancient archetypes of the atoning victim. [Wilder 1960:109]

More than one observer has found Spain to be a veritable museum of such horrors. From the fifteenth to the twentieth centuries, says Bennassar, every diary-keeping traveler in Spain has attended Holy Week processions and has been alternately entranced or disgusted by the vision of barefoot penitents dragging chains, flagellating each other, and groaning under enormous crosses (1985:40–41).

Most disturbing of all have been the Andalusian representations of the Passion, which, according to Domínguez Morano, express a popular religiosity whose "pathological" and "infantile" aspects can hardly by ignored (1985:171). Wilder, more cautious, simply points out that Spanish Catholicism's hyperbolic and overstrained prolongation of Christ's agony can "easily pass over into forms that are more than suspect" (1960:113).

The Passion of Christ lends itself to innumerable "readings." It may constitute an Oedipal drama, a reworking of Neolithic nature myths, or, as Girard argues, the ultimate unmasking of the victimage mechanism; sacrificial Christianity "fetishized" the Passion and thereby fell back into the same state of mythological paganism that Christ had come to subvert (1978a:266–373). But one thing is the script and another is the performance. To measure the degree of emotional or cultural maturity attaining to the ritual reenactment of Christ's death is a risky and complicated undertaking. One's own sociocentric prejudices can easily enter into the process of condemnation or exoneration. How are we to know, for example, what the people participating in a Passion procession really experience at an unconscious level? To what extent are Spaniards beholden to sacrificial or sadomasochistic archetypes of violence? To what extent does the general cultural "style" of Spain reflect an excessive or morbid preoccupation with suffering?

In this chapter I will attempt to provide definitive answers to these questions. To better explore the persecutory structure of processions that dramatize the Passion of Christ, I will first review the major social and psychological functions of other ritual dramas that revolve around mock victimization.

Scapegoating as Popular Theatre

The role of scapegoat in a Spanish festal representation is not always played by an inanimate effigy or an animal. In Villanueva's trial and execution of Pero-Palo, it will be recalled, two "actors" impersonate the arch-traitor—a flesh-and-blood volunteer on donkey-back and the man of straw, with the latter standing in for the former in front of the firing squad. Fifty years ago in Villanueva de

Odra (Burgos), the young man playing Judas was actually killed by his overenthusiastic neighbors, but such occurrences are fortunately very uncommon (Caro 1965a:132). In the district of San Pedro Manrique (Soria), in the days before the construction of an effigy became standard procedure, the most recent arrival had to play Judas in the burlesque ceremonies of Easter Sunday, receiving his share of physical and verbal abuse from the youngsters; if the newest neighbor happened to be the schoolteacher, he usually found some excellent excuse to leave town that day (Manrique 1952:503–506). A similar initiation of strangers appears to be the main social function of the *Fiesta de la Vaca* in San Pablo de los Montes (Toledo). On the feast-day of Saint Paul in late January, neighbors solemnly carrying the icon of the patron in procession are continually bedeviled by a transvestite, a cow-boy (*mozo-vaca*) armed with a long pole topped with two huge horns, and two "bullocks" who jangle cowbells and shout "there goes the cow!" every time they rush past the main group. After a Mass is said in honor of the saint, the good people of San Pablo line the street from the church to the plaza in a mood of jubilant expectation, for every outsider present at the fiesta will now be chased from one end of the long gantlet to the other by the strange coterie; the hapless visitor is held fast by the two bullocks while the cow-boy pokes and prods him along with his inordinate horns. The outsider is considered an insider once the ordeal is over and is regaled with lemonade and candy in the town plaza (Pan 1945:194–199; González Casarrubios 1985:24–25).

Other scapegoating representations that employ human actors serve a different function. On Carnival Tuesday in San Benito (Ciudad Real), for example, a group of neighbors armed with shotguns ceremoniously leaves town and returns with a manacled man mounted on a burro. This "*faccioso*" or rebel is given a mock trial in the town square and condemned to death, whereupon his "mother," played by another local man, comes forward to beg her son to repent and pardon his debtors; the *faccioso* only agrees to a fifty percent reduction in the imaginary debts owed him. So, beginning with the most notorious skinflints, everyone is eventually obliged to make a contribution—a novel way to finance the fiestas—until the vast quantities of wine consumed by all make the rebel's execution impossible (González Casarrubios 1985:42).

In the more isolated regions of Spain, fiestas are almost synonymous with the masked, tricksterlike figures who have come to be known over the centuries by some of the strangest appellatives in the Spanish language: *cachimorros, choqueiros, madamas, mozorros, muradanas, tazarrones, vexigueos,* and *zaharrones,* to name only a few (García Sanz 1953; Caro 1963:148–216; Blanco 1983: 144–146; González Casarrubios 1985:23–24, 40–41). Under the generic title of *botargas,* they have fulfilled a wide variety of functions throughout the festal year, most notably in the winter months. They can be fund-raisers, auctioneers, minstrels, dance directors, or generalized disturbers of the peace. They are often associated with the popular censure or satire described extensively by García de Diego (1960). They impersonate animals, virtues, vices, saints, and devils in popular dramas. Sometimes what they do is too enigmatic for classification. Scholars disagree as to whether the *botargas* has his origins in Roman times or "only" goes back as far as the Middle Ages. A *botargas* enjoys a particularly paradoxical relationship with women and children: in some towns he scares and chases them and in other towns they chase him, following the appropriate provocations (Caro 1965b; González Casarrubios 1985:40).

The young man chosen by lot to play the *zangarrón* of Sanzoles (Zamora) incarnates many of the above mentioned functions and behaviors. Stockings of two different tones, a gaudy checkered suit, a black leather mask with a red nose, and a multicolored headdress comprise his outfit; a stick festooned with swollen bladders is his "weapon." He is accompanied by a retinue that includes a drummer, two pipers, two butlers, two bakers, and two transvestites. The fiesta begins on Christmas Day. After interpreting a traditional dance known as *"El Niño"* in honor of the newborn Savior, the *zangarrón's* retinue goes all over town asking for donations, while the *zangarrón* himself steals everything he can stuff into a large sack tied to his back. Children hurl rotten fruit to provoke him into frenetic pursuits. The actors then seek out the local priest and accompany him to the church; a high Mass is celebrated while the *zangarrón* waits outside. The image of Saint Stephen is then brought out in procession, and, while the 800-odd citizens of Sanzoles insult and pretend to attack the holy icon, the suddenly pious *zangarrón* fends them off with his bladder-stick.

No clear explanation for this behavior exists. Some say that the town re-enacts Saint Stephen's martyrdom; others relate that the town was once stricken with plague and commended itself to the saint, but when their prayers and processions did not end the problem they began to pummel the icon, whereupon a neighbor disguised as a billy goat drove them away with a horsewhip. [Blanco 1983:149–150]

Such are the unlikely derivations of persecutory mytho- and rito-poesis. In any case, Christianity's first martyr undergoes a fresh persecution every year in Sanzoles, with the neighbors happy to portray a mob and a garish *botargas* charged with defending the target of their righteous wrath.

Violence and piety converge in an even more remarkable way in the fiesta of the *Cascamorras*, a unique blend of *romería*, popular theatre, and feud elaborated around a Virgin whose tutelary protection is disputed by two small towns in rural Granada. According to the legend, the first *Cascamorras* was a descendant of the stone-mason of Guadix who in 1490 discovered a miraculous Romanic icon of the Madonna while working near the town of Baza, some fifteen kilometers distant. The Child in the Virgin's arms cried out for mercy; "Juan Pedernal" placed the portrait in his wheelbarrow to carry it back to Guadix but the wheelbarrow refused to budge; when he pointed it towards Baza, it sped right along (Sánchez Carrillo 1951:341–342; Marín 1986). The people of Baza built a church to house the portrait (reputed to have been painted in Jerusalem from life) but the people of Guadix never forgot that one of their own had rightfully discovered it. So for the past few centuries Guadix has honored a standing vow to annually send one of its sons on a true "mission impossible": to Baza to recover the icon. A given individual volunteers for the job (as the result of some private vow or penance), dons the traditional multicolored costume bestudded with stars, and makes the journey on foot, carrying an enormous flag festooned with *exvotos*. The citizens of Guadix follow at a discreet distance. In the meantime, the citizens of Baza assemble and wait at their city limits; no sooner does the *Cascamorras* appear when the young people of Baza attack—in legitimate self-defense, naturally. The *Cascamorras* breaks into a run and defends himself as best he can with his huge banner; his personal promise-fulfilling *via crucis* has begun in earnest—"the harsh game of one man alone against hundreds of youngsters" (Sánchez Carrillo 1951:345), except that some of the youngsters are grown men. The *Cascamorras'* goal is to make it in one piece to the sanctuary that houses the icon while being subjected to extreme verbal and physical abuse. He is pushed, shoved, cursed, punched, and covered with nauseous substances. One rule of "fair play" is observed: when the *Cascamorras* falls, his many attackers are obliged to wait until he gets up again to continue the game. But there is no stopping, and any broken bones must be borne with true Christian perseverance. The popular persecution (in the primary sense of *chase*) comes to an end when the *Cascamorras* enters the church and throws himself at the feet of the appropriately named Virgin of Pity. If hospitalization is not required, the *Cascamorras* cleans up and presides over the fiesta along with the local authorities; but the poor fellow is doomed to return to Guadix empty-handed, and, ostensibly as punishment for this failure to recover the icon, his own townspeople receive him in much the same way as the citizens of Baza (Sánchez Carrillo 1951:347–348; Marín 1986).

This enigmatic folk phenomenon confirms once again that the ritual canalization of violence is one of the great creative forces of Spanish culture. *Cascamorras* can be considered the archetypal fiesta, not because it is common or widespread—far from it—but because it so uniquely synthesizes the major features of Spanish folk religion I have discussed heretofore. Velasco's view of saints as "ritualizations of sociocentric attitudes" (1981:102), Lisón's emphasis on cultural canalizations of intercommunity strife (1980:96), and Gómez-Tabanera's insistence upon the centrality of vows (1968:164–165), are all in evidence in the case of the *Cascamorras*. The relevance of *botargas* to traditional Spanish fetes (García Sanz 1953) and the purificatory functionality of same (Caro Baroja 1963:289–290; 1965b) are likewise borne out. The fetishistic dispute over possession of the Virgin amply confirms both Father Llompart's misgivings over his country's popular piety (1968:234) and theologian Maldonado's celebration of its "nostalgia for the magical" (1975:67–89). The fiesta of *Cascamorras* ceremoniously marks the enemy horizon for each of the participating towns and focuses the "hostility vectors" of both on an appropriate, time-honored target. Girard's notions regarding scapegoats, sacrificial feuding, catharsis, and even persecutory mimesis among children are all essential, in my view, to a fuller understanding of the sacral/festal rite of *Cascamorras*. Finally, the reformulation of magico-persecutory thought that I have suggested is borne out as well, for in most cases a man's own "persecutory" pangs of conscience lie behind his decision to don an eye-catching festal outfit and offer himself up, Christ-like, to be ritually persecuted. The private guilt of the *Cascamorras* and the aggressive fantasies of everyone else collaborate to purge each other.

Careful consideration of the *Cascamorras* of Granada, the *Zangarrón* of Zamora, and other rites that employ animate or inanimate scapegoats suggest that the borders between religious festival and popular theatre are well-nigh imperceptible in Spain. The "script" typically reflects some past identity crisis that elicited a violent response and was subsequently subjected to centuries of folk-work. The performance entails the active participation of all, either as protagonists or "supporting" characters. Popular participation is the essence of both folk drama and fiesta: what indeed is a fiesta but the show a town puts on for itself and about itself? The script is traditional, the assignation of roles is traditional, the time and place of performance is traditional—these factors in themselves promote that pleasing sense of group harmony that is as functional as any expulsion of evil or ritual integration of outsiders. Sometimes the script calls for vehement and seemingly sacrilegious behaviors: the solemn procession of Saint Paul is programmed to be interrupted by rude and rather obscene young men disguised as cattle; the sacred icon of Saint Stephen is to be assaulted and insulted. But sacrilege is in the eye of the beholder, not of the participants, who understand their actions as the time-honored way to pay homage to their mystical protector. When a group has had a personal supernatural friend for the past few centuries, sacrilege would consist of *not* making him an active participant in his or her own fiesta, and no friendly local saint is so stiff and formal as to take offense at a few practical jokes. To the contrary, villagers take for granted that their patron enters into the spirit of the festivities just as they do. The bond that unites a town to its patron is a very personal one, and an intense personal bond is an emotional one, full of ambiguities; these ambiguous emotions seek expression and release precisely on the day set aside for the renewal of the personal bond.

This does not imply that the villagers of San Pablo or Sanzoles or Guadix somehow contrive to lose contact with reality on an annual basis. It does mean that they personalize reality to the maximum. The saint is treated with familiarity, individual personalities meld with the sacralized personality of the group, and appropriate emotions are expressed within a traditional format. The format would probably not have become traditional in the first place if it were not emotionally gratifying. And, in view of the popular festal dramas discussed above, it can be affirmed that the simulation of persecution is an inherently satisfying vehicle of emotional gratification. Thus, what began as crisis-induced mythogenesis eventually flowers into a collective aesthetics conducive to *communitas*. This is the final and formidable function of asymmetric ritual violence.

Note that I am not attempting to account for the entire emotional/festal repertoire of the Spanish folk. Some of Spain's most moving fiestas have nothing whatever to do with persecution or martyrdom (the Nativity, the feast of the Immaculate Conception, the numerous Virgins of August, etc.). Still less do I affirm that the aesthetic sense of the peasant requires violence to become operative in a festal context. The processional pilgrimage of the *romería*, for example, bases its emotive appeal on the natural beauties of the countryside surrounding the sanctuary. In the *Romería de la Pastora* of Cantillana (Sevilla), the people returning from the sanctuary with their Virgin deliberately slow down the procession in order to cross the river at nightfall; at the right moment, those on horseback ignite flares that illuminate the silver accouterments of the "sinless one" while the shimmering waters mirror the whole *tableau vivant*—"the effect is overwhelmingly beautiful" (Rodríguez Becerra 1985:38–39). Similarly, fiestas that revolve around the collective interpretation of traditional dances exhibit an energetic but hardly persecutory brand of aesthetic enjoyment. Nevertheless, the prominent place occupied by the fiestas of Holy Week, with their popular representations of the betrayal, crucifixion, and resurrection of Christ in nearly every population nucleus of the Peninsula, will indeed confirm the centrality of asymmetric ritual violence to Spanish folklore and popular tastes.

The Ethnography of Holy Week

The Passion can be represented with living actors or with statues; though the first possibility is actually increasing in popularity (González Casarrubios 1985:53–54), the latter remains the dominant dramatic mode and the one most conducive to sociocentric diversification, for the following reason: In any given city or town, the representation is always the responsibility of one or more *cofradías* (confraternities). The only natural limit to the number of such brotherhoods is the size of the local population, inasmuch as the motifs or moments of the Passion that lend themselves to organized devotion are almost unlimited. Thus, in Ciudad Real there is one *cofradía* named The Prayer in the Garden; another is called The Holy Sepulcher; another, The Nailing; another, Jesus Fallen; another, *Ecce Homo* (Ramírez Rodrigo 1985:359).

Pasos are groups of life-sized sculptured images depicting some moment of the Passion that are mounted on portable platforms and carried by the confraternity's *costaleros*. In most cases, the *pasos* date from the sixteenth, seventeenth, or eighteenth centuries, are valuable works of art in their own right, and are heavy enough to require fifteen to fifty *costaleros* to carry them. A *cofradía* possesses at least one *paso* and usually several; the confreres not charged with carrying the *pasos* accompany them as penitents, musicians, or biblical personages. In Baena (Córdoba), for example, there are two competing confraternities, popularly known as white-tailed Jews and black-tailed Jews, whose *pasos* portray events such as the betrayal of Christ or the (apocryphal) attempt to prevent the writing of the Gospels. Another *cofradía*, that of The Holy Christ of Blood, carries scenes of the Last Supper or the trial of Jesus and equips its members as Roman soldiers, trumpeteers, drummers, and so forth. That of Jesús Nazareno is subdivided into groups of confreres dressed as Apostles or Prophets (Larrea Palacín 1968:348).

The processional representations can take place on any day between Palm Sunday and Easter Monday but are usually reserved for Holy Thursday and especially Good Friday. Several processions with numerous *pasos* and thousands of penitents are common in larger cities. But the Passion as experienced in a humble village will often make up in intensity what it may lack in splendor. The

940 neighbors of Bercianos de Aliste (Zamora), for example, who all belong to the confraternity of The Holy Cross, achieve notable degrees of religious/aesthetic emotion with the help of a life-sized, sixteenth-century Christ with articulated shoulders. On the morning of Good Friday, the Christ is "nailed" to a cross erected in the plaza not far from an image of the *Mater Dolorosa*. The procession as such begins at nightfall, when the brothers solemnly take the Christ down from the cross, collocate his arms by his sides, and place him in a transparent glass coffin; the people light candles and proceed to reenact the Holy Interment, while dressed in linen robes that will one day serve as their winding sheets (Blanco 1983 : 43–46).

The urge for realism that seems to characterize these acts acquires a different tenor in Priego (Córdoba). There, the *paso* of the Nazarene is ritually wrested from the control of the local clergy and *cofradía* by the young men of the town, whose preordained role is that of persecutory mob. In an atmosphere of vehement passion, they literally race the image along the tortuous road to "Calvary," along with implements of crucifixion such as hammers, nails, crown of thorns, and so on. At the end, the Christ is manipulated in such a way that he seems to impart a blessing on his persecutors, who burst into shouts of "*Viva Jesús Nazareno*" (Briones 1985 : 54–58; Domínguez Morano 1985 : 166–169). In Tobarra (Alicante), a similar simulated benediction is acknowledged with the frenzied beating of dozens of drums (González Casarrubios 1985 : 52–53). Meanwhile, in Calzada de Calatrava (Ciudad Real), people gamble away large sums of money with *el juego de las caras*, in commemoration of the Roman soldiers who cast lots for Christ's vestments (Ramírez Rodrigo 1985 : 360).

A different sort of festal excess is practiced in certain cities of central and northern Spain whose citizens choose to represent the Passion during the first frigid hours of Good Friday. Zamora's most popular procession (there are three others) leaves the temple with nine onerous *pasos* before daybreak, accompanied by no less than three thousand black-robed, black-hooded penitents. The *costaleros* "dance" their *pasos* to the rhythm of the funeral march played by the band that accompanies them, and pause at regular intervals to rest, distribute almonds to the spectators, and fight off the cold with brandy and garlic soup. After several hours, those penitents unable to control their ructation or cursing are brusquely ejected from the procession, sometimes by the dozens (Blanco 1983 : 46–48). Another so-called Procession of the Drunks takes place in Cuenca. As they accompany a *paso* of the Nazarene, *los turbos* ceaselessly bang their drums, blare their trumpets, and imbibe an autochthonous liquor known as *resoli* in order to fight off the early morning cold, thereby "producing the inebriation of the majority" (González Casarrubios 1985 : 52).

These examples indicate that the decorum of Holy Week is not uniform throughout Spain. In some places the overriding festal mood is one of majesty and solemnity; in others, sorrow and pain are the watchwords; in still others, light-hearted and even light-headed behaviors seem to predominate. Part of the ambiguity may be traceable to the liturgy itself; after all, Christ is in the process of saving all humanity and this infuses an encouraging ray of hope into the most somber ceremonies. Any Passion performance is inextricably bound up with group reactions and group tastes; if it were really improper to gamble or to drink on Good Friday, it would not be done. What are considered appropriate reactions vary from here to there and from day to day. Thus, the same festal episode can elicit two entirely different moods when performed at two different moments of the Paschal cycle. This is what happens in the ubiquitous processions that arrange for the *paso* of Jesus to "meet" that of His mother. The *pasos* and their retinues, usually divided according to the sex of the image they transport, start out from different churches or from the same church at different times, proceeding along different routes until they converge in some agreed-upon plaza. If the ceremony takes place on Tuesday or Wednesday of Holy Week, then Jesus is the Nazarene and Mary is the *Dolorosa*, and their *encuentro* (meeting) produces an exquisite sensation of grief. But if a *procesión del encuentro* takes place on Easter Sunday, the Virgin is no longer sorrowful and her Son, more often than not, has now assumed the guise of the Child Jesus; flocks of doves are flung skywards at the moment of their joyful reunion (Larrea Palacín 1968 : 342). The artificial postponement of the climactic *encuentro* serves to heighten its thrill in Los Hinojosos (Cuenca), where the young men hide Jesus from the Virgin and the young women who are seeking Him; the pious search can last all day (González Casarrubios 1985 : 56).

As it turns out, the most common way to express or augment the emotions that attend to the reunion of Mary and the Child Jesus is to put the torch to an effigy of Judas. Some folklorists have expressed surprise that an element that "ought to" belong to Carnival should show up on Easter Sunday (Gómez-Tabanera 1968:175; González Casarrubios 1985:56), as if Spanish peasants were an absent-minded lot who cannot remember which customs belong to which cycle. In view of the inner logic of persecutory mythopoesis, nothing could be more appropriate than to set Judas on fire at the very moment that Christ is discovered to be alive. For unlike the Christ of the New Testament, the Christ who is ritually "re-murdered" every year in Spain is an archetypal martyr, whose death is not merely unjustified but is also a criminal aggression that cries out for vengeance. One needs only the slightest acquaintance with psychology and Spanish history to conclude that the mock elimination of Judas at Easter time most likely reflects a projective and purgative mechanism closely related to the one that provoked the real elimination of Jews during the Middle Ages. The community *identifies* with Christ, in both a psychological and a sociological sense, and thus takes His martyrdom personally; indeed, Christ is taken as the very father of the in-group, which infuses a whole new dynamics of rage and guilt into the martyrological framework. The *coplas* that celebrate the burning of *Pero-Palo* in Villanueva de la Vera (Cáceres) are explicit in this respect:

Judíos, mi Padre es Cristo,	Jews, my Father is Christ,
vosotros me le matásteis;	you killed Him on me;
cada día que amanece	with every day that dawns
veo quien mató a mi Padre.	I see who killed my Father.
[Ramón y Fernández 1950:94]	

Small wonder, then, that children in Navarre go around chanting "¡Judas murió, Cristo resucitó!" on Easter Sunday, as if the destruction of the arch-traitor were instrumental to Christ's victory over death (Caro 1965a:134). The Oedipal dimension of persecutory mythopoesis is likewise evidenced by the countless confreres who assume the identities and supposed attitudes of Jews during Holy Week processions. Just as in Sanzoles' feigned attack on their own patron saint, people take advantage of the chance to impersonate a parricidal rabble in the very ceremony organized to lament the crime and mourn its victim. The popular obsession/identification with Judas reached a complex level of artistic development in Burgos and several towns of its province during the nineteenth century; neighbors got together to put on a representation reminiscent of the Passion itself, a *Celebrated Critical-Burlesque Drama of Judas Iscariot: His Arrest, Presentation to the Tribunal, Proclamation of Scourging, Sermon, Accusation, Defense, Conviction, and Execution, Capable of Making the Dead Laugh* (García de Diego 1953:63; Bergua 1934:590). A similar note of humor is injected into the Passion Play of Villanueva del Segura (Murcia), where Judas is transformed into a devilish *botargas* following his hanging (Caro 1965a:134). The utilization of sacred genres for satirical purposes has its structural converse in the *testamentos de Cristo* uncovered and apologized for by García de Diego (1953:65–66). The chief vehicle of comic popular censure is herein adapted for pious and didactic intentions by the anonymous blind bards of Spain. The themes of Judas's betrayal and Christ's Passion behave like Toelken's multiform folk ideas (1979:171–179) as they drift from one generic guise to the other—including the dance! (Bergua 1934: 468–469).

Psychodrama, Spanish-style

That the Passion representations of Andalusia constitute a popular mise-en-scène of the Oedipus complex is taken as self-evident by Domínguez Morano, who psychoanalyzes the Holy Week of Priego (Córdoba) and finds the classic symptom: Christ the Son is converted into the arbitrary and repressive Father-figure of the primal mob that seizes His *paso* and thrusts it along on the *via crucis* (1985:165–175). Domínguez recognizes the social usefulness of Holy Week and its role in the maintenance of the cultural identity of the Andalusians, but considers these functions to be secondary side-effects.

From a psychoanalytic approach, we can affirm that the affective ambivalence vis-à-vis the paternal that leads to violence, and from there to culpability and the need for reconciliation, constitutes the deepest psychological motivation for the celebration of Holy Week in Andalusia. In some way, the dramaturgy of death in Holy Week is an imaginary and ritual representation of parricide.   [1985:164]

The evidence that can be adduced in support of an Oedipal reading of Holy Week in Andalusia and elsewhere is virtually unlimited. We know that Spanish folk religion in general has tended to conceive of God as an idol of violence, always poised to punish sinners in the most exemplary ways (Caro 1969:122–129). We also know that Christ the Son has often been assimilated to this punitive paternal archetype. In a folk ballad entitled "*Jesucristo y el incrédulo,*" for example, the Savior is pictured as going around incognito to ferret out unbelievers and send them to the depths of hell (Piñero and Atero 1986:180). I have already discussed the manner in which popular impersonation of Jews on Good Friday and jubilant burnings of Judas on Easter Sunday can be understood in terms of parricidal guilt projection. We have another piece of damning circumstantial evidence in the fact that Jesus reappears as an infant in the many *procesiones del encuentro,* which can easily be seen in terms of Oedipal wish-fulfillment: now that the harsh and arbitrary Father-figure has been done away with, the Child can have Mother to Himself. Such an interpretation would have to postulate that people shift their libidinal identifications from one figure to another with celerity, but perhaps anything is possible in dreamwork and folk-work. In sum, it would seem that all over Spain communities give themselves up to their secret urges during Holy Week, glorying in the gruesomely realistic *pasos* of their heavenly Father's destruction, willing to impersonate penitents or persecutors with equal aplomb, dancing, gambling, and drinking to excess.

It is not adventurous to suppose that Holy Week processions became traditional in the first place because people found them to be emotionally gratifying; and to associate this emotional gratification with the major themes of the Freudian "family romance" is easily done. So far, so plausible. But then what? Are we now obliged to conclude that Spaniards are spectacularly neurotic? Domínguez does not hesitate to cast this first stone at the "infantile" and "pathological" aspects of the *Semana Santa* in Andalusia, that serve to "retard the development and maturity of a people" (1985 : 171). But such an evaluation is unwarranted for two reasons: 1) It negates the difference between normal and neurotic guilt feelings, and 2) it overlooks the fact that we are dealing with collective ritual representations, not individual thoughts or deeds. The Andalusian or any other Spaniard would only be open to the charge of pathology if he did *not* possess a culturally sanctioned apparatus for the dissipation of that normal quantity of guilt that is his lot as a human being. For anyone who is the son or daughter of a mother and a father, guilt is an unavoidable fact of life—this much can be granted psychoanalysis; the entire purpose of transcendent cultural symbols, as May points out, is to express, mediate, and dispel this guilt (1960 : 22–33). The many representations of scapegoating and collective violence that I have discussed heretofore, along with their highly wrought aesthetic elaborations, do not indicate a morbid obsession with cruelty, suffering, and murder. *The representations serve to prevent morbidity.* Holy Week processions in particular provide a classic psychoanalytic abreaction for the community involved, a de facto psychotherapy that is all the more effective because it remains unarticulated.

"Contemporary man suffers from the deterioration and breakdown of the central symbols in modern Western culture " (1960 : 22). But for most members of the popular classes in Spain, the drama of Christ's death and resurrection retains its cathartic power. For how long is uncertain; industrial growth with its new role models or life-styles has already begun to corrode the clear-cut, unambiguous cosmovision folk religion promotes. For the time being, however, neurosis (or pathology or morbidity or excess) will remain in the eye of the beholder. Domínguez congratulates those progressive, thoroughly aware Andalusian Christians who are able to take part in Passion processions with a wholesome and playful spirit "as if it were psychodrama" (1985 : 174), without understanding that it has always been psychodrama *avant la lettre* for the humble and unaware and no less playful masses.

The genius of the Spanish cultural "style" lies not only in the ritual canalization of collective violence but also in the ritual dissolution of whatever guilt may attach to this violence. Those individuals who happen to have an above average amount of guilt for whatever reason simply use the existing cultural formats with greater intensity. Most penitents in a given procession will wear shoes; some will feel a need to go barefoot; a few will want to drag chains as well. If this is "masochism," it is of a benign, group-approved, abreactive variety. Different folk enclaves evolve different ritual means for the expression and purging of guilt. The famous *empalaos* of Valverde de la Vera (Cáceres), for instance, are certain men who choose to commemorate the Passion by having their arms roped to a rough-hewn wooden beam slung across their shoulders; wandering through the streets all night long in severe pain, they receive constant encouragement from their neighbors (Pérez Gallego 1986 : 17).

Once the psychological dimension has been clarified and its utility established, it must be pointed out that the processions of Holy Week possess every bit of the *social* functionality that accrues to Spanish fiestas in general. No matter what inner psychic conflicts may animate them, the ability of the representations to mediate *outer* community conflicts is a matter of record. Consider the Holy Week of Priego that Domínguez uses to disparage the emotional maturity of Andalusians. Another observer of the same fiestas has produced an in-depth study that emphasizes factors such as group identity, group affirmation, and the ritual expression of intergroup competition (Briones 1985). It turns out that Priego's Holy Week functions as a powerful mechanism of integration for the very young, the very old, the sick, *quintos*, emigrants, and all other individuals whose sense of belonging to the community is threatened by natural or occupational factors (1985 : 54). Furthermore, Holy Week serves as a platform for the airing of grievances and the arbitration of disputes; the rituals themselves are the object of contention as different social classes struggle to assert their protagonism (1985 : 54–56). As in countless other Spanish fiestas, the rivalry takes place between groups of parallel importance, increases popular participation, produces finer fiestas, and potentiates the ongoing "invention of tradition" that characterizes folklore in general:

After several years of economic desolation—that were matched by the lethargy of the Holy Week processions—Priego is being revitalized through the initiative of middle and working classes of great dynamism, largely made up of returning emigrants. And it is precisely now that Holy Week is beginning to resurge with new *cofradías*—formed by the same ones who are behind the economic resurgence of Priego—who seek to renew and revitalize Holy Week by taking charge of the tradition.   [Briones 1985:57]

Taken all together, these factors suggest that the need for solid symbols of identity is at least as important as the ritual undoing of guilt. So much so, in fact, that those Prieguenses who have had to emigrate to Barcelona and elsewhere to earn a living are easily identified by the images of Jesus they wear around their necks and hang on their walls—the same Nazarene Jesus whose *paso* is the object of such vehement fascination on Good Friday (1985:54). Just as the renewed significance conferred upon Holy Week by the prospering citizens of Priego can be traced to pure sociocentrism, the Nazarene identity badges point to the existence of psychological gratifications that have little to do with the Oedipus complex.

By way of summary, it might be useful to picture the popular religious dramas of Spain as the central link in a chain of cultural conditioning. The various psychological and sociological functions that I have reviewed above serve to reinforce (i.e., make durable) diverse representations of a scapegoating or martyrological nature, and these in turn function to reinforce 1) cultural worldview, 2) traditional morality, 3) group identity, and 4) group tastes. A number of final observations are in order. To begin with, the role played by asymmetric violence in both phases of the reinforcement process has been patent. Insofar as popular Christianity in Spain manifests continuity, not rupture, with the religious systems in vogue long before the coming of Christ, this conditioning chain might well be portrayed as a vicious circle of sacrificial culture in the Girardian sense. The Oedipal elements observable in so many different rituals seem to form part of this sacrificial matrix, along with the healing catharsis the same rituals promote. It is this abreactive aspect that keeps Spanish tradition from being "neurotic" in the modern sense of the term. Outside of a ritual framework, of course, persecutory violence can have thoroughly indefensible consequences. To the degree that mythological or ritual systems have their origins in episodes of genuine scapegoating violence, as Girard affirms with no lack of evidence, then they can be seen as unwitting "accomplices" to such violence. Girard has stressed, however, that the blame is never to be laid on any particular doorstep, but to be understood as the tragic flaw of the *condition humaine* itself (1978a:7–68). In the final analysis, religion only adores victimizing violence because it seems to bring peace.

With these insights assimilated, we are now in a position to draw some definitive conclusions with regard to the Spanish cultural "style" and its supposed obsession with images of violence and death. For when we see certain *tastes* being reinforced generation after generation in religious fiestas that are themselves reinforced by clearly definable or demonstrable sociopsychological functions, then we are no longer beholden to romantic or mystagogic exegeses of the "Spanish soul." Such interpretations, which have been legion in certain spheres of discourse, can now be seen as a special kind of poetry that is itself traceable to the above mentioned conditioning process. Violence and death, after all, are not in short supply in any nation; to describe them as the distinguishing characteristics of any one culture is an exercise in shortsightedness or projection. To say that Spaniards have acquired a taste for the spectacle of death or death-as-spectacle is to state the obvious; but this does not authorize us to diagnose morbidity, nor to conclude that they harbor some unconscious stoic philosophy or some mysterious "cult of death." Spain's most influential religious psychologist was quick to point out the autonomy of purely aesthetic factors: Once you become accustomed to the bloody or livid Christs of Iberia, Miguel de Unamuno told a friend, other Christs seem "insipid" (1967[1909]: 275). Similarly, Castón has asserted that Andalusia's traditional preference for plastic portrayals of pain and horror can be traced directly to the prevailing aesthetic canons of the Baroque period in which the outward vehicles of popular piety were forged (1985: 125–126). Once popular tastes have become conditioned and established, in other words, they lead an independent and extremely tenacious life of their own.

8

In keeping with the dual nature of their magico-persecutory matrix, aesthetic elaborations of violence will adopt two parallel and sometimes convergent approaches: 1) a victim will be camouflaged; 2) a victim will be ostentatiously displayed. The first procedure tends to present itself as joyful popular justice (the witch is ritually expelled, Judas is burned in effigy, Saint Stephen is given a good thrashing, a murderous bull is skillfully dispatched). The second prefers to adopt a mournful martyrological decorum (a brave man or woman undergoes unbelievable tortures at the hands of wicked Turks, a *paso* is created for every moment of Christ's Passion, a flamenco singer turns his uncommon Angst into a musical arabesque).

Until now I have been concerned with revealing the ways in which these two subvarieties of persecutory mythopoesis structure the festal representations of Spanish folk religion; but other cultural formats have been characterized by a conscientious, if not conscious, exploitation of one mode or the other. The time has come to explore a major secular institution that has taken *both* to an extreme point of aesthetic development.

Bullfighting is an activity that overflows the traditional categories of folklore. It exhibits characteristics of a folk craft, a ritual, a game, and a festival. It paradoxically meets Toelken's criteria for both folk arts and fine arts (1979:182–186). It is a mass spectacle and an agribusiness at the same time. For two centuries it has been the source or subject matter of countless ballads, legends, poems,

plays, paintings, novels, and films. It has been, with the possible
exception of the Inquisition, the main focus of other nations' "exoteric" lore about Spaniards and their alleged national character.
And it has generated a vast number of erudite and ambitious interpretations on the part of scholars and literati alike. This chapter is
primarily devoted to the demolition of what may be termed the
"erotic" school of taurine exegesis. In the next I will seek to situate
the bullfight-event inside the same complex of magico-persecutory
mechanisms that structures the rites and pious legends discussed
earlier.

Bullfighting: The Ritual Origin of Scholarly Myths

Early scholarly "myths" of bullfighting were, appropriately enough,
myths of origin. The eighteenth and nineteenth centuries witnessed the struggle between the Roman Circus theory originally
propagated by Golden Age theologians and the Moorish thesis pro-
pounded by Moratín and popularized by Goya. A nativist position
eventually found an apologist in the Count of Las Navas (López-
Valdemoro 1900). But all three hypotheses were to be eclipsed following a major exposition of ancient bovine artifacts organized in
1918 by the Count of Las Almenas and several archaeologists,
thanks to which man's fight with the bull came to be seen as pre-
Castilian, pre-Moorish, pre-Roman, and altogether prehistoric. For
the first time, the bullfight was linked to the sacrifices primitive
peoples had made to their divinities, and, according to Alvarez de
Miranda (1962:40), the revelation was nothing short of sensa-
tional. Only a few years later, Sir Arthur Evans' use of Spanish
terms to describe certain taurine images he had unearthed at
Knossos served to fan the fires of the revolutionary "Neolithic"
thesis. Archaeologists of several different nationalities subsequently elaborated the Cretan-origins hypothesis of Iberian tauromachy; one even argued that Theseus was the first bullfighter
and the Labyrinth was in reality the sacrificial dance of the
Minotaur (Alvarez de Miranda 1962: 45–46). The ritual explanation of the bullfight was well-entrenched among Spanish intellectuals active in the 1920s and 1930s. Some, like Unamuno, found

cause for malaise therein; others, like Lorca, adopted an attitude of mystical affirmation.

The bullfight was also a prime target for the libidinal hermeneutics of the early twentieth century. Maurice Barrés had already sung the voluptuous nature of bloody deaths in Spanish bullrings (Barrés 1894); by the 1920s Freudianism had been successfully welded onto the sacrificial view of tauromachy—"Gross comedy of blood, sex, dionysian and sadistic; the ancient rites of the brute and of the Christ meet here in the final image of stability" (Frank 1926:236). In his satirical *Relato inmoral*, Fernández Flórez saw bullfighting as the first and easiest demonstration of Freud's pertinence to Spanish life (1927:240–241). His tongue-in-cheek remarks on the essential femininity of the matador will be taken in deadly earnest by later exegetes. The climax was reached with Bataille's surrealist mélange of eyes, eggs, gorings, and orgasms in *Histoire d'oeil* (1928).

Another major line of attack was initiated by Pérez de Ayala and consolidated in 1930 by Bergamín, whose *El arte de birlibirloque* vindicates bullfighting as a fount of the most sublime aesthetic emotions, available to a chosen elect of spectators with properly cultivated sensibilities.

These diverse trends (the bullfight as sacrifice, fine art, sex act, or sex crime) were brilliantly fused by Michel Leiris in his *Miroir de la tauromachie* (1964, [1937]). This French ethnologist and belletrist took the bullfight as a starting point for a series of meditations concerning the role of transgression in the erotic, the aesthetic, and the sacred.

The romantic exaltation of Spain's sanguinary customs was (temporarily) laid to rest by the awesome destruction of her Civil War (1936–1939). Taurine studies entered a new era with the historical investigations of José María de Cossío, whose importance for later scholarship cannot be overestimated. It was not until Cossío published the first volume of his encyclopedia (1943), for example, that the bullfight came to be understood within the context of the hundreds of patronal festivals that form the backbone of Spanish folk religion (Cossío 1943:637–688). The many ways in which bulls are manhandled in these traditional fiestas was further explored by the *Revista de Dialectología y Tradiciones Populares*

(RDTP), founded in 1945, which published important studies by Julio Caro Baroja, Hoyos Saínz, García Matos, Vicente Risco, and other major Spanish folklorists. The idea that bulls were fundamental to magic rural fertility rites was first advanced by Casas Gaspar (1950) and found its most succinct formulation in Alvarez de Miranda (1962).

Alvarez de Miranda began by analyzing a number of defunct Spanish legends and folktales that associated the bull with miraculous transformations of women into men, or homosexuals into heterosexuals, and with magical antidotes for feminine infertility (1962:59–87). He found that such "myths" were outnumbered by similarly defunct Spanish folk rituals that actively and pragmatically sought to exploit the sexual magic of the bull that the stories expressed. One of these rites allowed him to develop the first coherent if not entirely plausible theory of the folk origins of the modern bullfight. Instead of tracing it to the aristocratic and equestrian one that preceded it, as did Cossío and other historians, Alvarez de Miranda traced both to an archaic wedding custom that called for bride and groom to infuriate a bull with darts and spot their garments with his blood (1962:89–113). He went on to argue that each of the three *suertes* or "acts" of the modern taurine performance derived from some element or episode of the fiesta of the nuptial bull (1962:115–131). However, since this custom did not lead to the death of the bull but was only intended to evoke his fecundating power by ritually spilling his blood, Alvarez de Miranda concluded that the *suerte de matar* (act of killing the bull) in modern bullfights really derived from the "internal logic" of knightly tauromachy, already a secularized, ludic deformation of the original folk ritual (1962:109). Thus he subverted one of the major "mythemes" of pre-Cossío taurine historians, especially the enthusiasts of the Neolithic and Cretan theses, who were sure that the bullfight reflected the archetypal blood sacrifice of one ancient "bull cult" or another. "The great paradox of Spanish bullfighting," Alvarez de Miranda asserted, "is that only when it ceased to be a sacral question did it begin to seem a sacrifice" (1962:110). This caveat has been ignored by more recent researchers who make the most of Alvarez de Miranda's data and magico-sexual hypotheses.

Nonetheless, modern bullfighting can more properly be understood as an unusually dynamic variety of folk craft rather than a profane survival of folk ritual. It constitutes a traditional body of knowledge and practices transmitted orally through something like an apprentice system. It requires a highly sophisticated understanding of animal behavior, adherence to very specific norms and procedures, and a fair degree of nerve in carrying them out. This is not an "interpretation" of bullfighting, but a definition; interpretation begins with the use each bullfighter makes of the tradition, his physical and mental abilities, his style, his capacity for innovation or his respect for orthodoxy. But this traditional craft or technology produces no artifact, and this would seem to exclude it from the sphere of material culture altogether. A dead bull is what remains at the end of the process, of course, but it is the skill with which that death is administered that constitutes the raison d'être of the matador's performance and its one valid aesthetic criteria. We are thus dealing with a folk craft that paradoxically belongs in the sphere of "temporal" culture. The bullfight is Bruce Jackson's on-line, non-replicable activity par excellence (Jackson 1985:132–138).

Bullfighting is possible in the first place because an isolated and frightened *toro bravo* usually flees head first in a straight line. Beyond this basic characteristic, individual bulls vary greatly in their behavior and no two are ever exactly alike. The history of bullfighting is the history of the development of ever-more efficient techniques for controlling the animal raw material. The first professional bullfighters were eighteenth-century slaughterhouse employees who already knew a lot about bovid behavior and who discovered that they could earn more money by doing their job in public. According to García-Baquero, Romero de Solís, and Vázquez Parladé (1980), it was the then-dominant guild system that served as the model for turning the original folk technology into a profession, as evidenced by 1) the drive to submit every one of the *suertes* of the bullfight to strict regulation; 2) hierarchism, with a particular nomenclature for each of the successive ranks or specializations (*picador, banderillero, mozo de estoques,* etc.), as well as rigid observance of seniority and a clearly defined period of apprenticeship for young *novilleros*; and 3) the drive to get governmental authorities to guarantee the exclusivism of the new profession and the strict imposition of the ordinances (García-Baquero et al. 1980:99–

109). Díaz-Yanes has argued that few other groups in eighteenth- and nineteenth-century Spain were as committed as bullfighters were to the ideal of professional perfection, pushed onwards by a ferocious degree of internal criticism and the will to submit every kind of bull to the intelligence of the bullfighter (Díaz Yanes 1983: 234–239). This ideal of technical progress eventually enabled bull-fighters to shift from basically defensive ways of handling the bull to more offensive ones. Generations of selective breeding changed the bull as well, making him increasingly "noble" (i.e., coopera-tive). With time bullfighters learned to correct the defects of the particular bull that emerged from the *chiquero* into the ring, teach-ing him, as it were, to charge in a way that permitted his human opponent to demonstrate his skill, valor, and *arte*.

Aesthetic concerns accompanied this evolution every step of the way, it must be added—ones derived directly from the nature of the craft: What kind of play is a specific bull capable of? With what de-gree of skill does the matador play upon this ever-changing quality? Aesthetic standards grow out of technical ones and are largely in-terchangeable for the "close group" of the matador and his party. The strictly masculine mini-society of the *cuadrilla*, rooted in the archaic laboral practices that still infiltrate so much of Spanish so-ciety, has yet to be given the attention it deserves in taurine "ex-egesis." The popular exaltation of the matador blinds many to the fact that tauromachy is always and everywhere a group activity—each man with a role to play, clear-cut obligations and privileges, and a semifeudal loyalty to his captain.

But many other groups participate in the bullfight-event, and it might be convenient to see them as so many concentric rings of seats surrounding the circular enclosure where the *cuadrilla* per-forms. The *aficionados* might be defined as the "closest group," one that understands the problems of the bullfighting craft and that shares the technical/aesthetic concerns of the bullfighters and their historic passion for perfection. This group is not to be con-fused, though it sometimes overlaps, with the *taurinos* or fans, the unconditional supporters of a single bullfighter who stake their group identity on his charisma. The "way to watch" a bullfight most in accord with its vocational essence is accessible to a minor-ity of spectators only. Specialized knowledge, an unimaginably rich and esoteric vocabulary, broad experience, and a discriminatng sensibility—these are the characteristics of the true *aficionado*. No anthropologist who wants to talk about sacrifice or sex will have much sympathy with the endless discussion of technical details *aficionados* are given to—bracing in the attack, the distinction between natural and changed bullfighting, the proper execution of such and such a *suerte*, whether or not the bull was properly picced, and so forth. But it is here that we will find, boring or not for outsiders, the real "essence" of bullfighting.

Yet another group has formed around this one, the critics and journalists whose livelihoods derive from bullfighting's economic dynamism; the best critics have played an essential role in the technical and artistic progress of the profession. It is precisely this progress that has enabled another group, chiefly comprised of twentieth-century belletrists, to "discover" that tauromachy is a fine art, a geometry, or a metaphysical combination of both. This group has managed to redeem bullfighting from its former ill repute among intellectuals; nevertheless, their high-flown aesthetic standards are basically foreign to those of the "closer groups." But it is yet another group of true outsiders, often nonnatives, who have developed interpretations of the bullfight-event that differ most radically from the explanations of the people actually involved in it. Earlier I discussed a number of fanciful theories pertaining to the genesis of tauromachy—veritable myths derived from the study of a ritual. But these excesses do not necessarily mean that outsiders' evaluations are bound to miss the mark. As long as the testimony of insiders is given some small measure of attention, there is a way in which outsiders' perspectives on the bullfight can be useful to a majority of Hispanists, folklorists, and social scientists in general: when they seek to establish broad comparisons between the bullfight and other institutions or values peculiar to Spanish culture or its Mediterranean context. Let us turn our attention to a number of studies that purport to do just that.

Bullfights and Metaphors

A recent article in *American Ethnologist* affirms that "the bullfight is a metaphor that makes a statement about the social order," inasmuch as the social order is often represented by a sexual one and "the bullfighter is to the bull as man is to woman" (Douglass 1984:242–243). Honor, construed in sexual terms, is "the key to the interpretation of the Spanish bullfight" (1984:242).

I argue that ideologically, at least, the bull is female, an animal structurally equivalent to a woman. The role of the male is to control, contain, and finally kill the bull. I show that the popular image of females in (southern) Spain is that if not controlled by men, they are extremely dangerous and upsetting to the social order due to their sexual nature. It is through the treatment of the bull and the transference of language usually reserved for the *toro bravo* and the bullfight to women and the erotic relations between the sexes that the parallels between the bull and the female can be seen. [Douglass 1984:243]

Note that although the ethnologist limits her purview to southern Spain and thereby eliminates most of the provinces where the bullfight is held, her hypothesis is still arresting enough to merit close consideration. Her evidence is mainly metaphorical and linguistic in nature and derives almost entirely from Spanish sociologist E. Tierno Galván, who pointed out various ways in which taurine vocabulary can be used in a sexual context (1961[1951]:60–64). Tierno found that "the Spaniard" often employs bullfight terminology to characterize a woman of striking physique or to refer to his urge to dominate her. Douglass attempts to buttress this information with the proverb *"toro muerto, vaca es,"* which she uses as the title for her article and translates as "the dead bull is a cow." "Through domination," explains Douglass, "the wildly potent and mortally dangerous bull is identified with what is socially female" (1984:251). But in actual usage this saying does not refer to the bullfight, nor to the *brave* bull, nor to male-female relations. Best translated as "dead bull is cow," the phrase derives from the fact that the meat of a dead bull is prepared, packaged, and sold in exactly the same way as cow meat, and is used in contexts similar to those of the English "six of one and a half-dozen of the other." It is cited to indicate the triviality of certain distinctions, and is the structural opposite of *"jabón e hilo negro, todo es para la ropa"* (soap or black thread, everything is for clothes), which is used to mock those who fail to discern differences that *are* important. But Douglass falls into graver error with the one-way metaphorical evidence she borrows from Tierno. "What does it mean," asks Tierno, "that *the Spaniard* sees the conquest and possession of a woman the same as he sees the conquest and defeat of a brave bull?" (1961: 61; emphasis added). Tierno does not inquire as to whether the Spanish *woman* sees matters in the same light, and neither does Douglass. But a cursory examination of Spanish folklore reveals that the metaphor is entirely interchangeable: both men and women can and do picture themselves as the bullfighter and the opposite sex as the bull. A few items from the taurine *cancionero:*

Ven aquí, torico;	Come here, little bull;
ven aquí, galán,	come here, gallant,
que soy la torera [fem.]	for I am the bullfighter
que te va a matar.	that is going to kill you.
Cuando me citas,	When you "cite" me,
me siento toro bravo,	I feel like a brave bull,
niña bonita.	pretty girl.
Con la capa el torero	With the cape the bullfighter
maneja al bicho,	handles the beast,
y la mujer al hombre	and the woman handles the man
con su abanico.	with her fan.
Si me ves con otro hablando,	If you see me with another man,
no dudes de mi querer,	do not doubt my love,
el hombre es siempre un toro	the man is always a bull
y un torero la mujer.	and the bullfighter a woman.
[Martínez Remis 1963:70, 111, 176]	

For every metaphor that pictures the woman as a wild creature who must be dominated and penetrated with a long instrument, there is another that pictures the man as a gullible patsy whose blind charges are easily governed by a woman. Moreover, only men can be called *"cornudos"* (horned ones or cuckolds).

But by no means should it be inferred, as Tierno and Douglass infer, that male-female relations constitute the main facet of life that taurine vocabulary has lent itself to. Cossío lists some 220 different sayings and metaphors derived from the bullfight, the characteristics of the bull, and the bullfighter, no more than ten of which make some connection with female appearance or sex relations (Cossío 1947:232–242). Far more common are phrases that refer to deception, difficult or dangerous situations in general, skill, anger, and so forth. Even Tierno recognizes the existence of other spheres of application (1961:51). To Cossío's list can be added the use that Catholic priests have made of taurine terms to portray the truths of the faith, a custom that goes back several centuries (Pereda 1965:24–32). The bullfight, for its part, has borrowed a number of ecclesiastical terms to refer to different aspects or moments of the performance (Araúz de Robles 1978:155–156). Pérez de Ayala (1918) described the Spanish political scene in taurine terms and vice-versa. Bullfighting and *arte flamenco* have exchanged a considerable number of concepts and terms (Quiñones and Vega 1982; González Climent 1953, 1964). Any sphere of culture can give and take words to and from any other; it does not follow that therefore some profound structural connection exists. Douglass refers to Tierno as the one scholar who "has seen the event of the bullfight in its fundamental and principal essence as a confrontation between male and female" (Douglass 1984:252). Yet in fact Tierno does nothing of the sort; while indicating that taurine vocabulary lends itself to sex relations, he does not turn around and assert that therefore sex relations are the essence of the bullfight. This is Douglass' own hasty non sequitur, compounded by a tortuous analysis of "the Spanish Honor Code" (1984:254). "The bull is not female," she explains. "Rather, in the relationship with the *torero*, it has the same *structural* position as woman in the Honor Code relationship between the sexes" (1984:254; emphasis in original). The bullfight serves to reaffirm all social hierarchies, reasons Douglass, *because* it reaffirms the sexual one (1984:243). But does it indeed? The only hierarchy that can be seen is a man's victory over an animal. From this real (not symbolic) domination, the notion of domination itself can be abstracted and applied to other relationships: man over woman or woman over man—depending upon your informant or which folk song you listen to; light over darkness; good over evil; guile over force; vertical over horizontal; plebeian over aristocrat; son over father; Christian over Moor; sacrificer over victim; life over death and death over life. I have encountered every one of these possibilities in one author or another, each claiming that his particular equation is the "key" to the bullfight.

Julian Pitt-Rivers has managed to include several of these hermeneutic possibilities in an analysis of the bullfight that eschews mundane attention to evidence for the higher proofs of anthropo-logical intuition, artfully combining every twentieth-century reli-gious or sexual comparison made seriously or in jest with a few more he has discovered on his own. Contrary to Alvarez de Miranda, Pitt-Rivers maintains that the *suerte de matar* is truly a sacrifice and that the *corrida* in general is a religious rite (1984:27–47). The bullfighter initially appears as a feminine figure who artfully tricks the totally masculine bull into wasting his energy in useless charges; in the final *suerte*, this prepotent virility has passed into the bullfighter, who now dominates (at least in theory) the bull's every movement (1984:35). But if the matador kills clumsily, what-ever points he may have earned earlier with elegant cape-work will not prevent the jeers of the crowd. "This demonstrates that we are not dealing with a sport or a theatrical representation but with a sacrifice" (1984:36).When the matador finally plunges his sword into the bull's withers, he completes the process of humiliation and feminization with a symbolic rape (1984:38). But that is not all: since the "vagina-wound" between the bull's shoulder blades is thoroughly bloodied (from the pic and the *banderillas*), Pitt-Rivers concludes that the bullfighter heroically breaks the taboo against copulation during menstruation at the moment he perpetrates his "rape" (1984:38–39).

The symbolic violation of the [menstrual] taboo restores the natural rights of both sexes: freed of cultural bonds by the deed of the outlaw/hero, who allies himself with Nature, men are once again true men and, no longer fearful of women, the latter become authentic females, able to sign the peace in the war between the sexes. . . .   [Pitt-Rivers 1984:40]

With Pitt-Rivers, the most prestigious modern anthropologist to take an interest in bullfighting, taurine studies have taken a major step backwards. He effectively resurrects the mystagogy and vulgar Freudianism of the 1920s under a thin veneer of structuralist ter-minology. He utilizes Alvarez de Miranda's research into the magic rites of the bull (Pitt-Rivers 1984:40–42) but omits mention of his predecessor's refusal to see any sexual or sacrificial significance in modern bullfighting (Alvarez de Miranda 1962:106–113)—a nega-tion shared, incidentally, by other Spanish folklorists (Gómez-Tabanera 1968:295; Blázquez 1975:74). The fact that this traditional temporal craft is executed in public, with the performers dressed in a specified way and following the same specific routines, makes the bullfight *seem* like a ritual. But the insiders—*cuadrilla, aficionados,* critics—do not attribute any sort of symbolic meaning to their actions. In a true ritual, like the Mass, the officiant and his communicants are engaged in symbolic activity; their every word and action has an agreed-upon spiritual referent. It would be ludicrous for the participants in a Mass to scrutinize the skillfulness with which the priest elevates the chalice, or his style in distributing hosts, or the aplomb with which he consecrates the blood of Christ. But in the "ritual" of the bullfight, the entire point is to evaluate the superficial behavior of the "officiant." Skill, grace, and sang-froid are precisely the qualities on display and they do not stand for anything beyond themselves. Thus it would be—and is—ludicrous to place the bullfight on the same spiritual plane as the Mass, to call it a religious rite, a sacrifice, or a daring violation of the menstrual taboo. Even Michel Leiris exercised greater caution in this regard than Pitt-Rivers: the former began with the bullfight-event and followed it through his risk, transgression, and erotic analogies to arrive at a novel conception of the sacred, emphasizing all along that he was constructing metaphors, searching for affinities, for resemblances, for mirrors (Leiris 1964:23, 24, et passim). Pitt-Rivers begins with an erotic theory of the sacred and proceeds through a mechanical distortion of the data to "reveal" the true essence of the bullfight, its hidden reality, its fundamental structure. Leiris, furthermore, was intent upon developing a series of personal meditations; his work belongs to the genre of essay. But Pitt-Rivers wants his essay to have the status of fieldwork; he simultaneously converts his meditations into accomplished facts and attributes their invention to the natives themselves:

It remains to be seen just how the Andalusians have found in the sacrifice of the bull the means to overcome the contradictions that complicate relations between the sexes in that region. [Pitt-Rivers 1984:44]

Quod erat demonstrandum!

Thus, to the logical error of taking the metaphor for the essence there corresponds the methodological error of inventing the informant. Douglass confides that "the upper classes no doubt enjoyed the bullfight as a covert metaphor for the relationship between the sexes and used the relationship between the sexes as a metaphor for the relationship between the classes" (1984:255). This is a succinct formulation of her own premise that she places into ribald aristocratic minds. Yet, in fairness to foreign anthropologists, it must be pointed out that Spanish sociologists have been no less predisposed to attribute their interpretations to hypothetical or ficticious subjects. I have already mentioned Tierno's coaction of "the Spaniard." Similarly, he claimed that "the taurine spectator" goes to bullfights in order to confirm his quasi-religious faith in *hombría* (manhood) (1961:74–76). *All* taurine spectators? For Araúz de Robles, it is the greater glory of the masculine sex that "the public" really comes to enjoy at a bullfight (1978:177), or, a little more specifically, a traditional "Spanish Man" whose days are numbered (1978:178). Every detail of tauromachy as well as the folklore it elicits are to be understood in terms of pure machismo. What makes Araúz de Robles more refreshing, if no more reliable, than other taurine exegetes is his emphasis on the bullfight as a "virility contest" (1978: 182), in which a totally masculine bull bests a totally masculine horse and is subsequently vanquished by a totally virile matador (1978:183). The bullfight is *"cosa de hombres,"* a narcissistic spectacle of, by, and for men wherein women are mere ornamental adjuncts (1978:185).

The abuse of the hypothetical subject has been constant in the many psychoanalytic interpretations that have been made of the bullfight over the years. Conrad asserted in *The Horn and the Sword* that it "may be thought of as a culturally sanctioned ritual through which culturally produced but repressed fears and frustrations find release and expression in displaced aggression against the bull as a symbol par excellence of power and authority" (1957:185). As the bullfighter dominates and dispatches the bull, "the Spaniards" unconsciously fantasize that their fathers, lords, bishops, and kings are all being done away with in the arena (1957:190–191). The Oedipus Complex, the primal horde, ritual parricide, totemic feasts, and other familiar Freudian themes have all been brought to bear on the bullfight in Desmonde 1952, Ingham 1964, Betancourt 1970, or Gómez Pin 1981. "Tauromachy implicates the public," affirms the last, "because it implies fraternity, it implies the identification of the multitude with one—the bullfighter—who by killing the bull symbolically repeats the founding act of humanity" (Gómez Pin 1981 : 417). Psychoanalytically minded researchers could search out the repressed reactions of real individuals who attend or have attended bullfights to discern what they might be projecting onto whom. But in practice they have preferred to project their own pre-conception of the bullfight's "meaning" onto an artificially con-structed recipient of said meaning, a fault they share with most other taurine exegetes.

Tauromachy and Virility

For the sake of argument, let us momentarily overlook the logical and methodological failings of taurine exegetes and conjecture that perhaps, for some Spaniards in some regions, the bullfight is taken as a celebration of male supremacy or even as a covert sexual innu-endo. Where might we look for such Spaniards? Following Pitt-Rivers and Douglass, we can initially confine our search to the eight provinces of Andalusia. We can then ask if attitudes akin to "machismo" are generalized there or if they are more prevalent in one social class than another. Gilmore and Gilmore have already provided a specific answer to this question: Andalusian machismo is found almost exclusively in "the subordinate lower class of land-less day laborers" and constitutes a mechanism whereby impover-ished, uneducated, and politically impotent men "seek to disiden-tify from the powerful Andalusian mother figure and thereby to resolve intrapsychic gender identity conflict" (Gilmore and Gil-more 1979 : 281–283). In reviewing studies from the Mediterranean area in general, Saunders notes that it is mainly among proletarians that the idea of women as aggressive creatures who must be domi-nated receives greatest elaboration (1981 : 451). "If man cannot vali-date his masculinity through the exercise of authority in the home," concludes Saunders, "he may—at least in theory—explore other ways of doing so" (1981 : 451). One of these ways may be the Car-nival ritual. Gilmore and Gilmore analyze the Carnival songs com-posed by male proletarians and find them to be obsessed with images of women (usually mothers-in-law) who are as powerful and hypersexual as wild beasts (1979:292–297). It might be inferred that such men could find in the bullfight another ritual statement of their anxieties and a ritual vindication of their threatened sense of manliness. This is precisely the inference that Pitt-Rivers and Douglass elevate to the status of ontology when they sever it from its one possible social base. Meanwhile, Pérez Delgado finds that fantasy elaborations about the bullfighter are most intense among those Andalusians who cannot afford to go to bullfights (1978: 863). So for the moment all we have is a hypothetical connection between a fantasy image of male domination and a fantasy image of the bullfight that *might* exist—consciously or unconsciously?—in the minds of an impossible-to-determine number of poor men in southern Spain. Furthermore, Caro Baroja has emphasized that it is not the *profession*, but the *situation*, of bullfighting that popular culture in Andalusia has elaborated: taurine heroes are almost always 1) very young *novilleros* or 2) martyrs fatally gored in the bullring (1983:18). Contrary to what we might have been led to suspect, totally virile, domineering types are as absent from Andalusian taurine mythopoesis as are realistic, professional types. Women, for their part, are commonly pictured as either remote beauties one glimpses in the *palco* of the aristocrats or maternal figures who worry about or mourn for the child-bullfighter (González Climent 1982:125–131)—not uncontrollable, devouring shrews thirsting for domination. The female companions of bullfighters are, in fantasy *and* "real life," flamenco singers and dancers (Quiñones and Vega 1982:704–705).

But let us suppose, for the sake of argument, that certain cultural notions of what it takes to be a real man lie behind a young man's decision to become a bullfighter. Suppose that these factors operate more intensely if he belongs to a social class that greatly prizes virility, male prepotence, feminine submission, and simultaneously suffers poverty and social margination. Spanish Gypsies, for example; here Douglass could find a group of (mostly southern) Spaniards for whom the "Honor Code" is most directly related to virility in an almost exaggerated way (San Román 1976). Furthermore, the list of Spanish Gypsies who have become major matadors is long and glorious. But *aficionados* and critics all agree that Gypsy bullfighting places very little emphasis on virility or valor (Sureda Molina 1967; Araúz de Robles 1978:28–30; Quiñones and Vega 1982: 706–708; Bergamín 1985:31–34). Hemingway noted of a great Gypsy bullfighter named Cagancho that "his cowardice at the moment of killing is disgusting . . . a cold-blooded gypsy defrauding of the public by the most shameless, anger-arousing obtainer of money under false pretenses, that ever went into a bullring" (1932:250). It turns out that Gypsies interpret bullfighting as a matter of style, of astuteness, of grace—all values that form an important part of their culture (San Román 1976:254–255). Even moments of panic and flight are prone to aesthetic elaboration. Machismo does not enter into the picture at all, but an elusive artistic/spiritual quality known as "*duende.*"

Andalusia is overrepresented in the ethnographic literature and this unfortunately enhances a longstanding tendency to see it as "typical Spain." But other areas of the Peninsula with climates less agreeable to tourists and researchers have a great many dealings with bulls; perhaps in these other regions we will find evidence of Tierno's generalized Spanish "faith in manhood," of some ideal concept of true masculinity or vulgar concept of *cojones* (slang for testicles). Such evidence might reasonably be sought in the *fiestas de toros* popular in rural and urban areas of northern, central, and eastern Spain. The "running of the bulls" in Pamplona is only the most famous example of what takes place in hundreds of folk festivals throughout both Castiles, León, La Mancha, Extremadura, Aragon, and Valencia, where communities ostensibly pay homage to their patron saints by stampeding and harassing bovids before slaughtering them and partaking of their flesh. Despite their diverse theoretical approaches, Spanish ethnographers and folklorists have tended to consider these fiestas as the historical/psychological basis of the modern bullfight (Ortíz-Cañavate 1931; Alvarez de Miranda 1962:31–58; Gómez-Tabanera 1968:167, 293–295; Herrera Casado 1973; Maldonado 1975:54–56; Caro Baroja 1984: 17–19). The great anti-taurine prophet, Eugenio Noel, saw them as the barbarous reservoir of all the distorted ideas of masculinity that find their quintessential expression in the bullfight (1967[1914]: 119–125). Araúz de Robles caps his view of bullfighting as a "virility contest" by a reference to certain primitive festivals that featured the jubilant excision of the bull's sex organs (1978:184).

A different picture emerges when these *encierros* (bull runnings) are studied more closely. Though a certain amount of courage is required to run alongside a group of bulls or to approach a *toro de fuego* at night (a bull with two burning torches attached to his horns by a metal apparatus), courage is never considered sufficient in itself. Even those who oppose such events on grounds of cruelty recognize that the chief values involved from the natives' point of view are courage *and* dexterity (Martínez 1986:14). In a study of the *toro de fuego* festival in Valencia, Mira found that "macho" qualities like raw courage and willingness to take risks took a definite back seat to another quality, *coneixement* (roughly know-how), which stipulates that the risks taken must be calculated ones and resolved with skill and agility (Mira 1976:122). "When someone does not show *coneixement,* his possible bravery is simply considered a form of useless risk and only provokes criticism and angry protests" (Mira 1976:122). Ingenuity, not manliness, is the foundation of the folk aesthetics that presides over this archaic folk ritual. Pamplona's *sanfermines* provide an even more striking example: the development of a body of techniques for participating in the traditional *encierros* has reached such a degree of sophistication that there are now several informal "schools" or styles that compete with each other in strategic maneuvers and artistic ambitions in what only appears to be several minutes of chaos (Echeverría 1983). More dangerous than the bulls, it turns out, are the many tourists who do not share close group knowledge and aesthetic criteria, take the *encierro* to be a simple question of guts, and simultaneously risk trampling and obstruct native artists by "running their own fear" (Echeverría 1983:138–139). Echeverría concludes that the current "state of the art" of bull-running is analogous to the formative stage of modern bullfighting, wherein a number of individuals began to invent the diverse *suertes* that would one day become standard procedure (1983:123–124). And the point is an important one because, as I discussed earlier, the history of the urban bullfight is the history of the slow but steady rationalization of the various ways that the peoples of Spain have played with bulls. The artistic elaboration of the *burla,* wherein a human being eludes a beast's blind charge through ingenuity and grace, was and is clearly present, perhaps dominant, in the taurine rituals of the

Spanish folk. And it is this element, not the necessary but insufficient one of valor, that has governed the development of tauromachy to this very day. If bullfighting really were Araúz de Robles' "virility contest," the bullfighter would not stand a chance. But tauromachy, as defined by numerous matadors and *aficionados*, is nothing more nor less than a standardized set of norms and procedures, which, if executed properly and with a certain degree of nerve, will lead to the swift demise of the bovid with something approaching mathematical certainty. Note that I say nerve, not valor or courage or bravery. These terms are best reserved for a lofty quality of the human spirit, the will to confront some spontaneous or unpredictable danger to achieve some social good. Nerve can be defined, at least in the case of bullfighting, as the quality required for carrying out a series of prearranged acts that have been developed to *reduce* personal risk. No spectator who understands the nature of the craft will blame the matador for being *unnerved* by certain bulls—the unpredictable ones that throw their heads around or turn sharply or "learn" too quickly during the course of the fight. By the same token, a bullfighter is expected to perform with a double measure of artistry with an easy, cooperative bull. The ideal bullfighter, according to the foremost taurine critic of the twentieth century, is simply the one who can deal successfully with the most varied kinds of bulls (Corrochano 1961 : 40).

In practice, some bullfighters do much better with bulls that permit a maximum demonstration of *arte*. Others prefer to pit their technical dominion and ingenuity against problematic bulls. Spanish Gypsy bullfighters can be considered an extreme development of the first group; the second has been the historical breeding ground for certain bullfighters who have chosen to emphasize (and exaggerate) the dangers of their profession and their own superior "valor." In such bullfighters, and more probably in their fans, it might be possible to find some evidence of that deeply rooted faith in manhood that Tierno found in "the Spaniard." Consider the case of Ignacio Sánchez Mejías, Lorca's much lamented matador of the 1930s. Cossío situated him among the bullfighters who had "achieved fame for their valor above any other consideration or cause" (1961 : 975). Even a critic as obsessed with getting his money's worth of courage as Hemingway was found him unpalatable: "He laid his bravery on as with a trowel. It was as though he were constantly showing you the quantity of hair on his chest or the way in which he was built in his more private parts" (1932:94). The historian Bennassar ranks Sánchez Mejías first in his gallery of prototypical Spaniards, talented men who dedicated their lives "to the service of an irrational impulse" (1985:17–18). His death in the bullring at age forty-three and Lorca's lyrical gifts made Sánchez Mejías one of the best known matadors outside of Spain and something of a demigod in his own country. But two points need to be borne in mind. First, Sánchez Mejías was not a kamikaze. It was paradoxically his mastery of technical resources and ingenious tricks that enabled him to make such a convincing show of his "careless" courage (Bergamín 1981:71). Secondly, no matter how many bullfighters choose to ham up their virile valor or how many spectators come to worship them, the fact remains that the craft itself has been shaped cerebrally, by the precedence of intelligence over strength, strategy over raw courage, brains over brawn. Jerry Lee Lewis can play the piano in a macho style but that does not convert the piano into an instrument of machismo. Virile valor, like Gypsy *duende,* is only an interpretive mode. As a technology bullfighting is sexless; as a form of art, both sexes have something to contribute. The many dozens of women who have become bullfighters have conclusively demonstrated this point (Boado and Cebolla 1976).

Each bullfighter interprets the craft in accordance with his or her degree of expertise, reflexes, physical ability or defects, imagination, ingenuity, and in accordance with the particular cultural values (they are legion) that his or her personality has selected. Likewise, each spectator of the bullfight "interprets" the spectacle according to his or her competence in matters taurine, social class, values, personality, mood, etc. "The public" varies enormously according to province, time of year, condition of the bulls, weather, presence or absence of food and alcohol, number of tourists, and other even more intangible factors (Claramunt 1982:118–125). And the public or publics change over time as well, with one generation more demanding or indulgent that its parents, more or less circumspect, more or less knowledgeable (Díaz-Cañabate 1970: 105–108).

Bullfighting and Cultural Complexity

The bullfight-event constitutes a perfect model of the four main varieties of cultural complexity enunciated by Saunders (1981:437) in that people can plug into—or reject—it at one of several ideational levels, as a function of their social status, in terms of consciously held attitudes regarding "traditional" and "modern," and as a function of unconscious ambivalence stemming from their personal lives. If we add one more factor to the list, their relative familiarity with the close group criteria of the taurine performers, then we have all the ingredients for the broadest variety of possible reactions. Just as taurine vocabulary lends itself to many cultural spheres, only one of which is sexuality, the bullfight-event is complex enough to generate an almost unlimited number of cultural and psychological resonances. A brief review of such psychocultural elaborations will demonstrate the extent to which social scientists with sexual axes to grind have distorted the data.

To begin with, a great deal of ideational culture has grown out of an aspect I mentioned earlier, the radical temporality of this idiosyncratic folk craft. Pérez de Ayala argued that bullfighting was "the only strictly temporal art," inasmuch as its unfolding is the act of creation itself, not just the effect or illusion of such creation that obtains with music or ballet (Pérez de Ayala 1963:1276). The impermanence of a matador's performance paradoxically potentiates its durability, in the form of mythicizing remembrances that convert the bullring into the privileged domain of *laudator temporis acti* (1963:793–798). These "praisers of times past" tend to locate the finest and most artistic moments of bullfighting in its so-called Golden Age (1914–1920), whose brevity was entirely in keeping with the ephemeral nature of the taurine performance itself. The heroic/aesthetic exploits of Joselito and Belmonte, the two great rivals of the period, form the "enemy-twins" nucleus of twentieth-century taurine mythology. Similar rivalries have provoked similar mythologies in every "age" of bullfighting (Vila 1947; Corrochano 1961:45–51). At times taurine culture's built-in penchant for nostalgia evokes the bitterest sort of disillusionment in *aficionados*—especially those, says Savater, whose deficient knowledge of metaphysics keeps them from seeing that the perfect bullfight they dream about never existed and cannot exist (Savater 1983: 119–124). At other times it provides grounds for a quasi-religious reverence for the giants of the past; taurine writers offer ecstatic descriptions of the immortal *faenas* that took place long before they were born (for example, Ríos Mozos 1985:33, 38, 46, 59 et passim). Though Bergamín, unquestionably the most prestigious philosopher of the "planet of the bulls," has contributed to this mythic nostalgia, he nevertheless underlines the aesthetic miracle of tauromachy that is available at any time to the right sensibilities (1981:39–41, 1985:25–34 et passim). One of Bergamín's firmest tenets held that bullfighters who melodramatically flaunt their virile valor effectively falsify the artistic truth of bullfighting, turning it into a kind of sadomasochistic pornography for the ignorant multitudes (1930:41–45, 1981:50–58, 1985:106–107). That this attitude enjoyed wide currency among taurine insiders was evidenced by their almost total rejection of the last great idol of said multitudes, *El Cordobés*, whose suicidal antics in the ring made him a "legend in his own time" and simultaneously provoked an outpouring of nostalgic counter-mythology on the part of disgusted *aficionados* (Collins and Lapierre 1968; Pozo and Bardón 1980; Díaz Cañabate 1970:134–145).

It can be stated in general that "the public" is the villain of the piece for most *aficionados* and serious critics. The public—or so goes the exoteric lore—wants only for thrills (the cheaper the better), is easily fooled, is given to base proclivities, and has a way of capriciously exalting certain matadors only for the pleasure of destroying them afterwards (Bergamín 1981:42–46; Ríos Mozo 1985:50–53; Claramunt 1982:148–150). Worst of all, it is alleged, the public no longer pays heed to the inner core of *aficionados* that have traditionally watched over the purity of the bullfighter's art. This informal but formerly powerful "senate," which has an exact parallel in the so-called *cabales* of flamenco, has at times been too swift to judge and condemn heterodoxy (González Climent 1964: 48–49, 419–429). Ironically, innovators who have taken steps along the road to rationalization—which is the essential historical thrust of bullfighting itself—have been routinely damned at first as the corruptors of the "eternal essence" of tauromachy. It is my contention that said rationalism is the basis of the twentieth-century discovery of tauromachy's artistic appeal.

With this brief survey of aesthetic elaborations we have only begun to describe the ideational possibilities of taurine culture. During the nineteenth-century "Heroic Age," bullfighting was seen not so much as a fine art as a martial art. Bullfighters were identified as warriors or gladiators and their performances as so many episodes of a grandiose popular saga (Bleu 1983 [1913]; Altabella 1965: 7–47). A related psychocultural development has portrayed the matador as the archetypal Spanish stoic or as the reincarnation of a Classical heroic ethos (Fernández Suárez 1961: 302–303; Pérez de Ayala 1963: 1271–1276). The bulls themselves have undergone an intense anthropomorphism in Spanish culture: on the one hand, certain bulls have become "legends in their own time" on the basis of size, strength, number of horses killed, strange or amusing behaviors, number of innocent bystanders killed, etc. (Cossío 1943: 323–406). On the other, those bulls that were able to get the best of an unfortunate matador have been branded assassins, cowards, and traitors in the popular ballads that recount the tragic goring (Gil 1964: 62, 72, 89, 92, 94 et passim). Praised for his heroic deeds or vilified for his homicidal tendencies, the bull has generally been considered anything but a victim.

The "outsider myths" of the nineteenth century were essentially literary and romantic, not anthropological or psychoanalytic, and they established a group of archetypes that have dominated bullfighting's image in novels, paintings, music, and films to this day (Lasker 1976; Delgado-Iribarren 1982; Fernández Cuenca 1982; González García 1983; González Troyano 1983). The tragic death of the matador has been *de rigueur* in these middle-brow and high-brow spheres of cultural resonance, despite the fact that, statistically, the *picador* and the *banderillero* are more likely to be killed in the line of duty (Carande 1964). It is here that taurine culture effortlessly bridges the social or ideational gaps between landless day laborers and belletrists, between oral poetry and cinema, between men and women, between insiders and outsiders. For few events are as productive in psychocultural responses of all kinds as the death of a prestigious bullfighter. That of Manuel Rodríguez "Manolete", for example, was unquestionably a major sociocultural event of the post-Civil War period and the reverberations continue to this day (Vizcaíno Casas 1971: 57–58; Araúz de Robles 1978: 11–12; Soto Viñolo 1986: 7–66).

The abuse of linguistic and folkloristic data, the confusion of metaphor with essence and fantasy with explanation, the willful disregard for the explanations of insiders, vulgar Freudianism, reductionism—these logical and methodological errors have characterized outsiders' interpretations of bullfighting. But the principal defect to be deplored is their one-sidedness. Unilateral interpretations of a cultural phenomenon that is as multilateral, dense, and contradictory as the bullfight cannot help but miss the mark. Rather than developing a tolerance for this ambiguity, taurine exegetes have tended to reduce it to some simple monolithic sign that can be equated to some other. They illicitly generalize a belief or a fantasy that may only belong to a few members of a social class or to a single level of culture as perceived by a few masculine informants in a given province. The resultant distortions of reality deserve to be branded "scholarly myths" and unhesitatingly grouped with other outsider myths of a romantic or archaeological hue.

I do not believe that it is easier for a camel to pass through the eye of a needle than for a foreigner to understand bullfighting, as one elderly *aficionado* told me. But research will only advance when 1) the body of techniques that constitutes the entirely unambiguous essence of tauromachy is distinguished from the highly ambiguous psychological and cultural resonances of the bullfight-event, and 2) when these psychocultural resonances are sorted out according to the specific groups, classes, levels of culture, etc. that may harbor them at one moment or another. Folkloristic, sociological, and anthropological investigations can then proceed productively in many possible directions. Caro Baroja has already indicated four concrete ways in which our information about rural *encierros* and their connection to civil and religious institutions needs to be improved (1984 : 18–19). Arévalo has outlined ten major enigmas relating to the history, politics, sociology, and biotechnology of bullfighting that have yet to be resolved (1984 : 56–59). Psychologically minded folklorists may wish to look more closely into the intricate web of rituals and superstitions that many bullfighters rely upon to one degree or another or the mimetico-charismatic chemistry between matadors and their *peñas*. Little attention has been paid thus far to the structural connections between comic bullfighting and the serious kind, with reference to the different groups who enjoy or condemn either one. A systematic exploration of the matador as a hero of modern mass culture in Spain and Latin America has yet to be undertaken. The manner in which the folk aesthetics and forms of *arte flamenco* have influenced those of bullfighting is another promising area for research, provided it is henceforth carried out on a less mystical plane. And it would be extremely useful to know more about the ways in which women of diverse backgrounds and personalities have joined in or opted out of taurine culture over the years.

I hope to have established that we do not need another "interpretation" of bullfighting. We have dozens, each more strained than the last. Nor is it a question of affording a vague, open-minded tolerance to the ones that exist. It is a question of seeing the limits of all interpretations, their arbitrariness, their perverse blind spots. It is, finally, a question of recognizing that several hundred years and several thousand books have left questions of vital import untouched. As Bergamín put it in one of his final taurine essays (1985:114), "Will we ever be able to learn all that bullfighting teaches us?"

9

Bullfighting and Identity

Few areas of life and culture in Spain fail to intersect in some way with the bullfight-event. Its structural connections with Spanish folk religion, for instance, are more striking and a good deal more solid than Pitt-Rivers' mystagogic misrendering of bullfighting itself as religious ritual complete with sexually ambiguous priests and victims. The bullfighting calendar is basically identical to the calendar of summertime patronal festivals. The prestige of a town is symbolically expressed by the caliber of the bullfighters it can contract to honor its supernatural protector. "Cults" of matadors—usually local boys who have made good—are almost as ubiquitous as local cults of saints and answer to the same logic of community differentiation. Like the numerous fiestas of "Moors and Christians" or the *Fallas* in Levante, bullfights represent urban festival/spectacles that serve old "sociocentric" needs in new circumstances. Spain's hundreds of *peñas* or taurine clubs provide suppers and socialization for their members in much the same way as the religious *cofradías* (Zúmel 1982). The rivalries of the bullring have always been overshadowed by the rivalries among supporters of different matadors, apologists for different styles, promoters of neighboring towns; in exactly the same way as the conflicting story traditions between the clans of primitive societies (Fischer 1963: 260), people in Spain use their particular versions of taurine myths and legends as badges of identity. Taurine culture as a vehicle of sociocentrism functions on many levels: Córdoba, for example, prides herself on the disproportionate number of great matadors born in that city or nearby (Sánchez Garrido 1985); the cities of Ronda and Seville each dispute the other's claim to be the *fons et origo* of modern bullfighting (García-Baquero et al. 1980:93—94)—which Cossío attributes to the region of the Pyrenees (1961:850—854). At a more inclusive level, the bullfight has been utilized by the defenders and definers of Andalusia's cultural singularity, some of whom claim that it owes its existence to what might be termed a flamenco *Volksgeist* (González Climent 1964:449—461). Meanwhile, Madrid's *aficionados* pride themselves on being the definitive connoisseurs of taurine art and the supreme arbiters of Andalusian pretensions (Bleu 1983:12; Arévalo and Moral 1985:100—101). Finally, at a nationalistic level, the institution of tauromachy has been one of the most powerful generators of cultural specificity Spain has known, the very essence of the Spanish *raza* (race), *casta* (caste), or *sangre* (blood)—all the naturalistic metaphors that Handler and Linnekin find at work in processes of "traditionalization" (1984:277—278). And, fully in keeping with Saunders' third category of cultural complexity, bullfighting has lent itself to the opposite process: the most famous group of "modernizers" in Spanish history, the Generation of 1898, was determined to extirpate the bullfight, and precisely because they identified it with the traditional essence of their country! (Prado 1973:11—61; Cambria 1974:48—100).

Taurine Martyrology

Numerous monographs establish beyond a doubt that what we might call "scape-bulls" are as central to Spanish popular piety as the saints, Virgins, and Christs in whose fiestas they are sacrificed (Pan 1945:194—199; Gutiérrez Macías 1959:471—485; Gómez-Tabanera 1968:269—295; Maldonado 1975:54—57; Caro Baroja 1948b:9—26; González Casarrubios 1985:111—135). The number of witches ritually exorcised and Judases symbolically executed pales into insignificance alongside the spring, summer, and autumn holocaust of bovids. In certain ancient religions the bull was thought to generate life itself; in contemporary Spain he can be observed to generate all manner of rites, romances, legends, and songs. That most of this folklore should disguise the fact that the bull is a victim can come as no surprise, in view of the major mechanisms of persecutory mythopoesis outlined in earlier chapters.

From a magico-persecutory point of view, the bull constitutes a perfect victim. Two centuries of de facto genetic engineering have taken full advantage of the natural bovine tendency to "flee head-first" and the result is the *toro bravo*—a true domestic animal that with sufficient stimulation will act out a culturally created role. The dozens of adjectives used to describe the fighting bull revolve around the central fiction of *bravura* (García-Baquero et al. 1980: 115–148), an imaginary ferocity that is analogous with the fabrications naive persecutors adopt to justify their actions. The common thread is the idea of legitimate self-defense; the bull must be portrayed as the fierce aggressor for the same reason that the Jew must be seen as the nefarious instigator of sacrilege. Both representations exemplify the persecutory mythopoesis that permits a group to reify, project, and expel its own violence. Self-defense is the basic justifiction for persecution and popular justice and it never fails to show up in the festal texts that mimic them. The Moors of the *moros y cristianos* festivals always attack first; Judas betrayed Christ without provocation and now his effigy pays the price of his perfidy. But the bull is an even better candidate for mythic disguise because everyone can *see* how he deliberately tries to destroy an initially unarmed man who weighs 400 kilograms less.

That the bullfight exemplifies the typical Spanish propension for cruelty is a charge as old as it is widespread; it is based on the conviction that said cruelty is self-evident for all observers of a *corrida de toros* and that disgust or sadistic delight are the only reactions possible. But if sadism is understood as the wholly conscious and morbid enjoyment of another's pain, the term does not fit the ethnographic reality. The cruelty of the bullfight is *not* in plain sight; in spite of the fact that, statistically, the matador almost always "wins," Spanish spectators have traditionally regarded the bullfight as a fair and evenly matched encounter between man and beast. Dozens of matadors fatally gored in the line of duty have only reinforced this conception. Those individual bulls who do not live up to the desired image instantly arouse the disgust of many spectators. A true *toro bravo* must play his culturally assigned role with dignity; he must seem to deserve his own death by "wanting" to kill the men with the capes. More than any other contemporary mass spectacle, tauromachy attests to the timeless tendency of human beings "to transfer their anxieties and conflicts onto arbitrary victims" (Girard 1978a: 201). The bull is not, of course, the *victime émissaire*—that time-bound social phenomenon that, in Girard's system, has forever departed our purview; but in his own sphere (or ring), the archetypal bull is the target of a mimetic polarization and the source of a burgeoning polysemy reminiscent of those Girard attributes to the *victime émissaire* (1978a: 71–72).

For people who possess this elementary but effective worldview, the notion that there could be something inherently cruel about the bullfight is simply unthinkable. Only when it becomes thinkable, in relatively more sophisticated members of the public, will it become susceptible to rationalization. Then it will be argued, for example, that the corrida is cruel but no crueler than many activities or sports practiced in other countries. Or it will be observed that fifteen minutes of misery is a small price to pay for the life of pampered luxury a *toro bravo* leads during four years. A third mechanism of defense will accuse the accusers of unwholesome curiosity, ill-disguised repression, or hypocrisy. And if all these tactics fail, taurine apologists can always fall back on the argument of "lesser evil": as Father Pereda put it, people who can attend a good rousing bullfight are likely to have little interest in protest meetings or social agitation (1965: 216–217).

Both the naive and the conscious rationales of bullfighting were rejected out of hand by the Regenerationist movement of the latter part of the nineteenth century and the Generation of 1898 afterwards. The bull came to be seen as an innocent victim—but only to be immediately assimilated to the martyrological genre of persecutory mythopoesis. Eugenio Noel tirelessly "martyrized" the bull in his essays and lectures, anthropomorphized him to the maximum, and even carried on long imaginary conversations with brave bovids on their way to be slaughtered by scoundrels in front of drunk and cowardly mobs (Noel 1967: 37–40, 90–100, et passim). More philosophical, Unamuno recurred to the bull by means of explaining the bloody and livid Christs that fill Spanish churches:

"If you should see a bullfight," I told him, "then you will understand these Christs. The poor bull is also a sort of irrational Christ, a propitiatory victim whose blood washes us of quite a few barbarous sins. And induces us, nevertheless, to others." [1967[1909]:274]

But the anti-taurine eloquence of the generation of reformers did not prevail, and by 1935 a new literary generation had actually come to celebrate what the earlier one had abhorred.

The real protagonist of the martyrological lore generated by tauromachy has not been the bull, of course, but the bullfighter. The sheer volume of ballads, legends, *coplas,* and hagiographical novels that sacralize the lives and tragic deaths of great matadors disposes one to believe that the bullfighter is as "appropriate" a victim as the bull, his blood as necessary to the ongoing functionality of the fiesta. The mythic nature of these psychocultural elaborations is easily demonstrated. Unlike a true martyr, the matador does not die for a religious or nationalistic cause; he risks his life for nothing beyond himself. A fatal goring, as Bergamín pointed out, is nothing more than a lamentable accident. Bergamín was an eyewitness to the goring of Sánchez Mejías in Manzanares and remained at his friend's bedside to the end, but he differed sharply with Lorca regarding the ultimate significance of such events. The only tragedy that can possibly occur in a bullring, Bergamín affirmed, is that of the bull; the bullfighter's death is not tragic, nor honorable, nor glorious, but simply . . . irrelevant (1930:32, 1985:107). Over the years Bergamín will heap abuse on anything and anyone that threatens to betray bullfighting's aesthetic raison d'être—including the matador himself, whenever he seeks to curry favor with the base multitudes by melodramatically underlining the dangers of his profession. Such a bullfighter does not even deserve a "clean mortal wound," according to Bergamín, and if he receives one, intelligent spectators can only turn away in disgust (1930:32). Bergamín had all the purgative zeal of a Noel, though he employed it to reform tauromachy from the inside. And just as Noel struggled in vain to show that the bull was a martyr, Bargamín did little to convince people that the bullfighter was not.

Significantly, the ballads and legends that mourn martyred matadors serve to occult the victimization of the bull even more effectively. A blind beggar ballad cited by Gil is typical of the tendency:

A José Gómez, Gallito,	José Gómez, Gallito,
la gran figura torera,	the great taurine figure,
lo ha matado en Talavera	has been killed in Talavera
la cornada de una fiera	by the horn-thrust of a
mansa y criminal.	meek and criminal monster.
[Gil 1964:89]	

Another example from the oral tradition of Badajoz:

Al sonar los clarines	When the clarions sounded,
salió el primero	the first [bull] came out
y el valiente Montano	and the valiant Montano
salió a los medios,	strode to the center,
dio un capotazo	gave him one pass with the cape
y echó a correr,	and started to run,
y la maldita fiera	and the damned monster
se fue tras él.	went after him.
[Martínez Remis 1963:146]	

Gil concludes that the Spanish people must have been especially affected by the deaths of Pepete (1862), Espartero (1894), Joselito, also known as Gallito (1920), and Manolete (1947), judging by the vast number of the popular songs that commemorate their exemplary personal qualities and lament their tragic ends (1964:10). Many other martyred matadors have been immortalized in *coplas necrológicas* as well, beginning with José Cándido, who died in 1771, and including Pepe-Hillo (1801), Chiclanero (1853), Cúchares (1868), Bernardo Gaviño (1886), Reverte (1903), Granero (1922), Ignacio Sánchez Mejías (1934), etc. (Gil 1964:13–130). The death of Paquirri in 1984 provoked a veritable outpouring of national grief, as anyone who was in Spain at the time can attest. He was laid to rest in the cemetery of Seville, not far from the tomb of Joselito, while the city collapsed into a funeral procession eight kilometers long (Arévalo and Moral 1985:245).

The numerous rural *encierros* or *capeas* have been a no less fecund source of martyrological folklore; a moment of carelessness or bad luck and the presence of someone with a modicum of literary ambition combine to produce a poem that enters the local tradition and stays there for years. The ballad that recounts the tragic demise of one Mariano Mera during the patronal festival of Matapozuelos (Valladolid) may serve as an example. The mishap occurred in 1935 and a folklorist recorded the coplas in 1981:

Tarde muy triste de toros.   A very sad afternoon of bulls.
Pueblo de Matapozuelos.   Town of Matapozuelos.
Muy tristes quedamos todos   We were all very sad
por la muerte de este obrero.   at the death of this worker.
De Valladolid llegaba   From Valladolid he arrived
el pobre Mariano Mera,   poor Mariano Mera,
sin pensar que le acechaba   without thinking that a
esa muerte traicionera.   traitorous death lurked for him.
Apenas llegó a la plaza   Hardly had he got to the plaza
el toro le atravesó   when the bull pierced him
y la cornada le alcanza   and the horn thrust penetrated
hasta el mismo corazón.   to the very heart of him.
Ninguno culpa ha tenido,   No one can be blamed.
Sólo la fatalidad.   Just fate.
Pero Mariano ha venido,   But Mariano has come,
y ya no vuelve a su hogar.   and will not be going home.
¿Cómo creerá su esposa   How will his wife believe
ni su niñito tampoco   or his little boy either
que sin vida ya reposa   that lifeless he now reposes
el que contento hace poco   the erstwhile happy man
llevó la muerte alevosa? . . .   whom perfidious death has
                                          taken? . . .

[Delfín Val 1981 : 32]

If unfortunate men are sometimes killed by bulls in urban bull-rings or rural plazas and subsequently mourned in time-honored forms, their unfortunate wives and mothers are culturally programmed to act out the role of *Dolorosa*. The aesthetic possibilities of violence are redoubled in the innumerable popular songs and novels that dwell on the maternal anxieties, the unrequited passion of beautiful but poor seamstresses, or the bitter tears of young widows (Lasker 1976 : 69–71; Claramunt López 1982 : 125–133). A number of particularly popular ballads tell of young *novilleros* under the tutelage of nuns who behave much like fairy godmothers as they care for and educate their ward, sew and border his first suit of lights, pray fervently for his success, and sorely bemoan his inevitable goring; the reiteration of motifs like youth, inexperience, roses, blood, and horn-wounds leads Claramunt to see defloration anxieties as central to this particular genre of taurine mythology (1982 : 128).

The ballads of blind beggars or the rondelets of flamenco singers contribute to an ongoing elegiac tradition that is best known outside of Spain through poets such as Rafael Alberti, Gerardo Diego, and especially Federico García Lorca. The latter functions like a theologian of folklore, taking the aesthetic standards and conventions of Gypsies and Flamencos and elaborating them into a higher-order sacro-erotic theory of the bullfight whose unifying principle is religious sacrifice:

In the middle of the Iberian summer the plazas are opened, or rather the altars. Men sacrifice the brave bull, son of the sweet cow, goddess of the dawn that lives in the dew. The immense celestial cow, a mother losing blood continually, requests the holocaust of man and naturally obtains it. Every year the best bullfighters fall, destroyed, lacerated, by the sharp horns of a few bulls that for one terrible moment exchange the role of victim for that of sacrificer. . . . From Pepe-Hillo to my unforgettable Ignacio Sánchez Mejías, embracing Espartero, Antonio Montes, and Joselito, there is a chain of glorious deaths, of Spaniards sacrificed to an obscure religion, incomprehensible for almost everyone . . . [Cited by Soberanas 1984 : 726–727]

The lyrical prose of Lorca communicates an important lesson with regard to persecutory mythopoesis: one can *see* the mythological parallels without seeing *through* them. In presenting what he takes to be the profound essence of the bullfight, Lorca has only succeeded in giving it a beautiful new décor. The exploitation of sacrifice as theme does not entail the exposure of the sacrificial mechanism. Thus it does not matter whether Lorca really believed that "a sweet mother goddess of all the cows" regularly demands human victims in return for the ritual slaughter of her "sons." Even in the guise of poetic metaphor such notions remain anchored in a closed system of persecutory representations. The mythmaking machine of collective violence acquires a more persuasive poetic camouflage; awkward questions of an ethical nature need not be asked, for blind fate is beyond good and evil and immune to moral correction. Rather than a callous disregard for human or animal suffering, it is an unquestioning acceptance of the inevitability of it all that informs Lorca's attitude, totally consonant in this regard with the fatalistic cosmovision of Andalusian Gypsies.

What distinguishes Lorca from his contemporaries is not the martyrological interpretation of the bullfight itself, which most shared in one way or another, but the perspective adopted thereupon. Like Lorca, Unamuno contemplates the spectacle of his compatriots being sacrificed to an obscure religion, but his attitude is one of horror, not mystical affirmation. And the mythological parallels he draws are not to the classic beauties of Greece or Crete but to the anthropophagous Aztec war god, Huitzilipóchtli (1967: 981–983). Lorca's mythopoesis is even more beguiling and internally coherent than the representational system fabricated by sacrificial culture itself: the bullfight becomes a sublime religious ceremony; the bullfighter does what he does because it is "in his blood"; his technique is governed by the mystical aesthetics of *duende*; and the rural poverty that drives adolescents into the profession becomes "the desire for a beautiful death" (cited by Soberanas 1984:727, 729). Unamuno's malaise was a necessary first step in the right direction, but it cannot be claimed that he transcended the martyrological mind-set of his culture. Furthermore, the righteous indignation that constituted a veritable trademark of the reformers sometimes impeded a just appraisal of Spanish cultural institutions. The bullfight is neither the fount of all virtues nor the triumph of cruelty and fanaticism. Stable sacrificial systems, such as that comprised by the bullfight-event and the reservoir of values, myths, and artistic forms that it generates or maintains, do possess, after all, functional validity. As long as violence is being channeled onto "appropriate" targets—a bull, occasionally a bullfighter—its potential for destruction will be neutralized. The anonymous and pathological forms of violence that characterize modern societies hardly represent an improvement over this systematic ritual containment.

Matadors, Magic, and Marianism

The actual beliefs and religious practices of bullfighters have never received as much scholarly or literary attention as the supposedly religious essence of the "rite" they protagonize. Speculation and poetry aside, it can be affirmed that the vast majority of bull-fighters have no interest in becoming demigods after a timely death in the ring. Survival, not martyrdom, structures their relationship with supernatural powers.

In view of the risks of the profession, it is not surprising to find that superstitions and magical rituals abound among matadors and their *cuadrillas.* The belief in the *gafe* or "jinx," for example, is widespread, and many bullfighters have had experiences that seem to confirm its validity. The anecdote of one bullfighter interviewed by Claramunt is typical:

In a provincial bullfight I did everything possible to avoid contracting a certain *banderillero* who was said to be *gafe.* He insisted but I was firm. When I got to the plaza I found him at the door of the *paseíllo*—he had managed to get hired for the *cuadrilla* of another matador. When he saw me he came up quickly and clapped me on the shoulder. "Good luck," he said, with that *gafe* face of his. As soon as I opened my cape the bull tossed me. The other matador got gored.   [1982:56–57]

Any number of stimuli can come to be considered unlucky by a given matador, but there is a generalized corpus of superstitious lore that most subscribe to—seeing a corpse on the day of the bull-fight, lending one's suit of lights to another, or the one referred to in a popular *siguidiya:*

Campanita, no repiques   Little Bell, don't chime
si salgo de la posá,   when I come out of the inn,
que esas cosas dan mal fario   such things bring bad fortune
y tengo que torear.   and I have a bull to fight.
   [Martínez Remis 1963:118]

In some cases, Claramunt reports, a bullfighter will come to adopt rigid counterphobic rituals to symbolically "undo" the bad luck he feels threatened by, but in most cases superstitions function as a sort of identity lore for the close groups of the bull planet (1982: 58). The famous and fearsome cattle ranch of the Miura family developed a ritual early in the nineteenth century that continues to this day: they light candles every time a *corrida* or group of six

Miura bulls is to be fought in any bullring in Spain or Latin America. When the great Espartero was killed by a Miura bull in Madrid, it was later revealed that the candles had been lit twenty minutes too late by an absentminded maid (Soto Viñolo 1986:15–16).

Moving on to a "higher" plane of religiosity, it is standard practice for bullfighters to take a little portable shrine with them on their trips. The shrine is set up on a table in the hotel room while the sword-keeper helps the matador into his suit of lights.

Then comes a moving moment. The friends have left the room and, alone with his sword-keeper, the matador lights a little oil lamp in front of the images of his devotion on the table. How beautiful and how spiritual is this situation in which the bullfighter invokes the Christs and Virgins of his devotion so that all will go as he wishes!   [Ríos Mozo 1985:182]

Ríos Mozo is not the only person to be inspired by the simple piety of the matador; "The Prayer of the Bullfighter," a quartet composed by Joaquín Turina, is considered to be one of the most important and perfect pieces of contemporary Spanish music (Delgado-Iribarren 1982:657–659). In the heart or on the lips of a working matador, the prayer is understandably brief and to the point. Asked what he says to God before a bullfight, Rafael de Paula responded

"Lord, give me luck, may everything go well for me. Give me valor and strength so that I will be up to the condition of the bull." I never ask Him to let me cut ears or be carried out on shoulders.   [Fidalgo 1986:10]

It can be affirmed in general that there are no atheists in bullrings, at least among the men who must come face to face with the bull.

A bullfighter's piety is entirely in accord with the standard operating procedures of Spanish folk religion, whereby a supernatural figure protects his or her client as part of a tacit collective or personal contract. The number of miraculous rescues in the bullring or miraculous cures after some bloody mishap have been legion during the past two centuries (Cossío 1947:225–231). In rural Spain, the saints in whose honor the *encierros* are held are traditionally expected to look out for the safety of the neighbors. A similar belief reassures the men and boys of Pamplona during their famous *sanfermines:*

En la calle de la Estafeta
nadie se puede morir,
que cuando vienen los toros
hace el quite San Fermín.
   [Martínez Remis 1963:88]

On Estafeta Street
nobody can get killed,
for when the bulls come
Saint Fermín keeps them off.

Spanish sanctuaries are full of bullfighters' *exvotos*, material evidence that the particular supernatural benefactor housed therein granted his or her aid at a crucial moment. Cossío reproduces one of these *exvotos*, a crude drawing made by a picador as proof of and in thanksgiving for a taurine miracle: the bull had thrown picador and horse to the ground during the first *suerte*; the bull was almost upon the picador when a crucified Christ appeared, with one arm down from the cross, flapping a cape to distract the bull and keep him off the man on the ground (1947:229).

Taurine piety, however, does not center around any saint or Christ; bullfighters great and mediocre have always looked to the Virgin to assist them in their hour of need. Folk songs, to name but one sphere of taurine cultural resonance, amply document the centrality of Marianism to tauromachy:

Todos quieren que haya toros,
porque si no los hubiera
se quedaría muy triste
la Virgen de la Salceda. . . .
A la Virgen de los Reyes
rezo al salir a la plaza,
y parece que la Virgen
en el ruedo me acompaña. . . .
Cuando salen los toreros
entre músicas y palmas,
la Virgen se queda sola
rezando por los espadas. . . .
Por Dios no me desampares,
Señora de los Remedios,
que cuando medie la tarde
ya estará el torito en medio.
[Martínez Remis 1963:78, 116, 124, 166]

Everyone wants the bullfight,
because if there weren't one
the Virgin of the Salceda
would be very sad. . . .
To the Virgin of the Kings
I pray upon entering the plaza,
and it seems that the Virgin
accompanies me in the ring. . . .
When the bullfighters come out
among music and applause,
the Virgin stays behind alone
praying for the swordsmen. . . .
For Godsake don't forsake me,
Our Lady of the Remedies,
for in the middle of the afternoon
I'll be in the middle with the bull.

The tutelage of the Madonna over the planet of the bulls is also attested to by the numerous *plazas de toros* dedicated to her in any of her advocations, by the popular imagery that pictures her accompanied by docile bovids, and by the great number of patronal festivals in which bullfights are held in her honor (Delgado Ruiz 1986:203–204).

This demonstrated Virgin-torero link has led Delgado to construct an audacious theory regarding the role of tauromachy in Spanish folk religion. Briefly, this anthropologist believes that the public sacrifice of bulls is nothing more nor less than a popular *variant* of the cult of María (1986:204–205), which is to be understood, in turn, as a "cult of tragic virility" (1986:210). In killing the bull, Delgado reasons, the matador carries out a symbolic excision of the dangerous and indomitable male sexuality that the bull represents—completely analogous to the sacrifice made by Christ, Who meekly offered Himself up as a sacrificial animal to the greater glory of matriarchy (1986:212). Popular Christianity itself is to be seen as the unofficial ideology of the dominant force in popular society—mothers. In support of his thesis, Delgado adduces 1) the lore and images of the Holy Family that highlight Mary at the expense of Joseph; 2) the importance the Church concedes to mothers in the crucial domestic sphere of the community; 3) the subordination of men to the authority of the women in their lives and the resultant rage and blasphemy of the former; 4) and, above all, the systematic inculcation of the Christ archetype, whereby young males are socialized in accordance with a tame, self-castrating, tragic, fatalistic, and utterly manipulable concept of their masculinity (1986:220–224).

In Spanish popular culture, Christ symbolizes, like the bull, the masculine. His cult is the cult of that which grows in order to be destroyed. . . . The young men that sacrifice a bull or that lend themselves to pseudo-sacrifice imitate Christ in his frightening act of renunciation, in the collective crime of which he was the object. During Holy Week they have the opportunity to make their imitation explicit and can inflict public punishment upon themselves that dramatically recalls the suffering of the Redeemer. [1986:225]

Both the bullfight and the Passion processions constitute the ritual reenactment of any young man's sexual truncation, the painful but proud fulfillment of "the culture of mothers and the religion of mothers" (1986:256). Delgado proceeds to associate Christ, the Antichrist, the bull, and the matador—all four—with the archetypal bull deities sacrificed to a lunar-solar mother goddess, represented in Spain by María (1986:242–250). All these vigorous young bridegrooms are so many hermaphrodites who symbolically protagonize tragic carnal acts that facilitate their absorption into the relentless maternal order of things. In this sense, the torero-Christ is "hardly distinguishable" from the other juvenile bull-gods that animated tragic virility cults in earlier ages—Attis, Dionysus, Mythras, etc. (1986:247–248). Such is "the religion of Mary and the bull," in which "life and death are venerated for themselves" (1986:259).

The Dionysian Connection

Delgado is not the first to connect Spanish tauromachy with ancient mythology; the "Neolithic theory" in vogue during the first part of the century made much of the tauromorphic mate of the Great Mother whose regular sacrifice assured agricultural productivity. Similarly, the parallels between the *fiestas de toros* and Dionysian rituals have been exploited over the centuries by both the enthusiasts and the detractors of the bullfight. From the very beginning the devil had been portrayed in taurine/Dionysian terms by the fathers of the Church; from the Middle Ages onwards, Spanish theologians never ceased in their (rarely effective) condemnations of popular or aristocratic bullfights as pagan abominations, *agitatio taurorum*, and *spectaculum daemonum*—with Bacchus joining Mithras and other phallic taurine deities to corrupt the morality of the populace (Alvarez de Miranda 1962:37–39; Conrad 1957:165–175; García-Baquero et al. 1980:15–25; Pitt-Rivers 1984:45). Dionysus has been one of the most dynamic and versatile gods in history, according to Henrichs (1984:205–206), so it is not surprising to find him associated with the modern bullfight from a variety of perspectives. The positive aspects of the "Dionysian spirit," for instance, have been celebrated by Maldonado in his study of Spanish religious festivals (1975:346–349). From an archaeological standpoint, Gómez-Tabanera has associated Dionysus with the totemistic aspects of Spain's rural *encierros* (1968:274). On philosophical/aesthetic grounds, Arévalo has described the interplay of bull and bullfighter as the harmonious union of Dionysus and Apollo (1984:55). Waldo Frank exemplified the literary/journalistic use of the "orgiastic" Dionysus in relation to modern tauromachy (1926:236–237). Even García-Baquero and his fellow authors momentarily abandon their levelheaded historical approach in order to place Dionysus squarely in the bullring of Seville:

> We know . . . that in the course of cults in honor of Dionysus, the faithful managed to achieve total participation only after they were incited by the overwhelming howls with which the priestesses gave notice, seized by the wild furor that they called enthusiasm, of the transmuting moment in which they were possessed by their god. Now, as then, the people congregated for the taurine sacrifice unanimously oscillate between rejoicing and silence and between propriety and convulsion following upon the hysterical or sacred scream of the women present at the celebration. [García-Baquero et al. 1980:15]

The majority of the "Dionysian connections" that have been found in the bullfight are as superficial and farfetched as the examples I have cited. Serious attempts to trace real, historical links, like that of Caro Baroja and the "Bull of Saint Mark," are quite rare. In keeping with his longstanding ambition to trace certain Spanish customs to classical antiquity, Caro examines the festivity of San Marcos, which he takes to be a Christian continuation of the Roman *Rubigalia*, and the manner in which it was celebrated for centuries in many towns of Cáceres, Badajoz, and other provinces of western Spain (1974b:77–110). On the morning of April 25th, villagers sought out the fiercest bull available and beckoned him under the appellative of the saint, whereupon the bull meekly joined in the procession, suffered himself to be adorned with garlands by the women and girls, entered the temple to attend Mass, and so forth. On the following day, the bull recovered his natural *bravura*. The yearly miracle was apparently assisted by having the chosen bovid lap up enormous amounts of wine on the night of April 24th (1974b:94–97). Such a procedure would not imply disbelief among the people that at some time in the distant past, when their less-sinful ancestors walked the earth, the miracle really occurred in an "un-assisted" way. Nevertheless, García Matos reports that no one in any century ever believed that the particular bull involved in the ritual was really transformed into *manso* (the opposite of *bravo*); records from the old parishes reveal that in at least one town of northern Extremadura the people were only interested in making a sort of living iconography, and that moreover they viewed their idiosyncratic folk drama as pure divertissement (García Matos 1948). At any rate, Caro hypothesizes with all due caution that the rite harks back to the cult of Bacchus/Dionysus that was firmly entrenched in the Hispania of Roman days, buttressing his comparison with a number of solid archaeological data. *The Bacchae* of Euripides is considered by Caro to be the fundamental text for associating Dionysus with the bull, the procession, the temple, the enthusiastic women, and the inebriation that characterized the defunct Spanish fiesta (1974b:105–110).

In reviewing his study of *el toro de San Marcos* (originally published in 1945), Caro demotes the "Dionysian connection" to secondary importance inside a broader and more significant issue: the "double character" of the bull in Spanish archaeology, folklore, and folk life (1984b:11–18), where images of dynamic, aggressive bulls alternate with passive and peaceful ones. "The question would be to find out how both were formed and why, once formed, they alternate in the Hispanic popular mind" (1984b:15). Sometimes the alternation adopts the guise of an active transformation, as in the case of the bull of Saint Mark; the power to convert the bull from a wild state to a mild state is traditionally considered miraculous. Much of Saint Dominic's lore in Spain, reports Aitken (1953), derived from his ability to work such taurine wonders. "The ferocity of the bull will always humiliate itself before holiness and virtue," observes Cossío (1947:205), while noting that even Saint Teresa of Avila came to be included among the saintly bull-tamers of Spain (1947:212). The idea is also at the heart of an intriguing medieval legend, studied by Alvarez de Miranda (1962:71–81) and Blázquez (1975:69–70), whose protagonist is a Galician bishop accused of sodomy. Either as punishment or trial-by-torment (the twelfth-century sources are unclear), Bishop Ataúlfo is obliged by the king to expose himself to a *toro bravo*, one deliberately stirred up and made even more *bravo* by the barking of dogs and the blaring of trumpets. The bull halts in mid-charge, turns utterly tame, and humbly entrusts his horns into the hands of the bishop. The king and the entire city of Santiago de Compostela witness the awesome miracle, and Ataúlfo is formally absolved of the calumny. After a detailed analysis of the sources and their variations, Alvarez de Miranda concludes that the legend dimly reflects not a trial or a punishment but a *cure*, a magic remedy that seeks to transmit true virility to those found wanting. "The bull constitutes the most appropriate mimesis against sodomy," affirms Alvarez de Miranda (1962:79), and the success of the operation is symbolized by the bull's "gift" of the very emblem of his prepotent masculinity. Other legends and folktales associate the bull with miraculous metamorphoses of women into men or with magical cures for infertility (Alvarez de Miranda 1962:60–70; Blázquez 1975:69–71; Rodríguez Almodóvar 1982:190–194).

Delgado Ruiz appropriates all of this folklore and recasts it in the light of his idée fixe: matriarchy. Then and now, he asserts, the sexual magic of the bull is a transparent metaphor of the sexual domination of men by women. A wild bull becomes a mild bull for the same reason that a vigorous bridegroom becomes a henpecked husband; each is tricked by the community into protagonizing his own self-castrating rite of passage—bullfight or wedding night (1986: 170–177). Eschewing Caro's attempts at historical reconstruction, Delgado grasps *el toro de San Marcos* by the horns to demonstrate the validity of his own Dionysian thesis: The rite features a group of thoroughly domesticated men who identify with the meek and malleable bull that they ceremoniously entrust to the Church-community-matriarchy; the women take the four-footed "neophyte" in hand, adorn him with feminoid frills, and oblige him to attend "the liturgical evocation of the death of a young god" (1986: 206–210). These and other details "prove" that we are dealing with yet another cult of tragic virility, another ritual variant of the mother-dominated and masochistic folk religion of Spain. Ancient myths and defunct cults live again when their structure is found to be identical to that of the modern Spanish family, whose "marital bedrooms must be presided over by a crucifix that archetypifies what takes place there" (1986:229), i.e., the periodic destruction of male pretensions.

To even begin to accept such a reading of the bullfight—and of folk religion in Spain—we would have to dismiss dozens of studies that present the father as the dominant figure in the Spanish family and men in general as the dominant sex in Spanish society. Few anthropologists of the Mediterranean, moreover, would subscribe to the notion that female chastity and the maternal appetite for suffering represent values that an unwavering conspiracy of mothers has managed to impose upon Spain or any other society in southern Europe. Most would concede that such values originate in an economic-ecological system in which men have the upper hand and women can be socialized, with at least partial success, to accept the "official" male devaluation of their sex and the concomitant idealization of figures like the Madonna (Schneider 1971; Saunders 1981: 438–442; Juliano 1986:49–54). It is a fact that the Virgin is the preferred devotion of bullfighters, but this can be simply and efficiently accounted for by reference to the same patriarchal mind-set that makes women into the archetypal *onlookers* of serious (male) activities—war, business, law, or bullfighting. "The beauty of the woman in the stands is as indispensable as the valor of the bullfighter and the vigor of the bull" (Claramunt 1982:131). "Beautiful, distant, and static. In this way she has been portrayed by those who have attended bullfights with a sensitive pupil: poets and painters" (Araúz de Robles 1978:185). This is one of the two roles that taurine culture assigns to woman; the other is that of yearner, worrier, and sufferer, as seen in the songs and novels I discussed earlier. The ubiquitous nuns function as the literary link between earthbound wives and mothers and their heavenly projection, María. The bullfighter's maternal dependency, or the dependency upon the Virgin that replicates it, is entirely peripheral to his profession. And *if* the bullfight-event represents some sort of socialization process, it would be male socialization (Araúz de Robles 1978:163–185). Perhaps in some ideal realm of culture the majestic matador constitutes the kind of role model for young men that the Madonna plays for young women. It would be a grave mistake to define the bullfight as a symbolic expression of women's sexual subordination to man (Douglass 1984); to portray it as matriarchy's supreme castration ritual is an equally perverse abuse of the evidence. To see the Passion of Christ in precisely the same terms redoubles the impropriety. Delgado's version of Holy Week in Spain stands in sharp contrast to that of Domínguez, who emphasizes that the violence, guilt, and mortification dramatized therein reflect the ambivalent relationship with Christ as *Father-*figure (1985 : 160–169). Fathers of a supernatural or natural variety are glaringly absent from Delgado's theoretical world.

The main issue is this: Delgado's Jungian-style *aggiornamento* of the long-dormant Neolithic thesis participates in, without transcending, the closed sacrificial universe that it purports to explain. It comprises a scholarly reverberation of the same echo chamber in which taurine metaphors have resounded for two hundred years. It represents a protraction of the familiar procedures of persecutory mythopoesis, an admittedly daring variation on the Oedipal themes that form the psychological counterpart of victim camouflage/victim ostentation. What Lorca does in the sphere of literary discourse, Delgado replicates in the sphere of social science; Delgado is Lorca with footnotes. For a poet or an anthropologist to explain one form of sacrificial culture by reference to another is to leave sacrificial culture itself unexplained, and this is no way to escape the "Spanish labyrinth."

IO

Don Juan Tenorio *as Collective Culture*

The myth of Don Juan affords an irresistible opportunity to demonstrate the extent to which Spain's general cultural "style" has been shaped by an idiosyncratic fusion of violence and piety. The quintessential version of the myth, as far as Spaniards are concerned, was reached by José Zorrilla in his "drama religiosos-fantástico" of 1844. The inclusion of this famous play in a book devoted to folk rituals, saints' legends, and fiestas is warranted by the following.

1) The motif of a rash young man's confrontation with the dead, the nucleus of the myth of Don Juan, originally derives from a pious legend widely disseminated throughout Spain and the rest of Europe. The oral, theatrical, and literary elaborations of this motif, and those of seduction and dueling—what Rousset calls the *système donjuanesque* (1978:12)—are inseparable from the system of traditional moral reinforcement I discussed in an earlier chapter (whereby hardened sinners are punished and penitent ones are pardoned).

2) Every one of Zorrilla's "innovations," including the abduction of a nun, Don Juan's vision of his own funeral, and his eventual salvation via a supernatural female, can be found before 1844 in romances, blind beggar ballads, and other popular genres. Tracing such themes in antecedent oral or "subliterary" traditions does not sully the Spanish dramatist's brilliant synthesis of the same, nor is it incompatible with searching out the foreign literary models he

might have been heir to. It simply suggests that the Spanish folk might have been "Romantic" *avant la lettre.*

3) Zorrilla's formulation or reformulation of the myth became and remains the definitive version for Spaniards. No tragedy or comedy has ever stayed so popular for so long in the history of the Spanish theatre; to attend a representation of *Don Juan Tenorio* on or near All Saints' Day has been as traditional in Spain as jack-o'-lanterns and Halloween costumes in America (Aymerich 1963; Peña 1986:20). The aging Zorrilla's own harsh criticism of the work of his youth fell on deaf ears, and his attempt to rework it into a *zarzuela* in 1877 failed miserably—critics damned his "sacrilegious" interference with the already inveterate drama (Peña 1986:26). In the meantime, popular culture had been quick to digest *Don Juan Tenorio* and regurgitate it in the same forms and genres that had accumulated the main motifs prior to its première in 1844 (Marco 1977:II, 386–387).

For all of these reasons, Zorrilla's play can be studied as an anonymous, collective cultural product. In this chapter I will endeavor to demonstrate that *Don Juan Tenorio* became traditional because it was an aesthetically and emotionally pleasing synthesis of the social and religious values most important to the popular classes of Spain. In addition, I will attempt to correlate those values that pertain to more ideal realms of culture (divine justice, Marianism) with those that were collectively sanctioned or collectively condemned behavioral norms (martial valor, indulgent mothering, *majismo*, blasphemy).

The Social History of an Imaginary Personage

Caro Baroja has affirmed that folk religion in Spain rests upon two pillars: the punishment of God and the cult of the Virgin (1969: 126). Over the course of several hundred years, the myth of Don Juan evolved to accommodate both, developing and elaborating upon the story's pious or normative function. The nature of this functional norm is clearly set forth in an oral ballad Menéndez Pidal collected in the province of León in 1889. A young gentleman was on his way to church one fine day

no diba por oir misa
ni pa estar atento a ella,
que diba por ver las damas
las que van guapas y frescas.
En el medio del camino
encontró una calavera,
mirárala muy mirada
y un gran puntapié le diera;
arregañaba los dientes
como si ella se riera.
—Calavera, yo te brindo
esta noche a la mi fiesta.
—No hagas burla, el caballero;
mi palabra doy por prenda.
   [Bonachera and Piñero 1985:14]

not to listen to the Mass
nor to pay heed to it,
but to watch the ladies,
the saucy and beautiful ones.
In the middle of the road
he came upon a skull,
looked it through and through
and gave it a great kick;
the skull gritted its teeth
as if in laughter.
"Skull, I invite you
to come to my fiesta tonight."
"Mock me not, gentleman;
you can take my word on it."

The temerarious young man is much shaken by this unexpected turn of events. True to his word, the skull shows up at the fete, eats nothing, and calls upon the gallant to dine with him in the church at midnight:

En la iglesia hay en el medio
una sepultura abierta.
—Entra, entra, el caballero,
entra sin recelo'n ella;
dormirás aquí conmigo,
comerás de la mi cena.
—Yo aquí no me meteré,
no me ha dado Dios licencia.
—Si no fuera porque hay Dios
y al nombre de Dios apelas,
y por ese relicario
que sobre tu pecho cuelga,
aquí habrías de entrar vivo,
quisieras o no quisieras.
Vuélvete para tu casa,
villano y de mala tierra,
y otra vez que encuentres otra,
hácele la reverencia,
y rézale un pater noster,
y échale por la huesera;
así querrás que a tí t'hagan
cuando vayas desta tierra.
   [Bonachera and Piñero 1985:14]

In the middle of the church
there is an open sepulcher.
"Enter, enter, gentleman,
get into it without fear;
you will sleep here with me,
and eat my supper."
"I will not get in here,
God has not given me license."
"Were it not because God exists
and to God's name you appeal,
and for that reliquary
that hangs upon your breast,
here you would enter alive,
whether you wanted to or not.
Go back to your house,
lowborn and of evil land,
the next time you find a skull,
do it reverence,
say an Our Father for it,
and toss it onto the bone pile;
so you'll wish they do unto you
when you have left this earth."

Youth, temerity, impiety, and a fittingly sacral dénouement constitute the core of the legend of Don Juan and donjuanesque legends. In *El Burlador de Sevilla, y combidado de piedra* (ca. 1630), Tirso de Molina combined these themes with nobility, seduction, the Golden Age obsession with honor, and a sound theological message. For two centuries hence the theatrical or operatic Don Juan will carry his hubris to its ultimate consequences, mocking men, women, and God and receiving his just deserts—the flames of hell—until Zorrilla finds a way to bring about the scoundrel's last-minute salvation through the intercession of the ghost of Doña Inés. For Rousset, Zorrilla's replacement of punitive justice with tenderness and pity goes against tradition (1978:71); Don Juan remains a criminal in the eyes of society and

he owes his final recovery not to his virtues but to an undeserved love, to the intercession of a woman. Grace is always gratuitous; for the Romantics grace is feminine. [1978:72]

I will eventually show that Don Juan's salvation was not so gratuitous or undeserved as Rousset suggests, at least for those first enthusiastic audiences of Zorrilla's dramaturgy in Spain. But another of Rousset's affirmations must be dealt with at the outset; for by way of presenting his model of the *système donjuanesque* in a coherent and manageable fashion, he states that

The libertine that confronted, that still confronts the stone statue, could not have lived in Golden Age Seville, except in the imagination of Tirso and that of his spectators or readers, just as he still lives in ours. It is on these grounds that he can concern us today. [1978:17]

The considerable coherence that Rousset's investigation of the Don Juan theme and its variations thereby acquires is won at considerable cost. Stone statues do not really walk and talk, of course, but the sociohistorical origins of the legend and its sociocultural repercussions are hardly figments of the imagination. These repercussions include real acts of bloodshed committed by real young men under the influence of an imaginary or metaphysical concept of honor.

It is my conviction that Don Juan cannot be understood apart

from a specific historical period and a specific society that 1) up-
holds a series of strict religious norms, 2) associates female honor
with chastity, and 3) identifies male honor with aggressive virility
and a pugnacious sort of one-upmanship that can easily come to
jeopardize the first two. Don Juan is nothing more nor less than the
tip of an enormous cultural iceberg of *bravos, guapos, jaques, va-
lientes, majos, contrabandistas, bandoleros,* and other violently
honorable figures whose almost interchangeable exploits have
been sung by popular poets for centuries. The lore is simultaneously founded upon and influential over the lives and deaths of real
individuals and reflects the social mores they endeavored to copy
or to flaunt. Narcissistic posturing, rivalry, vengeance, love affairs,
murder, punishment, piety—these are the key themes of a "donjuanesque" world where reality stimulates fantasy and fantasies
govern actions.

The myth of Don Juan crystallizes in the same seventeenth century that beholds the transformation of many flesh-and-blood
"men of honor" into men of personalistic violence. This much can
be gathered, says Caro Baroja, from a reading of the memoirs or
autobiographies of noted aristocrats and military officers of the
period.

> With my apologies to those who make his behavior a problem of hormonal
> deficiency, I think it can be defended that Don Juan is the literary result of
> a society in which the individual *más* or *menos valer* has come to exercise
> an obsessive influence   [1964:444]

Más valer, it will be recalled, lay at the heart of the original Iberian
honor code. It was not an individual matter at first but a collective
one, the stakes in an ongoing competition between households or
blood lines, each striving to be "worth more" (*valer más*) than the
others. Three kinds of blood myths were involved: 1) There was
nothing like spilling the enemy's blood to show how valuable your
own was; 2) the prestige you earned in battle was automatically
transmitted to your blood descendants; and 3) noble blood was
something that, once polluted by some *agravio* or affront, could
only be washed by blood. *Más valer,* in sum, was something to be
gotten or defended through violence. Over the centuries, as Caro
relates, this bellicose notion of honor underwent a process of indi-

vidualization (1964:430–460). In the new context, the figure of Don Juan can be considered the paradigm of the conceited, defiant, and aggressive young man

who in order to demonstrate his superiority in everything connected with disorderly and juvenile living must not only be the one who risks his life more, kills more, gambles more, shows off more, but also the one who conquers more women and employs greater ingenuity in seducing them. . . . In other words: the principle of *más valer* through individual violence is always the ethics of the soldier which, as long as the risk and the venture last, are acceptable and even desirable, but which are inacceptable in civilian life. [1964:444–445]

Just as the wars of the *Reconquista* reinforced the martial piety of medieval Spain, the imperialistic wars of Spain's expansion reinforced the spirit of braggart amorality that Caro refers to. In contrast to the inertia and rigid stratification of Spanish society, wars in Europe and the New World provided the fluid ambience for social climbing, fortune-seeking, and honor winning. Marco cites the case of a famous Valencian *bandolero* named Josep Artús, who was reputed to have committed thirty-seven homicides before being captured and sent off to the Neapolitan front as "punishment." He returned to Spain in short order with the rank of captain and became a protégé of the vice-regent and a hero to his home town (1977: II, 436). Marco goes on to reproduce a number of Golden Age romances that reveal how the Spanish infantry campaigns in Flanders wrought a peculiar synthesis of the chivalric honor code and that of the macho bully (1977: II, 439–442).

The text of *Don Juan Tenorio* faithfully echoes the phenomena in question. Don Juan and his arch-rival, Don Luis, depart for the nearest battle zones to demonstrate their superior worth—not through combat or service to the nation, but through a self-serving exploitation of the social chaos that accompanies war. Don Juan opts for Italy—

De la guerra y del amor	Of war and of love
antigua y clásica tierra,	antique and classic land,
y en ella el emperador,	and there the Emperor,
con ella y con Francia en guerra,	with [Italy] and France at war,
díjeme: "¿Dónde mejor?	I said to myself: "Where better?

Donde hay soldados hay juego,	Where there are soldiers there
hay pendencias y amoríos."	is gambling, brawling, and
	[amour."

[Part One, Act 1, XII, 446–452]

Similar considerations lead Don Luis to Flanders:

Allí, puesto que empeñadas	There, since wars are being
guerras hay, a mis deseos	waged, my desires will be
habrá al par centuplicadas	matched a hundredfold
ocasiones extremadas	by extreme occasions
de riñas y galanteos.	of squabbles and gallantries.

[Part One, Act 1, XII, 541–545]

The final score will put Don Juan on top: thirty-two homicides to Don Luis's twenty-three, seventy-two seductions to the other's fifty-six (631–660).

Military campaigns were the apt setting for braggadocio, difference-settling, and licentious behavior of all sorts; but the antisocial customs reinforced therein eventually spread to any situation in which vehement young men had something to prove, from the jail of Seville to the University of Salamanca. From the seventeenth century onwards, notes Bennassar, masculine honor was slowly assimilated to the willingness to risk death, among all social classes and most notably among young Andalusians of noble birth (1985: 218–219)—such as Don Juan and Don Luis. Far removed from any sort of military or social utility, this exacerbated brand of honor is utterly reminiscent of the metaphysical desire described by Girard, the mimetic and potentially pathological struggle among rivals to incarnate a self-sufficient model/idol of violence (1978a: 419–474). The pertinence of Girardian theory is enhanced when we consider the "aesthetic" aspects of Spanish *más valer*.

Models of Violence

The readiness to kill or die for the sake of reputation was not sufficient in itself to make a man a "legend in his own time": he had to display this readiness with a maximum of nonchalance. He had to be willing to court destruction with the same easygoing self-possession that Don Juan evinces when he bets his life that he can usurp the conjugal rights of Don Luis (Part One, Act I, XII, 705). The mentality of the age was clear on this point: honor was nothing without style. Enemies, death, and even divine wrath were to be countenanced with composure; the valiant had to be gallant, dashing, and devil-may-care; the outlaw *guapo* had to be a consummate *majo* as well.

Majismo can be defined as the personal presentation style for both men and women of the lower classes of the eighteenth and nineteenth centuries that was characterized by a bold, self-assured, malapert, and patently erotic manner of dressing, walking, and talking. It represented a more-or-less conscious popular rejection of the alien and overrefined fashions and behaviors that the upper classes of the early eighteenth century had adopted, and was so overwhelmingly successful that by the end of the same century the upper classes were doing their best to imitate the *majos* and the *majas* of the proletariat (Martín Gaite 1981:98–109). *Majismo* was central to the same grand and somewhat reactionary "invention of tradition" that eventually served to make *arte flamenco* and bullfighting into paradigms of "authentic" Spanishness.

This ongoing traditionalization process was proto-Romantic, Romantic, and post-Romantic, and was given solid historical reinforcement during the War of Independence (1808–1814)—begun, waged, and won by the popular classes.

Those who like their history in neat packets find the Spanish resistance to Napoleon almost as hard to understand as did Napoleon himself. It was national, but not liberal, a super Vendée, peasant, Catholic, and royalist. Here the new mass army which fed itself on conquest met its first mass resistance, a combination of modern national fanaticism with the fanaticism of the Wars of Religion. . . . This was the war of Goya's famous *The Disasters of War.* Probably more people lost their lives in it than in any other war of the Napoleonic era. As many French officers were killed there as in Russia or Germany. [Ropp 1962:126–127]

A people given to the careful calculation of the odds would never have risen up against the greatest army in Europe. The revolt was Manichaean, expulsive, sacrificial, and even possessed millenarian overtones (Herr 1978). The main point I wish to convey is that the war not only reflected and gave new impetus to old-fashioned notions of valor but also to an entire constellation of popular values, including traditional religious beliefs and practices. The triumph over Napoleon meant the triumph of a conservative, nationalistic, and markedly plebeian cultural style as well. For the rest of the nineteenth century and for a good part of the twentieth the charismatic heroes of the people will be those who protagonize masterful public demonstrations of risk-taking. The borders between *majismo* and *más valer* will become well-nigh indistinguishable.

The archetypal figure of the bullfighter is a case in point. On the one hand, taurine chronicles from 1793 to 1883 demonstrate that, inside the bullring, the matador was to show all of the arrogant valor and willful dominance that any "martial art" required; the bullfight was understood as *lidia, brega, combate* (Cossío y Corral 1986:37–945). The development of the techniques of tauromachy, to be sure, responded far more to a modern or "bourgeois" concept of war than to the feudal variety (García-Baquero et al. 1980:97), but the fervor of the masses was oblivious to such fine distinctions. On the other hand, a vast corpus of popular songs and ballads demonstrates that, outside the bullring, the matador was celebrated as the very embodiment of insouciant elegance and sex appeal—in a word, *majismo* (Martínez Remis 1963; Quiñones and Vega 1982; Caro Baroja 1969:214–222).

Quien quiera ver torero	Whoever wants to see a torero
de fantasía,	from out of a dream,
aquí está este real mozo	here is this splendid lad
de Andalucía	from Andalusia,
sin deshecho ninguno	without a single flaw
de abajo arriba.	from head to toe.
¡Esta sí que es pierna!	Now this is a leg!
¡Este sí que es cuerpo!	Now this is a body!
¡Este sí es columpio	Now this is swing
y este sí es manejo!	and this is flair!
¡Vea usted qué fachenda	See what style
y qué meneo!	and what swagger!
[Caro 1969:216]	

Small wonder, then, that the *majas* of Embajadores, a working-class neighborhood of Madrid, divested themselves of their carnations and other appurtenances in order to throw them at the feet of

Pepe-Hillo during his triumphant promenades around the bullring (Martínez Remis 1963:28).

To understand the values and tastes that made bullfighting popular is to understand the popularity of Zorrilla's *Don Juan Tenorio.* Scholarly or literary exegetes of tauromachy have occasionally recurred to the figure of Don Juan for purposes of comparison but have tended to content themselves with superficial and misleading word-plays (Bergamín 1930:67–68, 1981:89–90; Leiris 1964: 33–34; Tierno Galván 1961:62–64, 69–70). Don Juan, we are told, sets out to *burlar* women; the bullfighter sets out to *burlar* bulls. The equation of taurine "deception" with amorous seduction can lead to an erotic theory of the bullfight whose pitfalls I have discussed at length in Chapter Seven. Only Fernández Suárez seems to have seen that the essential matador-Don Juan connection has nothing to do with sex and everything to do with their hubristic exhibition of serenity before the forces of death.

Don Juan confronts death with good style, without losing his nerve or his composure; and not only death but also supernatural powers, God, and hell—in which he believes—, and which he defies with the same style with which he defied his human rivals. Nevertheless, Don Juan knows that this time he will be vanquished, destroyed, hauled off to a frightful supernatural destiny, nothing less than eternal torment. But Don Juan would die of shame if he flinched before this horrendous danger. He faces the terrors of the other world with the same grace with which he faces those of this world. He is a madman.   [1961:307]

In this sense, the specific techniques of bullfighting—or of seduction or of sacrilege—are irrelevant to the psychocultural resonances of their public ostentation. What unites Don Juan and the bullfighter as *figures* or *performers,* in other words, is their "passionate pride" (Fernández Suárez 1961:309), identical to the hubris that Caro Baroja finds in the *bandoleros, guapos,* and spoiled young aristocrats of Andalusia (1969:212–218, 388–390). Such hubris can be referred in turn to some of the seminal concepts elaborated by Girard. In effect, everything indicates that the inordinate pride that characterizes the archetypal matador, bravo, or Don Juan is created and nourished by rivalry, that this rivalry is itself traceable to social crisis, and that a sacral dénouement is inevitably involved.

The upsurge of bullfighting on foot, *majismo, bandolerismo,* and many of the other phenomena associated with "typical Spain" took place during the long period of economic collapse and hierarchy effacement that followed fast upon Spain's imperial splendor. As social structures fell, violent men rose; aristocrats aped popular modes of speech and dress; the provincial bully could win "honor" with sword in hand; the bandit could hold his head high; the brave bullfighter could become the lover of a duchess—while the duke was pursuing the *maja* (Martín Gaite 1981:100–104). Bennassar describes how a veritable "contagion of honor" was accompanied by and contributed to the increasing internal violence of the seventeenth and eighteenth centuries in Spain (1984:196–206). Contagious honor implies contagious vengeance: the *venganza del honor* reached epidemic proportions in certain areas of the south (1985:207–208). The decline and fall of the Spanish Empire supports Girard's observation that, in a society of effaced hierarchies, men will soon succumb to the temptation to differentiate themselves through a tragically identical desire to have the last word on violence (1978a:429–430).

Folklore mirrors the exacerbated one-upmanship engendered thereby. *Jácaras,* or "bully ballads," are typically recounted in first person and commence wth a *de rigueur* denunciation of rival bullies:

Pedro Ponce fue una gallina,	Pedro Ponce was a chicken,
el Pelado fue vergüenza,	the "Pelado" was a shame,
Mateo Benet le respeto,	Mateo Benet I respect,
Corrales se colorea,	Corrales turns color,
Escobedo es un menguado,	Escobedo is a has-been,
Pedro Gil atrás se queda,	Pedro Gil is out of it,
Piquer fue muy corta pala,	Piquer was small potatoes,
Ganchet en guapos no entra,	Ganchet wasn't even a *guapo,*
Domingo Ribas es baba,	Domingo Ribas is drivel,
Miguel Aguilar no llega,	Miguel Aguilar doesn't make it,
Romero fue un mata moscas,	Romero was a fly-killer,
Juan de Lara fué una dueña,	Juan de Lara was a duenna,
Pedro Andrés no tuvo manos,	Pedro Andrés couldn't fight,
ni Cholvi el de Betjeléa,	nor could Cholvi of Betjeléa,
Leandro Escales fué un niño,	Leandro Escales was a boy,
Pedro Roxas no se cuenta	Pedro Roxas doesn't count,
ni Don Agustín Florencio,	nor Don Agustín Florencio,

ni el guapo Francisco Estevan,	nor the *guapo* Francisco Estevan,
¿Qué vale Martín Muñoz?	What is Martín Muñoz worth?
¿Mosén Senén, qué aprovecha?	What good is Mosén Senén?
Peñalver fué un pobrezuelo,	Peñalaver was a poor devil,
y lo mismo Juan de Vera,	the same goes for Juan de Vera,
Robira fue un poco guapo,	Robira was a little *guapo*,
el Mellado ya flaquea,	the "Mellado" is getting weak,
Martín Alonso qué mandria!	Martín Alonso what a jerk!
[Caro 1969:110]	

Marco reproduces similar examples (1977:II, 445–452).

Rivalry is the motor of Zorrilla's drama as well; its protagonist does not seduce seventy-two women nor slay thirty-two men for the sake of lust or bloodlust but solely in order to demonstrate his *más valer* to the world in general and to his rival Don Luis in particular. Peña observes that Don Juan invites the statue of Don Gonzalo to supper not out of sacrilege but in order to show his companions that he fears nothing (1986:202). Rivalry is nothing without publicity; one's exploits must be known or they do not count. Voilà the crucial role of taurine journalism.

Bullfighting and mimetic rivalry are inseparable, structurally and historically. There is, to begin with, the struggle between man and bull: great *faenas* are always as symmetrical as possible, and Claramunt has noted that the fascination a bullfighter can come to feel for his opponent may cause him to lose all notion of prudence (1982:165–166). Secondly, the institution that showcases this primary rivalry was itself the object of a prolonged class rivalry: the proletariat eventually wrested control of the taurine spectacle from the patriciate and imposed its own styles (Cossío 1961:842–890; Araúz de Robles 1978:71–78; Pérez Delgado 1978:862–873; García-Baquero et al. 1980:51–83). Subsequently, intense rivalries between matadors of different "schools" or styles caused bullfighting to thrive, year after year, decade after decade (Vila 1947; Cossío y Corral 1986:40–60). The decisive role played by real or imagined opponents in the career of the late Francisco Rivera has been explored at length by Arévalo and Moral (1985:37–40, 49–50, 81–82, et passim). A fourth type of rivalry needs to be mentioned, one that is even more "metaphysical" than the previous three: the sense of competition with great idols of the past. Claramunt refers to the keen envy that Ignacio Sánchez Mejías felt for Joselito, fatally gored in 1920, immortalized by the masses, and distressingly out of reach (1982:78). A similar phenomenon has been recorded among other model-obsessed men of violence: the foremost authority on nineteenth-century *bandolerismo*, Julián Zugasti, spoke of the "magic and prestige" that the legends of celebrated bandits held for their unsung successors and the resultant inferiority complex that more than one labored under (cited by Marcos 1977: II, 435).

Bullfighting, it must be pointed out, represents an effective canalization of mimetic rivalry. Unlike *guapos* or professional swashbucklers, matadors use their swords on the bull, not on each other. What prevents the entire affair from sliding into buffoonery is the fact that the bovid is a genuine and potentially deadly opponent. The spectators of a bullfight admire the matador because they hold the bull to be a just measure of his pretensions. Admiration can become idolatry if his skill is accompanied by a metaphysical sense of honor intense enough to supplant the survival instinct. Savater has attempted to account for the bullfighter's charisma by reference to ancient myths of heroes who return from their ritual confrontations with telluric fertility gods to spread regenerated life among the needy masses; hence the matador's image as a hard-drinking, free-spending womanizer and his faithful fans' idolatrous behaviors (1981:413–414). A less mythic explanation can be formulated by reference to Girard's *psychologie interdividuelle* (1978a:399–592): Desire tends to polarize around any expert manipulator of violence, seemingly autosufficient and *sans modèle* in his charisma (or his *guapeza* or his *majeza*, to employ the autochthonous Spanish terms).

The supercharged emotional bond that unites idol and idolizers can have comic and highly revealing consequencs, as shown by some of the anecdotes Belmonte told of his fans—how they mobbed him on every occasion, how they sought to parade him around on a platform like a patron saint, how their moods of elation or despair were totally synchronized with the matador's luck on any one afternoon (Chaves 1969[1935]:184–198). Not surprisingly, this hero-worship often went hand in hand with sociocentrism; in traditional Spain, the honor achieved by practitioners of valiant violence always engrossed the collective pride of their home towns or neighborhoods, which tacitly praised themselves in praising their favorite sons—even when the latter were murderous *bandoleros* (Marco 1977 : II, 447). The dramatic death of a *guapo* or a matador in the line of duty and his subsequent deification in folklore only served to carry the whole idolatrous process to its logical conclusion. Elevation to eternal glory is the most fitting reward for a charismatic hero, as long as his parting fulfills certain traditional expectations. Enter Don Juan.

Stern Fathers and Gentle Mothers

In one important respect the matador and Don Juan differ sharply. The former does nothing that the public considers morally wrong and, ninety-nine percent of the time, the death of the bull resolves the mimetic conflict and restores the right order of things. But the admiration Don Juan elicits is always tempered by the knowledge that he has gone too far. Some sort of sacral dénouement is therefore in order, for both Don Juan and the legendary blasphemers and hubristic transgressors that he epitomizes. Even the folk ballads that exude a primitive esteem for the daring-do of valiant sinners never fail to derive the appropriate moral lesson from their protagonist's inexorable fate. The moralistic finale can take one of two forms—damnation or salvation (with an optional probationary period in Purgatory). Marco reproduces a number of early nineteenth-century *pliegos* that feature these typical outcomes. The title of one is sufficiently illustrative:

Exemplary Relation of the manifest punishment that Divine Justice has executed with a Gentleman, who in order to establish lascivious communication with a Nun, with gifts and presents he convinced her; and going to take her from the Convent in order to achieve his desire, devils appeared to him in the form of dogs, and attacking him they tore his body apart, and carried off his soul to Hell: and all other details that the curious reader will see. [1977 : II, 494–495]

The seduction of a nun is not the only proto-donjuanesque theme contained in this truculent narration; in addition, the gallant but sacrilegious protagonist is temporarily stayed by the vision of his

own funeral (1977:II, 495–497). Don Miguel de Mañara, a seven-
teenth-century Sevillian nobleman considered by some to have
been the real-life model for Tirso's Don Juan, is said to have abandoned his dissolute life following just such a vision (Bonachera and
Piñero 1985:111–116). Another blind beggar ballad of 1831 fore-
shadows Zorrilla's most decisive innovation:

New Romance of Julián de Paredes, in which the famous and amazing history of Julián de Paredes is recounted, a miller of Triana, neighborhood of
Seville, who as a child was taught to pray every day seven Our Fathers and
seven Hail Marys to the Most Holy Virgin of Atocha, and although in the
course of his life he fell in with bad company that dragged him into vice
and evil to the point that he was sentenced to death by hanging, he never
neglected the devotion of María Santísima: and this enabled him to survive such a fatal predicament, and in his last infirmity he managed to see
the very Mother of God seven days before dying; with every other detail
that the curious reader will see.   [Marco 1977:II, 497]

A classic romance cited by Caro Baroja is equally pertinent in this
context of saintly ex-sinners: Don Miguel de Arenales began his
career of infamy as a university student in Salamanca, graduating
to homicidal duels all over Spain until meeting the beautiful Doña
Rosa; he is eventually obliged to kill her father and a rival para-
mour before carrying her off to Portugal. At the end, Doña Rosa
convinces Don Miguel to repent; she enters a convent and he becomes a Franciscan friar (1969:109–110).

Rousset's assertion that Don Juan's salvation-through-female-
intervention was "against tradition" (1978:71) is contradicted by
the foregoing. Spanish popular culture, Romantic *avant la lettre*,
had already shown the way. It is also inaccurate to claim that the
grace shown Don Juan was gratuitous and undeserved (Rousset
1978:62, 72). He does show sincere contrition for his crimes, after
all, and from the viewpoint of official and folk Catholicism alike,
that is enough to make him merit salvation. In addition, Don Juan's
willingness to confront death and damnation with all of the stylized composure of a *majo* or a *torero* affords him a parallel saving
grace for the popular mind. Don Juan is deserving of pardon, affirms Fernández Suárez, "because his impudent pride, in spite of
everything, is not satanic pride, but the rebellion of a courageous
boy" (1961:307). Zorrilla's finale is thus an ingenious satisfaction

of literary, theological, cultural, and emotional requirements—all mediated and fused together by a *femme redemptrice*. It may well be that the redemptive role of Doña Inés was largely inspired by European Romanticism (Peña 1986:58–59), but the popular tastes that acclaimed the new twist on Tirso's libertine and rapidly "traditionalized" Zorrilla's play responded in accordance with a different system of reference—Marianism, Spain's great cultural counterweight to the just wrath of God the Father. Even Peña refers repeatedly to Doña Inés as a "mediating Virgin Mary" (1986:31, 56, et passim).

Unamuno's interpretation of the importance of María to Spanish popular religiosity accurately conveys the emotional charge of maternal salvation:

God was and is masculine in our minds; His way of judging and condemning mankind is not that of a human person above sex, but that of a man, a Father. And to compensate for it the Mother was necessary, the Mother who always forgives, the Mother who always opens her arms to the son when he flees from the raised hand or wrinkled brow of the irritated Father, the Mother . . . who knows of no other justice than pardon, of no other law than love.   [1968[1905]:420]

Devotion itself is not sex-specific, of course; for help with matters grave and middling, Spaniards have been as likely to turn to male supernatural protectors as female ones—whichever was most specialized in a particular ailment or predicament. But it is a fact that the Virgin appears with unusual frequency in connection with men who make their living through violence, crime, or frequent contact with awesome or deadly elements (fishermen, for example). The predilection of bullfighters for one cult of the Virgin or another was established in the previous chapter, and duly associated with the culturally sanctioned solicitude of wives, mothers, and nuns. In the romance of Julián de Paredes cited above, the condemned outlaw does not pray directly to Mary; significantly, he prays to the spirit of his dead mother to ask her to plead his case with the Mother of God. And the vision granted to him on his deathbed demonstrates the success of this doubly maternal route to salvation:

Una mañanita hermosa,	One beautiful little morning,
que apenas nacía el alba,	just at daybreak,

de luces y resplandores	full of lights and resplendence
ví llena toda la sala.	I saw my hospital room.
Y como si en medio de ella	And as if in the middle of it
una gran Reyna llegara,	a grand Queen had arrived,
ví la muger más hermosa,	I saw the most beautiful woman,
que se vió en figura humana.	that ever took human form.
Que era la virgen Maria	That it was the Virgin Mary
al punto me anunció el alma,	my soul announced to me at once
y me puse de rodillas,	and I got down on my knees,
aunque sin fuerzas estaba.	although I had no strength.
Me pareció oir entónces	Then I seem to have heard
una voz suave y blanda,	a soft and smooth voice
que me dijo: "Ya tus culpas	that said to me: "Your faults
quedan, Julián, perdonadas.	are already, Julián, forgiven.
Del Cielo irás a gozar	You will go to rejoice in Heaven
que yo rogué por tu alma,	since I pleaded for your soul,
y á pesar de tus delitos	and in spite of your crimes
tu devoción hoy te salva.	today your devotion saves you.
Siete días vivirás,	You will live seven more days,
y despues de ellos te aguarda	and after them will await you
la madre de pecadores	the mother of sinners
en su corte soberana."	in her sovereign court."

[Marco 1977 : II, 499–500; original orthography]

Conflicts with fathers and supernatural Father-figures comprise the other side of this family romance *a la española*. It can hardly be coincidental that Andalusia, the privileged reserve of *guapos, majos,* Don Juan and other aristocratic libertines, *bandoleros,* and bullfighters, simultaneously nourishes a fervent devotion to the Virgin and the ancestral fear of an Old Testament type of choleric divinity. And, according to Domínguez Morano,

Affective ambivalence necessary surges with enormous intensity. That fatalist God induces one to submission, but also to blasphemy (let us not forget that Andalusia is the region of Spain that blasphemes the most). In this intense affective ambivalence vis-à-vis God and in the attachment to the maternal can be found, we believe, the two fundamental keys for understanding traditional Andalusian religiosity. [1985 : 141]

Bennassar finds that blasphemy is frequent, widespread throughout Spain, very old, and primarily a masculine activity (1985 : 82). Of the 644 blasphemy trials held at Toledo's Tribunal of the Inqui-

sition during the sixteenth century, 596 of the accused were men
(1985 : 83).

If blasphemy were defined as a willful and personalistic insulting
of a supreme idol of (potential) violence and punishment, its frequency among men obsessed with the exaltation of their own honor
through violence would not be surprising. It can be inferred that an
exaggerated concept of virile *más valer* carries the seeds of blasphemy within it—or of Oedipal conflicts of an earthly nature. Caro
finds both "the severity of the father" and "the adoration of the
mother" as the ultimate motivations of *majismo* in Málaga (1969 :
391). Appropriately, the first threat of divine punishment that
Zorrilla's Don Juan is obliged to listen to comes from Don Diego,
his father:

No puedo más escucharte,	I can listen to you no more,
vil don Juan, porque recelo	vile Don Juan, for I suspect
que hay algún rayo en el cielo	that some heavenly thunderbolt
preparado a aniquilarte. . . .	is ready to annihilate you. . . .
Adiós, pues: mas no te olvides	Goodbye, then: but don't forget
de que hay un Dios justiciero.	that there is an exacting God.
[Part One, Act 4, XII, 752–755; 772–773]	

It is thus quite coherent from an ethnopsychological point of
view that Don Juan's most clearly blasphemous speech follows fast
on his slaying of Don Gonzalo (the father of his beloved novitiate
and future guest of stone), which was itself provoked by the man's
rigid and hard-hearted rejection of Don Juan's sincere attempt at
contrition:

Escucha, pues, don Gonzalo,	Listen, then, Don Gonzalo,
lo que te puede ofrecer	what can be offered you by
el audaz don Juan Tenorio	the audacious Don Juan Tenorio
de rodillas a tus pies.	on his knees at your feet.
Yo seré esclavo de tu hija,	I'll be your daughter's slave,
en tu casa viviré,	and in your house I'll live,
tú gobernarás mi hacienda,	you'll govern my inheritance,
diciéndome esto ha de ser.	telling me "this is to be so."
[Part One, Act 4, IX, 2512–2519]	

Don Gonzalo, convinced by his own self-righteous hubris that Don
Juan is terrified, remains adamant in a most un-Christian way:

¡Nunca, nunca! ¿Tú su esposo?	Never, never! You her husband?
Primero la mataré.	I would rather kill her.
¡Ea! Entrégamela al punto,	Come, hand her over to me now,
o sin poderme valer,	or in spite of myself,
en esa postura vil	in that vile posture
el pecho te cruzaré.	I will run you through.
[Part One. Act 4, IX, 2544–2549]	

Don Juan has no choice but to eliminate his elder with a pistol shot (the intrusive Don Luis is dispatched with a sword thrust). The scene ends with Don Juan's blasphemy, pronounced with all of his legendary *majeza* and aplomb:

Llamé al cielo y no me oyó,	I called to heaven but it heard me [not,
y pues sus puertas me cierra,	and since it shuts its doors to me,
de mis pasos en la tierra	for my acts on this earth
responda el cielo, y no yo.	let heaven respond, not me.
[Part One, Act 4, X, 2620–2624]	

Don Juan's self-serving insolence towards matters sacred is the direct result of his frustrated attempt to gain salvation *por vía paterna*. And it is only through the saintly figure of Doña Inés that he will be reconciled to God the Father at the end—God the *forgiving* Father. Throughout the seven acts of the drama, Zorrilla recreates the major archetypes of popular religion in Spain, relates them to the characters in a psychologically valid way (valid for Spain and perhaps the Mediterranean in general), and deploys an abreactive apparatus analogous to that of other popular representations, such as Holy Week processions, that feature a mise-en-scène of parricidal guilt, virginal/maternal anxiety, and eventual forgiveness and regeneration.

None of this is necessarily immune to criticism. Zorrilla's finale could be described as magical or even demagogic, since all it takes to counteract a lifetime of sin is a second of repentance. Even Don Juan himself finds this hard to believe at first:

Tarde la luz de la fe	Too late the light of faith
penetra en mi corazón,	penetrates my heart,
pues crímenes mi razón	for only crimes does my reason
a su luz tan sólo ve. . . .	see by its light. . . .

y pues tal mi vida fue,   and since such was my life,
no, no hay perdón para mí.   no, there is no pardon for me.
[Part Two, Act 3, II, 3720–3723; 3736–3737]

Apart from this, it might be argued that Don Juan manifests no genuine spiritual growth or process of psychic maturation. Or that the sort of transcendence he achieves at the end is really the thinly disguised apotheosis of an outmoded brand of heroism that leaves the mimetic mechanics of his errors in the dark. The text of the drama itself, however—and in spite of its lushly Romantic surface—does not lend itself so easily to such negative interpretations. After carrying out a careful collation of ecclesiastical doctrines and practices with the final scenes of the play, Peña concludes that the playwright "had not forgotten his catechism" (1986:69); the dénouement of *Don Juan Tenorio* is entirely in keeping with the teaching of the Church regarding the last minutes of life, the sacrament of Extreme Unction, and so on (1986:61–69). The charge of demagogy would thus have to be placed at the door of Catholicism itself. Furthermore, Don Juan does not die with his retrograde *imago* of a vengeful Old Testament deity intact—arguably the very basis of his blasphemy and a major stimulus to his overweening honor. This is clear from the very last lines of the play, which constitute a bona fide prayer of thanksgiving to "el Dios de la clemencia/el Dios de don Juan Tenorio" (Part Two, Act 3, IV, 3806–3815). The *système donjuanesque* as completed by Zorrilla leaves the ex-sinner in good standing with his almighty (Oedipal) Father-figure. It might even communicate the sort of renunciation of metaphysical rivalry that Girard has considered to be incompatible with Romanticism (1961). Or can an outcome that is truly Christian in the evangelical sense of the word somehow remain a mystification of human desire and a *mensonge romantique*? But this is a question that falls outside the scope of my study.

My purpose has been to identify the major reasons behind the mass appeal of *Don Juan Tenorio*, to show why it can be considered the collective property of the Spanish people more than that of an individual author. Within the polarizing patriarchal mind-set I have described at length, Don Juan's salvation *por vía materna* functions. It broadcasts a message that may or may not stand up from an intellectual perspective but certainly "clicks" from an emotional one. The end, in other words, justifies the means—the only justice that matters for saintly mothers, as Unamuno said, is pity, and love is their only law. And this lies beyond the reach of mere reason, as Doña Inés herself points out:

Misterio es que en comprensión

no cabe de criatura:
y sólo en vida más pura
los justos comprenderán
que el amor salvó a don Juan
al pie de la sepultura.
 [Part Two, Act 3, III, 3790–3795]

'Tis a mystery whose
                    [comprehension
is beyond human capacity:
and only in a purer life
will the just understand
that love saved Don Juan
at the edge of his grave.

Conclusion: Sacrificial Civilization and Its Discontents

This book has focused on some of the mainstays of Spanish sacrificial civilization, i.e., the closed system of cultural representations and practices that have been structured by violence or by collective efforts to contain it. Time and again we have seen the stabilizing effects of folklore and folk rituals, which were themselves forged in instability; we have seen how projective and wholly utilitarian traditions invented in the heat of crisis evolved over the centuries to incorporate introjective and aesthetic features. I have attempted to depict the movement from identity crisis to identity consolidation, from folk terrorism to sociopsychological functionality, from accusation to self-accusation, from guilt to grace, from moral reinforcement to the reinforcement of popular tastes. I do not believe this movement to be unique to Spain, but I do believe that in Spain it is uniquely transparent. And, as fate would have it, Spain also provides us with the clearest contemporary example of what happens when the process reverses itself. The Civil War of 1936–1939 constitutes an exhaustively documented catastrophe in which a stable sacrificial ideology gives way to a highly unstable one, with results that take us back to the "hottest" and most primitive forms of stress-induced mythopoesis. This is not the place for a detailed examination, but a brief consideration of Spain's last great identity crisis and the lore it wrought will permit me to recapitulate the key findings of my study and further demonstrate the potential of its theoretical apparatus.

In a traditional sacrificial culture, power and prestige are associated with the expert manipulation of violence, the prerogative of certain well-defined figures (the matador, the swashbuckler, the outlaw). Their careers and exemplary deaths answer, in the last analysis, to a stable value system. But in a less traditional age, violence no longer kept in check by ritual or institutional means becomes the province of all. The chances of becoming a hero and a victim are multiplied and the archetypes generated will be less aesthetic and more sacred than ever—Anarchists in search of the millenium, crusaders for Christ, martyred poets, priests, workers, and peasants. An "apocalyptic-Manichean mentality" came to the fore in the Spain of the holy Civil War (Sperber 1974:xvii–xxvi), and every man could once again aspire to have the last word, figuratively and literally. For chaos was accompanied by logos in the form of thousands of songs and poems composed by people from every walk of life and especially by soldiers on the front lines, works that make almost exclusive use of the metrical scheme of Spanish folk ballads. In general, political considerations have guided the compilers and investigators of this unprecedented poetic output (Geist 1985; Puccini 1960; Ramos-Gascon 1978; Rodríguez Moñino 1977; Salaün 1971, 1985). It would be absurd to deny the objective social or political differences between the "two Spains" and the men who fought for each; but violence is the great equalizer, especially at an ideational level, and it is not difficult to see that both sides were caught in the thrall of a single closed system of sacrificial representations. The combined Civil War *romanceros* form one gigantic mythological corpus whose epicenter is none other than the victim, the glorious hero/martyr/victim who dies for us all and whose blood cries out for revenge.

The elements of martyrdom and vengeance that adhere to the spontaneous expressive culture of the Civil War are what most clearly distinguishes it from a "cooler" mythmaking machine like tauromachy. No bullfighter fatally gored in the ring can ever be considered a martyr, strictly speaking. The matador's motives are personal, not altruistic. He does not risk his life for any ideal as such, nor for any divinity, but to demonstrate his nerve and skill for money and applause. By the same token, the matador's death does not provoke an outpouring of righteous ire, only grief and tragic laments. But the multiplication of sacral/martial mythemes in an unstable sacrificial culture is propelled by the mimetic logic of the blood feud. One has only to compare the stable, elegiac legend of Ignacio Sánchez Mejías with the "hotter" or more dynamic one of his famous lamenter, Federico García Lorca.

Lorca's transfiguration of Sánchez Mejías in the well-known *Llanto* is mild indeed compared to the one he himself undergoes following his murder by Nationalist sympathizers. Though thousands died during the same period of bloody repression in Andalusia, Lorca was to become the magic symbol, assimilated to the archetype of a sacrificial Christ by well-meaning mourners like Pedro Salinas:

They killed him; but Federico emerged alive from the crime and they have emerged irremissibly dead. They, who wanted to free themselves of him by crime, will never free themselves of his most terrible vengeance, of the permanence of his wide peasant smile, of the permanence of his poetry. They will never free themselves of his life. Because crime does not kill. . . . In barbarous crime begins the triumph of the innocent victim.   [Salinas 1983:III, 293]

Naturally Lorca was an innocent victim, but the utilization of his legend in the grim years of the Civil War and afterwards only served to conceal the victim as *structure,* and hence to fan the flames of hatred and mutual destruction. The popular elegies Lorca inspired among the anonymous poets of the trenches document the overpowering urge to avenge the martyr:

Te mataron, poeta nuestro,	They killed you, our poet,
al nacer de una mañana	one morning at daybreak
y arrancaron de tu pecho	and the bullets tore
rosas de sangre las balas.	roses of blood from your chest.
Soy un gitano pequeño.	I am a little Gypsy.
Mi fortuna es una faca.	My fortune is a dagger.
¡Qué placer cuando la manche	What pleasure when I stain it
con sangre de los canallas!	with the blood of the scoundrels!
[Ramos-Gascon 1978:74]	

¡Ay si Federico os viera!	Oh if Federico could see you!
¡Con qué frases cantaría	With what phrases he would sing
vuestro arrojo en la pelea!	your boldness in battle!
¡Vengarlo, que él os lo pide	Avenge him, he asks it of you
con voz como el hielo, yerta!	with a voice like ice, inert!
[Ramos-Gascon 1978:77]	

Figures like Lorca provide a particularly economical means for grasping the "thermodynamics" of sacrificial civilization in Spain. In life he actively albeit unwittingly promoted the *méconnaissance* of the magico-persecutory culture of his native land. With his death he became a great mythical archetype himself, a genuine rallying point in a system of persecutory representations far more primary, violent, and hermetic than bullfighting ever was. In this new dimension his legend has much more in common with that of José Antonio Primo de Rivera (martyred founder of the Falange) than with any glorified Andalusian matador.

The Nationalists, to be sure, made constant and conscious use of religious symbols to advance their cause (Hernando 1977). But this should not blind us to the patently sacral nature of many songs and symbols seized upon by the Republic (cf. Palacio 1939). There were "saints" on the Left as well as on the Right, as Sperber reminds us (1974:xx). Both sides were engaged in a de facto internal crusade, and persecutory mythopoesis was the prime agglutinant in parallel and competing sociocentric ideologies that were identical in their obsession with difference. The incandescent sacrificial culture of the Civil War was not without its effects on the traditional one: the period from 1936–1939 saw an authentic revival of witchcraft fears and protective rituals in the insufficiently isolated rural regions of Spain (Caro Baroja 1961:294).

As with the other forms of persecutory mythopoesis I have dealt with in this book, point of view was everything in the generation of the archetypes. Lorca was no more an innocent victim for his slayers than José Antonio was for his. One group's martyr is another's culprit. What I wish to underline here is that the recognition of a victim's innocence does not automatically deliver people from the fetters of magico-persecutory thought nor does it guarantee that sacrificial logic will be transcended. "Scapegoat" as legendary motif can paradoxically serve the interests of counter-persecution. In a

dialectic that is thoroughly alien to the spirit of the Gospels but no
stranger to historical (sacrificial) Christianity, one victim leads to
another and another and another. As long as the urge to proclaim
the innocence of a victim is inseparably tied to the urge to blame
an out-group, we remain in a "Spanish" labyrinth.

For those readers who may be shifting uncomfortably in their
chairs, I repeat that I am not out to minimize objective social or
political differences between the victors and the vanquished of
Spain's last fratricidal conflict. My purpose, rather, is to point out
one more production run of the same mechanism that has manu-
factured folk and popular culture in *every* great crisis Spain has
known, quite independently of political factors. My objective
throughout this book has been to describe the workings of what
might be called "the poetics of violence." Once these workings are
grasped, we perceive the shortcomings of perspectives typically
adopted by those who have studied the popular myths of the Spanish Civil War. Salaün, for example, laments that the obstinate use
of traditional ballad meters by the Republic's soldiers prevented
them from attaining "authentic theoretical maturity"; this allows
him to judge and condemn the Anarchists as the greatest sinners—
even though they were the greatest contributors to the subliterary
corpus he studies (1985 : 367–383). A similar ideological bias leads
Amando De Miguel to account for the myth of Franco in terms of
cynical political manipulation (De Miguel 1976). While the *Gene-
ralísimo* was certainly surrounded by what we today would call
"image makers," the fact remains that frightened people shaken by
hunger and war require little prompting to mythify/sanctify a master of violence (as Franco undoubtedly was). The masses, not second-
guessing sociologists, determine the ingredients of charismatic
leadership. Mimetic psychology, not manipulation, is at work in
the following 1939 ode to Franco:

¡Oh genio portentoso,   Oh portentious genius,
por la gracia de Dios iluminado!   illuminated by the grace of God!
¡Fuiste maravilloso   You were marvelous
en tu gesto glorioso   in your glorious effort
contra el comunismo   against devilish Communism!
    [endemoniado!
El mundo, en loable   The world, in praiseworthy

declaración de tu talento y brillo,

a tu gesta admirable,
con cariño entrañable,
se rendirá de hinojos, ¡gran
                [Caudillo!
¡Bajad a los Infiernos,
rojos sangrientos de fatal ralea!

Salvamos los eternos
y siempre modernos
Mandamientos de Dios en la
                [pelea.
¡Mi patria querida!
¡Mil veces loado sea tu nombre!

¡Tu honor y tu vida
los salvó la aguerrida
majestad del Caudillo, tu Dios
                [Hombre!
        [De Miguel 1976: 119–120]

declaration of your talent and
                [glow,
before your amazing deed,
with endearing affection,
will render itself on bended knee,
                [great Caudillo!
Go down to Hell,
bloodthirsty Reds of accursed
                [breed!

We saved the eternal
and always modern
Commandments of God in the
                [fight!
My beloved Fatherland!
May your name be praised a thou-
                [sand times!

Your honor and your life
were saved by the valiant
majesty of the Caudillo, your God
                [Man!

The temptation to pass such paeans off as the handiwork of the dictator's lackeys must be resisted. However delirious or distasteful we may find them, the verses echo the feelings of great numbers of ordinary people, turned into true believers by the duress of one of history's worst wars.

When the fighting was over, the archetypes it had forged began to cool and stabilize in predictable ways. Outside of Spain, a vast exegetical industry grew up around the life and works of the martyred Lorca. Inside Spain, portraits of the martyred José Antonio became as ubiquitous as those of the Caudillo. Local Falangists who had fallen for the Nationalist cause were commemorated with monuments and plaques built into church walls. The cult of martyrs was finally crowned with an enormous cross (mimesis of Franco's "crusade"), built with prison labor in the Valley of the Fallen. The regime settled down to a paranoid obsession with the "Jewish-Masonic-Communist Conspiracy" and to the relentless ferreting out of its agents (Ferrer Benimeli 1982: 273–333). And, as a final ironic twist on Hobsbawm's invention of tradition, a legend born in the desperation of a tiny medieval kingdom came to justify a reactionary military rebellion a thousand years later. The ancient cult of Saint James the Moor-Slayer acquired fresh relevance in Franco's Spain, signifying as it did "the combative, militant, and violent affirmation of religious values for the sake of cultural unity" (Pérez Embid 1954:183).

But the most convincing evidence that Spain was safely returned to the traditional closed system of sacrificial representations came with an event that no wily apologist for the regime could have arranged. On 28 August 1947, a Miura bull named Islero severed the femoral artery of Manuel Rodríguez in the bullring of Linares, Córdoba. The thoroughly proletarian Manolete was one of the ablest bullfighters ever, without rivals in post-Civil War Spain. A man of irreproachable dignity and genuine popular appeal, his death sparked a national outpouring of cathartic—and apolitical—grief. The matador was mourned in dozens of *coplas*, literary elegies, chapbook biographies, and folk ballads (cf. Gil 1964:131−136; Cossío 1961: 992−997; Ríos Mozo 1985:111−122; Sánchez Garrido 1985:74− 77; Soto Viñolo 1986:234−255). This vast quantity of expressive culture carried out a "weak" sacralization of the fallen bullfighter, along the lines of prewar figures like Ignacio Sánchez Mejías, Granero, or Joselito. The epoch of "strong" sacralization that had elevated Lorca and José Antonio to semi-divine status had passed; the national mythmaking machine was back in operation once again, poised to produce nonsectarian sacrificial heroes at regular intervals to this very day.

It would be easy at this point to condemn the sanguinary imagination and escapist tendencies of the masses, to echo Philip Rahv's warning that "to look to myth for deliverance from history is altogether futile" (1953:647). The problem is that history has often been little more than a stage for the enactment of violent mythic impulses, a real-life theatre of the absurd and the cruel. To look to history for deliverance from myth would only compound the futility. Spaniards have not been so many Don Quixotes acting out deranged fantasies of honor and bloodshed. Rather, their fantasies—and their folklore—have been conditioned by their historical experiences, wars and feuds and vicissitudes of all kinds, economic and social inequalities, the greed of Napoleons and the self-righteousness of Caudillos. The psychocultural results (persecutory mythopoesis, ritual prophylaxes, mother-worship, the warrior fixation, etc.) subsequently shape collective history in gross and subtle ways. Gerald Brenan's choice of the word "labyrinth" to describe the sociopolitical background of the Spanish Civil War (Brenan 1960) takes on far broader connotations than those he intended. Every labyrinth, after all, has a Minotaur inside, a monstrous mélange of man and bull, sacrificer and victim, *Homo Ludens* and *Homo Necans*. Those who enter the labyrinth fall victim to a deadly game: the fortuitous and mechanical determination of who is right by who is left.

My study has been animated by the desire to unravel the relationship between collective values and collective violence, between social myth and social history. The suspicion that the *condition humaine* might be the Spanish labyrinth writ large has sustained my attempt to develop a research perspective with potential relevance to large group dynamics as well as to small, to anonymous cities as well as to agrotowns, for Mediterranean and non-Mediterranean countries, for every "level" of ethnicity, and for the entire folklore-popular culture continuum. To the degree that this new perspective is a valid one, there will be no need for nostalgia over the disappearing folk of Spain; the lessons they have taught us might tell us something vital about human behavior and prospects in general. In the last analysis, Spain's much-touted "difference" may reside in its rigorous replication of humanity's fascination with violence as well as its unceasing efforts to master or deceive it.

Bibliography

Aitken, B.
   1953   Las fiestas de Viloria, pueblo natal de San Domingo. *Revista de Dialectología y Tradiciones Populares (RDTP)* 9:499–503.
Altabella, José.
   Crónicas taurinas. Madrid: Taurus.
Alvarez, Carlos Luis.
   1964   The Public Square and the Bullring. In *Los toros/Bullfighting,* ed. F. Fernández Figueroa, pp. 41–43. Madrid: Indice.
Alvarez Arenas, Eliseo.
   1972   *Teoría bélica de España.* Madrid: Revista de Occidente.
Alvarez de Miranda, Angel.
   1962   *Ritos y juegos del toro.* Madrid: Taurus.
Amades, Juan.
   1959   El habla sin significado y la poesía popular disparatada. *RDTP* 15:274–291.
Andújar Espino, María del Socorro.
   1966   Fiestas y costumbres tradicionales de Peñaranda de Bracamonte. *RDTP* 22:350–377.
Araúz de Robles, Santiago.
   1978   *Sociología del toreo.* Madrid: Prensa Española.
Arévalo, José Carlos.
   1984   Ortega y los toros. *Revista de Occidente,* No. 36:49–59.
Arévalo, José Carlos, and José Antonio del Moral.
   1985   *Nacido para morir.* Madrid: Espasa-Calpe.
Attwater, Donald.
   1965   *The Penguin Dictionary of Saints.* Harmondsworth: Penguin.
Aymerich, José.
   1963   Sobre la popularidad de Don Juan Tenorio. *Insula* 204:1–10.

200   Bibliography

Badone, Ellen.
   1987   Ethnicity, Folklore, and Local Identity in Rural Brittany. *Journal of American Folklore* 100: 161–190.
Baring-Gould, Sabine.
   1967 [1866]   *Curious Myths of the Middle Ages.* New York: University Books.
Barrés, Maurice.
   1894   *Du sang, de la volupté et de la mort.* Paris: Librairie Plon.
Bataille, Georges.
   1928   *Histoire d'oeil.* Paris: Hachette.
Beatie, Bruce A.
   1976   Romances tradicionales and Spanish Traditional Ballads: Menéndez Pidal vs. Vladimir Propp. *Journal of the Folklore Institute* 13: 37–55.
Beltrán Martínez, Antonio.
   1979   *Introducción al folklore aragonés.* Zaragoza: Guara.
Ben-Ami, Issacher.
   1978   Miraculous Legends of Wartime. In *Folklore Studies in the Twentieth Century,* ed. V. J. Newall, pp. 123–127. Woodbridge, U.K.: Brewer.
Ben-Amos, Dan, ed.
   1976   *Folklore Genres.* Austin: University of Texas Press.
Bennassar, Bartolomé.
   1985 [1975]   *Los españoles. Actitudes y mentalidad desde el s. XVI al s. XIX.* San Lorenzo del Escorial (Madrid): Swan.
Bergamín, José.
   1930   *El arte de birlibirloque.* Madrid: Calpe.
   1981   *La música callada del toreo.* Madrid: Turner.
   1985   *La claridad del toreo.* Madrid: Turner.
Bergua, José.
   1934   *Psicología del pueblo español.* Madrid: Bergua.
Betancourt, Rafael.
   1970   *Psicoanálisis del toreo.* Madrid: Uguina.
Bettelheim, Bruno.
   1975   *The Uses of Enchantment.* New York: Vintage Books.
Blanco, Carlos.
   1983   *Las fiestas de aquí.* Valladolid: Ambito.
Blázquez, José María.
   1975   *Diccionario de las religiones prerromanas de Hispania.* Madrid: Istmo.
Bleu, F.
   1983 [1913]   *Antes y después del Guerra.* Madrid: Espasa-Calpe.
Boado, Emilia, and Fermín Cebolla.
   1976   *Las señoritas toreras. Historia, erótica y política del toreo femenino.* Madrid: Ediciones Felmar.

Bobadilla Conesa, María.
  1981   El fuego ritual de Navidad en un pueblo de la Ribagorza. In *I Congreso de Aragón de Etnología y Antropología*, pp. 139–151. Zaragoza: Instituto Fernando el Católico, C.S.I.C.
Boehm, Christopher.
  1987   *Blood Revenge. The Enactment and Management of Conflict in Montenegro and Other Tribal Societies.* Philadelphia: University of Pennsylvania Press.
Bonachera, Trinidad, and María Gracia Piñero.
  1985   *Hacia don Juan.* Sevilla: Servicio de Publicaciones del Excmo. Ayuntamiento de Sevilla.
Brandes, Stanley.
  1980   *Metaphors of Masculinity. Sex and Status in Andalusian Folklore.* Philadelphia: University of Pennsylvania Press.
Brenan, Gerald.
  1960   *The Spanish Labyrinth. An Account of the Social and Political Background of the Spanish Civil War.* Cambridge: Cambridge University Press.
Brenner, Charles.
  1974   *An Elementary Textbook of Psychoanalysis.* New York: Anchor Books.
Briones, Rafael.
  1985   La Semana Santa de Priego de Córdoba. Funciones antropológicas y dimensión cristiana de un ritual popular. In *La religión en Andalucía. Aproximación a la religiosidad popular*, ed. Centro de Estudios de Tradiciones Religiosas Andaluzas, pp. 43–71. Sevilla: Editoriales Andaluzas Unidas.
Burkert, Walter.
  1983 [1972]   *Homo Necans. The Anthropology of Ancient Greek Sacrificial Ritual and Myth.* Translated by Peter Bing. Berkeley: University of California Press.
Byock, Jesse.
  1982   *Feud in the Icelandic Saga.* Berkeley: University of California Press.
Cambria, Rosario.
  1974   *Los toros: tema polémico en el ensayo español del siglo XX.* Madrid: Gredos.
Campbell, Joseph.
  1968   *Creative Mythology.* Vol. 4 of *The Masks of God.* New York: Penguin Books.
Carande, Ramón.
  1964   Chronological Statistics of Victims of Bullfighting. In *Los toros/Bullfighting*, ed. F. Fernández Figueroa, pp. 188–195. Madrid: Indice.
Caro Baroja, Julio.
  1947   Las brujas de Fuenterrabía. *RDTP* 3 : 189–204.

1957　*Razas, pueblos y linajes.* Madrid: Revista de Occidente.

1961　*Las brujas y su mundo.* Madrid: Alianza.

1963　Mascaradas de invierno en España y en otras partes. *RDTP* 19: 139–296.

1964　Honor y vergüenza. *RDTP* 20:410–460.

1965a　*El Carnaval. Análisis histórico-cultural.* Madrid: Taurus.

1965b　A caza de botargas. *RDTP* 21:273–292.

1968　Modos de vivir hispánicos. In *El folklore español,* ed. J. M. Gómez-Tabanera, pp. 51–65. Madrid: Instituto Español de Antropología Aplicada.

1969　*Ensayo sobre la literatura de cordel.* Madrid: Revista de Occidente.

1970a　*El mito del carácter nacional. Meditaciones a contrapelo.* Madrid: Seminarios y Ediciones.

1970b　*Inquisición, brujería, y criptojudaismo.* Barcelona: Ariel.

1973　Mundos circundantes y contornos histórico-culturales. *RDTP* 29:23–47.

1974a　*Algunos mitos españoles.* Madrid: Ediciones del Centro.

1974b　*Ritos y mitos equívocos.* Madrid: Istmo.

1976　Algunas formas elementales de exposición y explicación de la historia. *RDTP* 32:103–122.

1978　*Los judíos en la España moderna y contemporánea.* 3 vol. 2d. ed. Madrid: Istmo.

1979　*Ensayos sobre la cultura popular española.* Madrid: Dosbe.

1980　*Introducción a una historia contemporánea del anticlericalismo español.* Madrid: Istmo.

1983　En torno a la literatura popular gaditana. *RDTP* 38:3–36.

1984a　*El estío festivo. Fiestas populares de verano.* Madrid: Taurus.

1984b　Toros y hombres, sin toreros. *Revista de Occidente,* No. 36: 7–26.

Carrasco Urgoiti, María Soledad.

1963　Aspectos folclóricos y literarios de la fiesta de moros y cristianos en España. *Publications of the Modern Language Association (PMLA)* 78:476–491.

Casas Gaspar, Enrique.

1950　*Ritos agrarios. Folklore campesino español.* Madrid: Escelicer.

Castillo de Lucas, Antonio.

1968　La medicina popular y su proyección en el folklore español. Concepto e importancia. In *El folklore español,* ed. J. M. Gómez-Tabanera, pp. 129–147. Madrid: Instituto Español de Antropología Aplicada.

Castón Boyer, Pedro.

1985　La religiosidad tradicional en Andalucía. Una aproximación sociológica. In *La religión en Andalucía,* ed. CETRA, pp. 97–129. Sevilla: Editoriales Andaluzas Unidas.

Castro, Américo.
  1954   *The Structure of Spanish History.* Trans. by E. King. Princeton,
         N.J.: Princeton University Press.
Cátedra Tomás, María.
  1976   Notas sobre la envidia: los ojos malos entre los Vaqueiros de Al-
         zada. In *Temas de antropología española,* ed. C. Lisón, pp. 9–48.
         Madrid: Akal.
Cháves Nogales, Manuel.
  1969[1935]   *Juan Belmonte, matador de toros.* Madrid: Alianza.
Christian, William A.
  1976   De los santos a María: panorama de las devociones a santuarios
         españoles desde el principio de la Edad Media hasta nuestros días.
         In *Temas de antropología española,* ed. C. Lisón Tolosana, pp. 49–
         105. Madrid: Akal.
Claramunt López, Fernando.
  1982   Los toros desde la psicología. In *Los toros. Tratado técnico e his-
         tórico,* Vol. VII, pp. 1–181. Madrid: Espasa-Calpe.
Cohn, Norman.
  1961   *The Pursuit of the Millennium. Revolutionary Messianism in
         Medieval and Renaissance Europe.* New York: Harper & Bros.
Collins, Larry, and Dominique Lapierre.
  1968   *The Extraordinary Life of El Cordobés.* London: Weidenfield &
         Nicolson.
Conquergood, Dwight.
  1984   Review of *Feud in the Icelandic Saga* by Jesse Byock. *Journal of
         American Folklore* 97:347–349.
Conrad, Jack Randolph.
  1957   *The Horn and the Sword. The History of the Bull as a Symbol of
         Power and Fertility.* New York: E. P. Dutton.
Cook, Albert.
  1980   *Myth and Language.* Bloomington: Indiana University Press.
Cook, Albert, and Edwin Dolin.
  1972   *An Anthology of Greek Tragedy.* Indianapolis: The Bobbs-Merrill
         Company.
Corrochano, Gregorio.
  1961   *Cuando suena el clarín.* Madrid: Alianza.
Cossío, José María de.
  1943   *Los toros. Tratado técnico e histórico,* Vol. I. Madrid: Espasa-
         Calpe.
  1947   Vol. II.
  1960   Vol. III.
  1961   Vol. IV.
Cossío y Corral, Francisco de.
  1986   *Los toros. Tratado técnico e histórico,* Vol VIII. Madrid: Espasa-
         Calpe.

Dégh, Linda.
 1972   Folk Narrative. In *Folklore and Folklife,* ed. Richard M. Dorson,
    pp. 53–84. Chicago: University of Chicago Press.
Delaruelle, Etienne.
 1975   *La piété populaire au Moyen Age.* Torino: Bottega d'Erasmo.
Delfín Val, José.
 1981   Donde en la vieja casa de la Sra. Flavia, se cuenta la triste histo-
    ria de la muerte de Mariano Mera. *Revista de Folklore* 2, No.
    6:31–32.
Delgado-Iribarren Negrao, Manuel.
 1982   Los toros en la música. In *Los toros. Tratado técnico e histórico,*
    Vol. VII, pp. 573–679. Madrid: Espasa-Calpe.
Delgado Ruiz, Manuel.
 1986   *De la muerte de un dios. La fiesta de toros en el universo sim-
    bólico de la cultura popular.* Barcelona: Península.
De Miguel, Amando.
 1976   *Franco, Franco Franco.* Madrid: Ediciones 99.
Denisoff, Harold.
 1969   The Proletarian Renascence: The Folkness of the Ideological
    Folk. *Journal of American Folklore* 82:51–65.
Desmonde, William H.
 1952   The Bullfight as a Religious Ritual. *American Imago* 9:173–195.
Díaz-Cañabate, Antonio.
 1970   *Paseíllo por el planeta de los toros.* Madrid: Salvat.
Díaz Roig, Mercedes, ed.
 1981   *El Romancero viejo.* Madrid: Cátedra.
Díaz Yanes, Agustín.
 1983   Joselito el Gallo: El último torero clásico. In *Arte y tauromaquia,*
    ed. UIMP, pp. 225–250. Madrid: Turner.
Domínguez Morano, Carlos.
 1985   Aproximación psicoanalítica a la religiosidad tradicional an-
    daluza. In *La religión en Andalucía,* ed. CETRA, pp. 131–175.
    Sevilla: Editoriales Andaluzas Unidas.
Dorfman, Eugene.
 1969   *The Narreme in Medieval Romance Narrative. An Introduction
    to Narrative Structures.* Toronto: University of Toronto Press.
Dorson, Richard M.
 1960   Theories of Myth and the Folklorist. In *Myth and Mythmaking,*
    ed. Henry Murray, pp. 76–89. New York: Braziller.
Douglass, Carrie B.
 1984   Toro muerto, vaca es: An Interpretation of the Spanish Bullfight.
    American Ethnologist 11:242–258.
Dundes, Alan, ed.
 1965   *The Study of Folklore.* Englewood Cliffs, N.J.: Prentice-Hall.

Durand, Gilbert.
    1968   *L'Imagination symbolique.* Paris: Presses Universitaires de
           France.
Echeverría, Javier.
    1983   Toros y juego. Del arte de correr toros a pie: el encierro de Pam-
           plona. In *Arte y tauromaquia,* ed. UIMP, pp. 127–185. Madrid:
           Turner.
Edmunds, Lowell.
    1985   *Oedipus. The Ancient Legend and Its Later Analogues.* Balti-
           more: The Johns Hopkins University Press.
Fernández Cuenca, Carlos.
    1982   Los toros en el cine. In *Los toros. Tratado técnico e histórico,*
           Vol. VII, pp. 763–937. Madrid: Espasa-Calpe.
Fernández Flores, Wenceslao.
    1927   *Relato inmoral.* Madrid: Atlántida.
Fernández Suárez, Alvaro.
    1961   *España, árbol vivo.* Madrid: Aguilar.
Ferrer Benimeli, J. A.
    1982   *El contubernio judeo-masónico-comunista.* Madrid: Istmo.
Fidalgo, Feliciano.
    1986   Rafael de Paula: "Quiero recuperar mi dignidad y mi honor." *El
           País,* 3 August 1986, p. 10.
Fischer, J. L.
    1963   The Sociopsychological Analysis of Folktales. *Current Anthro-
           pology* 4:235–295.
Frank, Waldo.
    1926   *Virgin Spain.* New York: Boni & Liveright.
Frye, Northrop.
    1976   *The Secular Scripture. A Study of the Structure of Romance.*
           Cambridge: Harvard University Press.
García-Baquero González, Antonio, Pedro Romero de Solís, and Ignacio
Vázquez Parladé.
    1980   *Sevilla y la fiesta de toros.* Sevilla: Servicio de Publicaciones del
           Excmo. Ayuntamiento de Sevilla.
García de Diego, Pilar.
    1953   El testamento en la tradición. *RDTP* 9:1–66.
    1954   El testamento en la tradición. *RDTP* 10:400–471.
    1960   Censura popular. *RDTP* 16:295–331.
García Matos, M.
    1948   Curiosa historia del "toro de San Marcos" en un pueblo de la alta
           Extemadura. *RDTP* 4:600–610.
García Sanz, S.
    1948   La quema del Judas en la provincia de Guadalajara. *RDTP* 4:
           619–625.
    1953   Botargas y enmascarados alcarreños. *RDTP* 9:467–492.

Geist, Anthony.
  1985   Popular Poetry in the Fascist Front During the Spanish Civil War. In *Fascismo y experiencia literaria,* ed. H. Vidal pp. 145–153. Minneapolis: Institute for the Study of Ideologies and Literature.
Gil, Bonifacio.
  1964   *Muertes de toreros según el romancero popular.* Madrid: Taurus.
Gilmore, David D.
  1987   *Aggression and Community. Paradoxes of Andalusian Culture.* New Haven: Yale University Press.
Gilmore, Margaret M., and David D. Gilmore.
  1979   "Machismo": A Psychodynamic Approach (Spain). *Journal of Psychological Anthropology* 2:281–300.
Girard, René.
  1961   *Mensonge romantique et vérité romanesque.* Paris: Grasset.
  1972   *La Violence et le sacré.* Paris: Grasset.
  1978a *Des choses cachées depuis la fondation du monde.* Paris: Grasset.
  1978b *To Double Business Bound: Essays on Literature, Mimesis, and Anthropology.* Baltimore: Johns Hopkins University Press.
  1982   *Le Bouc émissaire.* Paris: Grasset.
Gómez Pin, Victor.
  1981   Tauromaquia e interpretación freudiana del origen de la fiesta. In *Las Ventas. Cincuenta años de corridas,* ed. M. Kramer et al., pp. 416–424. Madrid: Excma. Diputación Provincial.
Gómez-Tabanera, J. M.
  1968   Fiestas populares y festejos tradicionales; Origen de las fiestas taurinas. In *El folklore español,* ed. J. M. Gómez-Tabanera, pp. 149–216, 269–295. Madrid: Instituto Español de Antropología Aplicada.
González Casarrubios, Consolación.
  1985   *Fiestas populares en Castilla-La Mancha.* Ciudad Real: Servicio de Publicaciones de la Junta de Comunidades de Castilla-La Mancha.
González Climent, Anselmo.
  1953   *Andalucía en los toros, el cante y la danza.* Madrid: Imprenta E. Sánchez Leal.
  1964   *Flamencología.* Madrid: Escelicer.
González García, Angel.
  1983   Pintura y toros. In *Arte y tauromaquia,* ed. UIMP, pp. 187–223. Madrid: Turner.
González Troyano, Alberto.
  1983   El torero como protagonista literario. In *Arte y tauromaquia,* ed. UIMP, pp. 93–109. Madrid: Turner.
Guinagh, Kevin, and Alfred Dorjahn.
  1942   *Latin Literature in Translation.* New York: Longmans, Green, & Company.

Gutiérrez Estevez, Manuel.
1981 *El incesto en el Romancero popular hispánico. Un ensayo de análisis estructural.* 3 vols. Madrid: Editorial de la Universidad Complutense de Madrid.

Gutiérrez Macías, Valeriano.
1959 Fiestas extremeñas. *RDTP* 15:457–494.
1960 Fiestas cacereñas. *RDTP* 16:335–357.

Handler, Richard, and Jocelyn Linnekin.
1984 Tradition, Genuine or Spurious. *Journal of American Folklore* 97:273–290.

Hasan-Rokem, Galit, and Alan Dundes, eds.
1986 *The Wandering Jew. Essays in the Interpretation of a Christian Legend.* Bloomington: Indiana University Press.

Hemingway, Ernest.
1932 *Death in the Afternoon.* New York: Charles Scribner's Sons.

Henrichs, Albert.
1984 Loss of Self, Suffering, Violence: The Modern View of Dionysus from Nietzche to Girard. *Harvard Studies in Classical Philology* 88:205–240.

Herm, Gerhard.
1977 *The Celts. The People Who Came Out of the Darkness.* New York: St. Martin's Press.

Hernando, Bernardino M.
1977 *Delirios de Cruzada.* Madrid: Ediciones 99.

Herr, Richard.
1978 El Bien, el Mal y el levantamiento de España contra Napoleón. In *Homenaje a Julio Caro Baroja*, ed. A. Carreira et al., pp. 595–616. Madrid: Centro de Investigaciones Sociológicas.

Herrera Casado, Antonio.
1973 San Agustín y el culto totémico. *RDTP* 29:427–433.

Hobsbawm, Eric.
1959 *Primitive Rebels.* Manchester: University of Manchester Press.
1983a Inventing Traditions. In *The Invention of Tradition*, eds. E. Hobsbawm and T. Ranger, pp. 1–14. Cambridge: Cambridge University Press.
1983b Mass-Producing Traditions: Europe, 1870–1914. In *The Invention of Tradition*, eds. E. Hobsbawm and T. Ranger, pp. 263–307. Cambridge: Cambridge University Press.

Holguín, Andrés, and Carlos Holguín.
1966 *Toros y religión.* Bogotá: Editorial Revista Colombiana.

Hyman, Stanley Edgar.
1955 The Ritual View of Myth and the Mythic. *Journal of American Folklore* 68:462–472.

Ingham, John.
1964 The Bullfighter. A Study in Sexual Dialectic. *American Imago* 21–22:95–102.

Jackson, Bruce.
  1985   Things That From a Long Way Off Look Like Flies. *Journal of American Folklore* 98:131–147.
Jansen, William Hugh.
  1965   The Esoteric-Exoteric Factor in Folklore. In *The Study of Folklore*, ed. Alan Dundes, pp. 43–51. Englewood Cliffs, N.J.: Prentice-Hall.
Jones, Ernest.
  1965   Psychoanalysis and Folklore. In *The Study of Folklore*, ed. Alan Dundes, pp. 88–102. Englewood Cliffs, N.J.: Prentice-Hall.
Jones, V. C.
  1948   *The Hatfields and the McCoys.* Chapel Hill: University of North Carolina Press.
Juliano, María Dolores.
  1986   *Cuadernos de antropología: Cultura popular.* Barcelona: Anthropos.
Kagan, Donald, ed.
  1975   *Problems in Ancient History, Vol. II: The Roman World.* New York: Macmillan.
Kamenetsky, Christa.
  1972   Folklore as a Political Tool in Nazi Germany. *Journal of American Folklore* 85:221–235.
Kirk, G. S.
  1970   *Myth: Its Meaning and Function in Ancient and Other Cultures.* Berkeley: University of California Press.
Kluckhohn, Clyde.
  1965   Recurrent Themes in Myth and Mythmaking. In *The Study of Folklore*, ed. Alan Dundes, pp. 158–168. Englewood Cliffs, N.J.: Prentice-Hall.
  1966[1942]   Myths and Rituals: A General Theory. In *Myth and Literature*, ed. J. B. Vickery, pp. 33–44. Lincoln: University of Nebraska Press.
Königshofen, Jacob von.
  1972[1930]   The Cremation of the Strasbourg Jewry. In *Social Textures of Western Civilization*, eds. M. Cherniavsky and A. Slavin, pp. 324–325. Lexington: Xerox College Publishing.
Krappe, Alexander Haggerty.
  1929   *The Science of Folklore.* New York: Barnes and Noble.
La Barre, Weston.
  1972   *The Ghost Dance: The Origins of Religion.* New York: Doubleday.
Larrea Palacín, Arcadio de.
  1968   El teatro popular en España. In *El folklore español*, ed. J. M. Gómez-Tabanera, pp. 339–352. Madrid: Instituto Español de Antropología Aplicada.

Lasker, Linda Gail.
  1976 *El tema de los toros en la novelística española contemporánea.*
         New York: Abra.
Lebreton, Jules, and Jacques Zeiller.
  1975 Religious Persecution. In *Problems in Ancient History, Vol. II:
         The Roman World,* ed. D. Kagan, pp. 379–382. New York: Mac-
         millan.
Leiris, Michel.
  1964[1937] *Miroir de la tauromachie, précédé de Tauromachies.*
         Paris: G. L. M.
Lévi-Strauss, Claude.
  1966 *The Savage Mind.* Chicago: University of Chicago Press.
Levin, Harry.
  1960 Some Meanings of Myth. In *Myth and Mythmaking,* ed. Henry
         Murray, pp. 103–114. New York: George Braziller.
Lewis, I. M.
  1976 *Social Anthropology in Perspective.* New York: Penguin.
Linenthal, Edward Tabor.
  1982 *Changing Images of the Warrior Hero in America: A History of
         Popular Symbolism.* New York: Edwin Mellen Press.
Lisón Tolosana, Carmelo.
  1974 *Perfiles simbólico-morales de la cultura gallega.* Madrid: Akal.
  1980 *Invitación a la antropología cultural de España.* Madrid: Akal.
  1983 *Antropología social y hermenéutica.* Madrid: Ediciones Fondo de
         Cultura Económica.
Livingstone, Frank B.
  1976 The Effects of Warfare on the Biology of the Human Species. In
         Physical Anthropology and Archaeology, 2d edition, ed. P. B.
         Hammond, pp. 150–158. New York: Macmillan.
Llompart, Gabriel.
  1968 La religiosidad popular. In *El folklore español,* ed. J. M. Gómez-
         Tabanera, pp. 217–246. Madrid: Instituto de Antropología
         Aplicada.
López-Valdemoro, Juan (Conde de las Navas).
  1900 *El espectáculo más nacional.* Madrid: Rivadeneyra.
Lüthi, Max.
  1976 Aspects of the Märchen and the Legend. In *Folklore Genres,* ed.
         Dan Ben-Amos, pp. 17–34. Austin: University of Texas Press.
Maldonado, Luis.
  1975 *Religiosidad popular.* Madrid: Editorial Cristiandad.
  1979 *Génesis del catolicismo popular.* Madrid: Cristiandad.
Manrique, G.
  1952 San Pedro Manrique: Cultura popular pastoril. *RDTP* 8:494–
         525.

210 Bibliography

Marco, Joaquín.
    1977 *Literatura popular en España en los siglos XVIII y XIX. Una aproximación a los pliegos de cordel.* 2 vol. Madrid: Taurus.
Marín, Karmentxu.
    1986 Aníbal y el Cascamorras. *El País*, 2 May 1986, p. 20.
Martín Gaite, Carmen.
    1981 *Usos amorosos del dieciocho en España.* Barcelona: Lumen.
Martínez, Luis.
    1986 Fiestas: Sacrificio y tortura de animales. *Natura*, No. 37 (April): 14–18.
Martínez Remis, Manuel, ed.
    1963 *Cancionero popular taurino.* Madrid: Taurus.
May, Rollo.
    1960 The Significance of Symbols. In *Symbolism in Religion and Literature*, ed. Rollo May, pp. 11–49. New York: Braziller.
Menéndez Pidal, Ramón.
    1925 *Floresta de leyendas heroicas españolas. Rodrigo, el último godo.* 3 vol. Madrid: La Lectura.
Mieder, Wolfgang.
    1982 Proverbs in Nazi Germany: The Promulgation of Anti-Semitism and Stereotypes through Folklore. *Journal of American Folklore* 95:435–464.
Mijares, José Luis.
    1968 *Civilización española.* Madrid: Editora Nacional.
Mira, Joan F.
    1976 Toros en el norte valenciano: notas para un análisis. In *Temas de antropología española*, ed. C. Lisón Tolosana, pp. 107–129. Madrid: Akal.
Narváez, Peter, and Martin Laba, eds.
    1986 *Media Sense: The Folklore-Popular Culture Continuum.* Bowling Green, Ohio: Bowling Green State University Popular Press.
Noel, Eugenio.
    1967[1914] Escritos antitaurinos. Madrid: Taurus.
Ortíz-Cañavate, Lorenzo.
    1931 El toreo español. In *Folklore y costumbres de España*, ed. F. Carreras y Candí, pp. 377–569. Barcelona: Casa Martín.
O'Sullivan, Sean, ed.
    1974 *The Folklore of Ireland.* New York: Hastings House.
Palacio, Carlos, ed.
    1939 *Colección de canciones de lucha.* Valencia: Tipografía Moderna.
Pan, Ismael del.
    1945 Recuerdo folklórico de algunas fiestas tradicionales. *RDTP* 1: 188–199.
Peña, Aniano, ed.
    1986 *Don Juan Tenorio de José Zorrilla.* Madrid: Cátedra.

Pereda, Julián.
  1965   *Los toros ante la iglesia y la moral.* 2d ed. Bilbao: El Mensajero del Corazón de Jesús.
Pérez de Ayala, Ramón.
  1963   *Política y toros.* In *Obras completas,* Vol. III (Book I: 1918; Book II: 1943). Madrid: Aguilar.
Pérez Delgado, Rafael.
  1978   Sobre las corridas de toros. Notas sociológicas. In *Homenaje a Julio Caro Baroja,* ed. A. Carreira et al., pp. 843–875. Madrid: Centro de Investigaciones Sociológicas.
Pérez Embid, Florentino.
  1954   El símbolo de Santiago en la cultura española. In *Santiago en la historia, la literatura y el arte,* ed. Colegio Mayor Universitario de la Estila, II, pp. 167–183. Madrid: Editora Nacional.
Pérez Gallego, J.
  1986   Semana Santa a la española. Desde la procesión de las palmas de Jerusalén a la desacralización de la fiesta. *El País,* 9 March 1986, pp. 17–18.
Piñero, Pedro M., and Virtudes Atero.
  1986   *Romancero andaluz de tradición oral.* Sevilla: Editoriales Andaluzas Unidas.
Pitt-Rivers, Julian.
  1979   *Antropología del honor o política de los sexos. Ensayos de antropología mediterránea.* Barcelona: Grijalbo.
  1984   El sacrificio del toro. *Revista de Occidente,* No. 36: 27–47.
Poliakov, Léon.
  1974   The Aryan Myth. *A History of Racist and Nationalist Ideas in Europe.* Trans. by Edmund Howard. New York: Basic Books.
Pozo, Raúl del, and Diego Bardón.
  1980   *El ataúd de astracán. El regreso de El Cordobés.* Barcelona: Ediciones Zeta.
Prado, Angeles.
  1973   *La literatura del casticismo.* Madrid: Moneda y Crédito.
Prat Canos, Joan.
  1982   Aspectos simbólicos de las fiestas. In *Tiempo de fiesta,* ed. H. Velasco, pp. 151–168. Madrid: Alatar.
Preston, James J.
  1982   New Perspectives on Mother Worship. In *Mother Worship: Themes and Variations,* ed. J. J. Preston pp. 325–343. Chapel Hill: University of North Carolina Press.
Puccini Dario, ed.
  1960   *Romancero de la resistencia española.* Mexico: Editorial Porrúa.
Pujol, Xavier, ed.
  1982   *Don Giovanni de Wolfgang A. Mozart.* Barcelona: Daimon.

Quiñones, Fernando, and José Blas Vega.

  1982   Toros y arte flamenco. In *Los toros. Tratado técnico e histórico,* Vol. VII, pp. 681–757. Madrid: Espasa-Calpe.

Rahv, Philip.

  1953   The Myth and the Powerhouse. *Partisan Review* 20:635–648.

Ramírez Rodrigo, María del Prado.

  1985   La cultura popular durante los siglos XVI al XX. In *El arte y la cultura de la provincia de Ciudad Real,* ed. F. Pillet Capdepón, pp. 341–375. Ciudad Real: Excma. Diputación de Ciudad Real.

Ramón y Fernández, José.

  1950   Costumbres cacereñas. *RDTP* 6:78–103.

Ramos-Gascon, Antonio, ed.

  1978   *El Romancero del Ejército Popular.* Madrid: Editorial Nuestra Cultura.

Rank, Otto.

  1959[1914]   *The Myth of the Birth of the Hero.* New York: Vintage.

Ricoeur, Paul.

  1969   *The Symbolism of Evil.* Translated by Emerson Buchanan. Boston: Beacon Press.

Ríos Mozo, Rafael.

  1985   *Tauromaquia fundamental.* Granada: Editoriales Andaluzas Unidas.

Risco, Vicente.

  1961   Apuntes sobre el mal de ojo en Galicia. *RDTP* 17:66–92.

Rodríguez Almodóvar, Antonio.

  1982   *Los cuentos maravillosos españoles.* Barcelona: Editorial Crítica.

Rodríguez Becerra, Salvador.

  1985   *Las fiestas de Andalucía.* Granada: Editoriales Andaluzas Unidas.

Rodríguez Moñino, Antonio, ed.

  1977   *Romancero General de la Guerra de España.* Madrid: Hispamérica.

Roma Riu, Josefina.

  1984   *Aragón y el Carnaval.* Zaragoza: Guara.

Ropp, Theodore.

  1962   *War in the Modern World.* New York: Collier Books.

Rousset, Jean.

  1978   *Le Mythe de Don Juan.* Paris: Armand Colin.

Sahlins, Marshall D.

  1976   The Origin of Society. In *Physical Anthropology and Archaeology,* ed. P. Hammond, pp. 58–64. New York: Macmillan.

Sáinz Rodríguez, Pedro, ed.

  1980   *Antología de la literatura espiritual española.* Vol I: *Edad Media.* Madrid: Fundación Universitaria Española.

Salaün, Serge.

  1971   *Romancero libertario.* Paris: Editions Seghers.

1985   *La poesía de la Guerra de España.* Madrid: Castalia.
Salinas, Pedro
1983   *Ensayos completos.* 3 vol. Madrid: Taurus.
Sánchez, María Angeles.
1981   *Guía de fiestas populares de España.* Madrid: Tania.
Sánchez Carrillo, Antonio.
1951   El Cascamorras. *RDTP* 7 : 341–348.
Sánchez Garrido, José Luis.
1985   *Córdoba en la historia del toreo.* Córdoba: Publicaciones del Monte de Piedad y Caja de Ahorros.
Sanmartín Arce, Ricardo.
1982   Ecología, economía, y fiesta. Algunos ejemplos del País Valenciano. In *Tiempo de fiesta,* ed. H. Velasco, pp. 43–69. Madrid: Alatar.
San Román, Teresa.
1976   El buen nombre del gitano. In *Temas de antropología española,* ed. C. Lisón, pp. 243–262. Madrid: Akal.
San Valero Aparisi, Julián.
1969   Notas para una teoría etnológica de las Fallas de Valencia. In *Etnología y tradiciones populares. I Congreso Nacional de Artes y Costumbres Populares,* pp. 213–231. Zaragoza: Instituto Fernando el Católico, C.S.I.C.
Sarasa Sánchez, Esteban.
1981   Mitos y ritos feudales en Aragón. El caso de doña Brianda de Luna. In *I Congreso de Aragón de Etnología y Antropología,* pp. 127–132. Zaragoza: Instituto Fernando el Católico, C.S.I.C.
Saunders, George R.
1981   Men and Women in Southern Europe: A Review of Some Aspects of Cultural Complexity. *Journal of Psychoanalytic Anthropology* 4 : 435–466.
Savater, Fernando.
1981   El torero como héroe. In *Las Ventas: Cincuenta años de corridas,* ed. M. Kramer et. al., pp. 410–414. Madrid: Excma. Diputación Provincial de Madrid.
1983   Caracterización del espectador taurino. In *Arte y tauromaquia,* ed. UIMP, pp. 111–125. Madrid: Turner.
Schneider, Jane.
1971   Of Vigilance and Virgins: Honor, Shame, and Access to Resources in Mediterranean Societies. *Ethnology* 10 : 1–24.
Siebers, Tobin.
1983   *The Mirror of Medusa.* Berkeley: University of California Press.
Simeone, Fabio.
1978   Fascists and Folklorists in Italy. *Journal of American Folklore* 91 : 543–562.
Smith, C. Colin
1964   *Spanish Ballads.* London: Pergamon Press.

Smith, Robert J.
 1972   Festivals and Celebrations. In *Folklore and Folklife*, ed. R. Dorson, pp. 159–172. Chicago: University of Chicago Press.
Soberanas, Amadeu J.
 1984   Ensayo o poema sobre el toro en España. Otro inédito de Federico García Lorca. *El Crotalón* 1:717–730.
Soto Viñolo, Juan.
 1986   *Manolete, torero para olvidar una guerra*. Madrid: Delfos.
Sperber, Murray A., ed.
 1974   *And I Remember Spain. A Spanish Civil War Anthology*. New York: Macmillan.
Sueiro, Daniel.
 1974   *La pena de muerte. Ceremonial, historia, procedimientos*. Madrid: Alianza.
Sureda Molina, Guillermo.
 1967   *El toreo gitano*. Palma de Mallorca: Imprenta Fullana.
Taboada, Jesús.
 1969   La matanza del cerdo en Galicia. *RDTP* 25:89–105.
Thomas, Hugh.
 1961   *The Spanish Civil War*. New York: Harper and Row.
Tierno Galván, Enrique.
 1961[1951]   Los toros, acontecimiento nacional. In *Desde el espectáculo a la trivialización*, pp. 53–77. Madrid: Taurus.
Toelken, Barre.
 1979   *The Dynamics of Folklore*. Boston: Houghton Mifflin.
Trachtenberg, Joshua.
 1983[1943]   *The Devil and the Jews. The Medieval Conception of the Jew and Its Relation to Modern Anti-Semitism*. Philadelphia: Jewish Publication Society of America.
Tripp, Edward.
 1970   *Crowell's Handbook of Classical Mythology*. New York: Thomas Y. Crowell.
Unamuno, Miguel de.
 1967[1909]   El cristo español. In *Obras completas*, Vol. III, pp. 273–276. Madrid: Escelicer.
 1968[1905]   Vida de Don Quijote y Sancho. In *Visión de España en la Generación del 98*, ed. J. L. Abellán, pp. 419–421. Madrid: Editorial Magisterio Español.
Velasco, Honorio M.
 1981   Textos sociocéntricos. Los mensajes de identificación y diferenciación entre comunidades rurales. *RDTP* 36:85–106.
 1982   Tiempo de fiesta. In *Tiempo de fiesta*, ed. H. Velasco, pp. 5–25. Madrid: Alatar.
Vergara, Gabriel María.
 1946   La Catorcena, tradición segoviana. *RDTP* 2:430–434.

Vila, Enrique.
  1947   *Historia de la rivalidad taurina (1777–1947)*. Madrid: Gráficas Tejario.

Vizcaíno Casas, F.
  1971   *Contando los cuarenta*. Madrid: Altamira.

Wang, Betty.
  1935   Folksongs as Regulators of Politics. *Sociology and Social Research* 20:61–66.

Warner, Marina.
  1976   *Alone of All Her Sex: The Myth and the Cult of the Virgin Mary*. New York: Alfred A. Knopf.

Wilder, Amos.
  1960   The Cross: Social Trauma or Redemption. In *Symbolism in Religion and Literature*, ed. Rollo May, pp. 99–117. New York: George Braziller.

Wolf, Eric R.
  1966   *Peasants*. Englewood Cliffs, New Jersey: Prentice-Hall.

Zorrilla, José.
  1986[1844]   *Don Juan Tenorio. Drama religioso-fantástico en dos partes*. Ed. Aniano Peña. Madrid: Cátedra.

Zúmel, Mariano F.
  1982   Peñas y asociaciones taurinas de todo el mundo. In *Los toros. Tratado técnico e histórico*, Vol. VII, pp. 1027–1088. Madrid: Espasa-Calpe.

Index